# The
# *Indeterminate World:*

## *A Study of the Novels of Joyce Cary*

*We are stale and dull. . . . The causes of this are not to be found in our stupidity, our lack of talent, or our insolence . . . but in a disease which for the artist is worse than syphilis or sexual exhaustion. . . . Let me remind you that the writers who we say are for all time or are simply good, and who intoxicate us, have one common and very important characteristic; they are going toward something and are summoning you toward it, too, and you feel not with your mind, but with your whole being, that they have some object, just like the ghost of Hamlet's father, who did not come and disturb the imagination for nothing. . . . The best of them are realists and paint life as it is, but through every line's being soaked in the consciousness of an object, you feel, besides life as it is, the life which ought to be, and that captivates you. And we? . . . We have neither immediate nor remote aims, and in our soul there is a great empty space.*

Anton Chekhov, 1892

# *The Indeterminate World:*

## A Study of the Novels of Joyce Cary

### Robert Bloom

*Philadelphia*
*University of Pennsylvania Press*

© 1962, by the Trustees of the University of Pennsylvania
Published in Great Britain, India, and Pakistan
by the Oxford University Press
London, Bombay, and Karachi

Library of Congress Catalog Card Number: 62-10745

7329

Printed in Great Britain
by Charles Birchall & Sons Ltd
Liverpool and London

For their kind permission to reproduce passages from works protected by copyright, thanks are due to the following:

The Estate of Joyce Cary, Curtis Brown Ltd., and Harper and Brothers for the following works of Joyce Cary: *An American Visitor,* Michael Joseph, Carfax edition, 1952; Harper, 1961; *Mister Johnson,* Michael Joseph, Carfax edition, 1952; Harper, 1951; *Charley Is My Darling,* Michael Joseph, Carfax edition, 1951; Harper, 1960; *A House of Children,* Michael Joseph, Carfax edition, 1951; Harper, 1956; *The Horse's Mouth,* Michael Joseph, Carfax edition, 1951; Harper, 1950; *The Moonlight,* Michael Joseph, Carfax edition, 1952; Harper, 1947; *A Fearful Joy,* Michael Joseph, Carfax edition, 1952; Harper, 1950; *Prisoner of Grace,* Michael Joseph, Carfax edition, 1954; Harper, 1952; *Except the Lord,* Michael Joseph, 1953; Harper, 1953; *Not Honour More,* Michael Joseph, 1955; Harper, 1955; *Art and Reality,* Cambridge University Press, 1958; Harper, 1958.

The Estate of Joyce Cary and Curtis Brown Ltd. for the following works of Joyce Cary: *Aissa Saved,* Michael Joseph, Carfax edition, 1952; *Castle Corner,* Michael Joseph, Carfax edition, 1952; *Power in Men,* Nicholson & Watson, 1939.

Harper and Brothers for *First Trilogy* by Joyce Cary, Harper, 1958.

Chatto & Windus and Harper and Brothers for *Joyce Cary: A Preface to His Novels* by Andrew Wright, Chatto & Windus, 1958; Harper, 1958.

*For Gloria,*
*who ministered*

# Preface

Any admirer of Joyce Cary must feel uneasy about the neglect that Cary has suffered at the hands of serious critics of contemporary fiction, and somewhat disconcerted, as well, by the extravagant recognition that he has had from his most enthusiastic admirers. The injured tone that Hazard Adams takes in his recent survey of Cary criticism, as he contemplates the "woefully small" body of intelligent and detailed comment now available,[1] threatens to become the characteristic way of thinking about, and dealing with, Cary. We have come to a point, at any rate, where to approach Cary's novels at all is to be concerned inescapably, if not woefully, with his failure, by and large, to interest the best critical minds of our time. The present study attempts to explore and to explain what I take to be the basis of this failure. The fault, we shall see, lies less with the critics than with Cary himself.

Cary's consistently impressive performances in the sixteen novels that he wrote in the period from 1932, when his first novel, *Aissa Saved*, appeared, to 1959, when the posthumous *The Captive and the Free* was issued, are enough to assure us that a problem exists. The fiction produced in England during this period does not, on the whole, make Cary's work suffer by comparison, and will not, in any event, entirely explain the silence about him in high places. The explanation, I think, must rather be looked for in the particular conception of reality in which his novels are

---

[1] "Joyce Cary: Posthumous Volumes and Criticism to Date," *Texas Studies in Literature and Language*, I (Summer 1959), 289.

grounded. It is this conception which gives them their shape, their purport, and their vitality. But more importantly, as the pages that follow try to indicate, it is this same conception which is responsible for Cary's frequent failure to impose genuinely meaningful shape on his fiction—a failure that has made his novels, despite his extraordinary gifts, fall short of the best work done in this century.

In this study, I define the view of reality which both generates and impairs Cary's novels as indeterminateness—a species of captivating but disquieting philosophical and moral largesse. Chapter I traces the indeterminate cast of Cary's mind in his nonfiction, as he discourses on a wide range of problems—political, philosophical, aesthetic, religious. We find him driven to a kind of intellectual reluctance because he is so loath to slight the infinite variety and multiplicity of reality. Chapter II examines all of Cary's novels, except those in the second trilogy, in an effort to indicate how indeterminateness has from the outset affected both the form and substance of his fiction. Chapters III, IV, and V are devoted to a detailed study of the second trilogy—*Prisoner of Grace, Except the Lord,* and *Not Honour More*—the last three novels published during Cary's lifetime. As Cary's culminating novelistic achievement, in scope, import, and technique, these works will serve as a focal text for our analysis of Cary's fictional world. In them we can discern most clearly the consequences for Cary's fiction of his indeterminate vision.[2]

The moral concern evinced in this study is neither inadvertent nor, I hope, naïve. We have lived through twenty-five years of a

[2] Frederick R. Karl's "Joyce Cary: The Moralist as Novelist," *Twentieth Century Literature,* V (January 1960), 183-196, is a recent attempt to account for Cary's failure to write fiction of the first rank; but Mr. Karl's explanation differs markedly from the one developed in the course of this study. I cannot consent to his view that Cary's characters lack sufficient irrationality to strike an acceptably modern note—surely to seem "really chaotic" is a questionable requirement to make of characterization in any period. Nor can I accept Mr. Karl's assertion that Cary's figures are creatures of passive will and inadequate intellectual power who are not sufficiently in conflict with one another. This is to misconstrue, it seems to me, the whole tenor of Cary's novels, which are grounded in mind, will, and antithesis.

formalistically preoccupied criticism which has achieved notable things for the study of literature, but which has had to do so, to some extent, at the expense of its relation to life and value—a particular misfortune for the novel. Either for this reason, or perhaps from sheer exhaustion, this formalism has hardened into triviality and jargon, and at present we can witness a number of attempts to reappraise the intent of criticism and to enlarge the scope of critical concern. Not enough account, however, is being taken, even now amongst the reconstructionists, of the essential and indestructible bond between the literary and the moral order.

We need to remember that today, as before, the writer—the novelist especially—apprehends his material meaningfully only as he judges it; the aesthetic choice arises out of, or is born together with, a moral cognition, a moral choice. All life cannot be for the serious writer, as it sometimes is for the tourist, simply and equally photographable. It is the novelist's intense conviction about, his assessment of, the quality of the life and conduct that he treats which determines his ordering and expression of it. That is to say, the business of the novel has always been, and continues to be, moral discrimination—no matter how difficult and subtle—and no great novelist has ever been indifferent to it, or more interested, for that matter, in other things. It is here that the individual novel begins—its very inspiration and substance consist of moral transactions—and in a sense, it is here that it ends as well, with all its action, all its figures, all its words made lucid, resonant, and urgent to the moral imagination. This process depends, of course, on the writer's power to convey and recreate experience; still, a work of fiction is addressed, at its best, not only to the emotions, but to the adult moral intelligence, which is to say that it exists in the service of life precisely because it enables us to measure, order, and master experience as well as merely to feel it. If the novelist's moral vision, his sense of human possibility, is shallow or slipshod, so too, inevitably, is his work. For all our aesthetic addictions in the past seventy-five years, no major writer has ever regarded art as an end in itself; and the classical program, to instruct and delight, is neither a jejune nor an obsolete formula for novelists, even if, with some, we may be forced to construe their intention to instruct largely as a means of their achieving a coherence that will delight. Our part, as critics and readers of fiction, is to perfect once again our response to, and estimate of, this subtle knot of value and feeling—and the ability to articulate them—which makes novels and novelists. The pressures of our age cannot fundamentally alter the classical and immutable character of this union, or its central importance to our well-being.

Of course, the widespread—perhaps much exaggerated—uncertainty about valid criteria for conduct in our century has been felt, disturbingly, in critical and creative practice, though one cannot help suspecting that difficult as life is, it is almost never so difficult, in this one particular, as we make it. Sophisticated critics have come to express a large and genial tolerance, an unwillingness to assess or proscribe behavior emphatically in our "fragmented" culture, or to hold a novelist accountable for his judgment of his matter, or even require him to make one, as though his novel had nothing really to do with human life, but were merely the execution of an exquisite autonomous design, or the liberation of wild, neutral energies. In this connection, the dubious dramatic ideal of the effaced author, and a tireless psychological delight in the analysis of consciousness for its own aimless, experiential sake, have both served only to aggravate an already regrettable habit of disclaiming responsibility. Mary McCarthy, reflecting on the modern novelists, herself included, who have succumbed to the enticement of total impersonality—ventriloquism, in fact—has recently put the matter well: "Certainly the common world that lies between the contemporary reader and the contemporary author remains unexplored, almost undescribed, just as queer and empty a place as Dickens' world would be if he had spent eight years recording the impressions of Fagin or the sensory data received by Uriah Heep in the slithery course of a morning's walk."[3] Occasionally, when they cut through such eccentric and trivial considerations, capable critics take preposterous pains to conceal from themselves that in interpreting and judging a work, they are, in some measure, making moral discriminations, not merely descanting *ad libitum* on "point of view," "structure," "texture," "controlling symbol," or, more recently, "society."

Criticism, however, can no longer afford to take refuge in the mere craft of fiction, in the nonhuman, nonnormative consideration. Our time demands better of us. Critics cannot help to restore sanity and balance to it, and to our literature, by pretending that there are no moral issues, that such issues reduce characteristic literary complexity, or that they have grown altogether too difficult or too elusive for rational consideration. The dogged escape from genuine, personal predication must cease to be our idiom, as novelists and critics; for Arnold's words are as timely as ever: "The question, *how to live,* is itself a moral idea; and it is the question which most interests every man, and with which, in some way or other, he is perpetually occupied." It must interest and occupy us today with an increased urgency, even a wholly new purport, in our art as in our lives, although some are able to speak to it only with earnest human injunctions in place of the hallowed formulations of a more confident age. Our novelists will not, of course, save us; but they can put us in a frame of mind where we wish to be saved and where we know something of what there is to save. There has perhaps never been a better occasion than the present for the novelist to be enjoined to speak in his own voice once again, in order that he may evaluate life as well as "render"

---

[3] "Characters in Fiction," *Partisan Review*, XXVIII, No. 2 (March-April 1961), 191. Wayne Booth's *The Rhetoric of Fiction* (Chicago: University of Chicago Press, 1961), which appeared, unfortunately, after my own book had gone to the printer, presents a comprehensive, perceptive account of the problems raised by the dramatic preoccupation of many novelists coming after Henry James. Booth's reservations about unreliable narrators and about the moral ambiguity that results from the effacement of the author may be portents of a welcome shift in critical thinking.

it; to tell us what we are and what we have done, but to preserve and enunciate for us also the knowledge of how to be human; to rejoice in, not regret, the contact between fiction and life and to confront in himself the relentless, endless succession of judgments which existence and art alike impose on us; in sum, to reach beyond the generalized prescriptions of the mere moralist and uncover for us, as only he can, the intricate reality of where we are in relation to the high exigency of where we should be. This is the peculiar work, not of science, philosophy, religion, psychology, or sociology, but of literature. For in one of its crucial aspects, literature, more than we have been willing to acknowledge—more, assuredly, than religion, whose sanctions lie elsewhere—is morality touched with emotion.

The moral component of literature is unquestionably a very old revenant indeed, haunting in our own century the work of Irving Babbitt and Paul Elmer More, and, in recent years, that of Yvor Winters, Dr. Leavis, and other distinguished critics more intermittently. But our experience of the full extent and import of the New Criticism, with its theoretical exaltation of the purely literary dimension—whatever that may be—has given us a means of exploring this component more explicitly, yet more subtly, more responsibly, and more fruitfully than ever before. I can only hope that my own partial adoption of a moral perspective in this study is flexible and sensitive enough not to discredit the principle, and to be worthy of Cary's work, which, again and again, manifests gifts of the highest order. In a sense, a critic is a man speaking to men about a man. There is no man's memory that I should be more loath to do violence to than Joyce Cary's.

Among the "woefully small" body of intelligent comment available on Cary, Barbara Hardy's "Form in the Novels of Joyce Cary" and Andrew Wright's pioneer book-length study, *Joyce Cary: A Preface to His Novels,* stand high indeed. My debt to Professor Wright may be somewhat belied by the frequent departures from his own views that occur in the following pages; but that debt is nonetheless a very real one.

Enrique Anderson-Imbert, Richard Ruland, and Norman E. Nelson read versions of this study in manuscript and made recommendations from which it has profited.

To Allan Seager I wish to express an obligation which goes beyond such matters as counsel and encouragement, precious as these have been. If it were possible to do such things, I should want to thank him, simply, profoundly, for being what he is, as a man and a novelist, and allowing me to know him. My debt to Mark Spilka for so much wise and passionate conversation, even before he employed his brilliant critical gifts in an effort to save this book from its most stubborn perversities, is immense. Lastly, I hope that to my wife, who during the writing heroically preserved a stable and beneficent universe about me, the dedication of this volume will give, perhaps, some feeble measure of a gratitude which is essentially immeasurable.

R. B.

Berkeley, California
August 1961

# CONTENTS

# The
# *Indeterminate World:*

## *A Study of the Novels of Joyce Cary*

# I

## The Reluctant Sage and the Objective Relative

In 1920, when he was thirty-two years old, Joyce Cary settled at
Oxford with his wife and began a course of study to prepare himself for writing novels. His earlier years had afforded him a rich
and varied experience of the world. As a young man he had studied
painting at the University of Edinburgh, read law at Trinity
College, Oxford, and spent time in Paris with his close friend and
schoolmate John Middleton Murry; later he fought in the Balkan
War of 1912-1913, served briefly as a member of Sir Horace
Plunkett's Cooperative Society in Ireland, joined the Nigerian
service as a magistrate, fought and was wounded in the Cameroons
campaign of 1915-1916, and, finally, served as District Officer of
Borgu in Nigeria, until his war injuries forced him out of the political service in 1920. Experience alone, however, was not in Cary's
view a sufficient preparation for serious fiction. Although in 1920
he had published ten stories in *The Saturday Evening Post* under
the pseudonym Thomas Joyce, when he turned to more ambitious
work he discovered that he was unable to satisy himself. "What, in
fact, I needed," he says of this period,

> was a new education, in ethics, in history, in philosophy.
> Although I did not know it, how could I, my mind was split.
> I had no real religion, no integrated idea of the world. I be-
> lieved vaguely in God and I believed vaguely in science, but
> I had never seen the need to reconcile the mechanism of the
> scientific idea and the free creative soul of the world, of which,
> in art especially, I was so intensely and continuously aware.
> And until I had made such reconciliation, I could not even

write dialogue. My characters perpetually raised questions I could not answer and yet I knew that I must not run away from them, I knew I must not falsify my characters and their speech in order to hide my own inadequacy. That was the way to bad and superficial work.[1]

From 1920 to 1932, when his first novel, *Aissa Saved,* was issued, Cary published nothing but worked steadily at re-educating himself, repairing his intellectual omissions, and achieving an "integrated idea of the world." His success was sufficiently meaningful, to himself at least, to allow him, in the interval from 1932 to his death in March 1957, to produce sixteen novels, more than thirty-five short stories, four political treatises, a book on aesthetics, some twenty-five literary essays and another twenty-nine on general subjects, together with an attic full of manuscripts which remain, for one reason or another, unpublished.[2] Having solved his intellectual problem, his only difficulty since 1932, he tells us, was to choose what he should write next, what aspect of the rich world he should explore.[3]

In discussions of his own work, Cary has repeatedly insisted upon this close connection between his systematic thought and his ability to write his mature fiction. He has been careful too, however, to point out that the novel is by no means a form which accommodates itself easily to philosophical discourse. "I don't care for philosophers in books," he says. "They are always bores. A novel should be an experience and convey an emotional truth rather than arguments."[4] A number of his most sympathetic critics, paying perhaps more attention to the connection than Cary's qualification will allow, have traced the appearance of some of Cary's leading ideas in his fiction. Walter Allen deals with Cary's

[1] Quoted in George Steinbrecher Jr., "Joyce Cary: Master Novelist," *College English*, XVIII, No. 8 (May 1957), 389.

[2] See Andrew Wright, "Joyce Cary's Unpublished Work," *London Magazine*, V, No. 1 (January 1958), 35-42.

[3] See Steinbrecher, p. 389.

[4] "An Interview with Joyce Cary," conducted by John Burroughs and Alex Hamilton, *Paris Review*, VIII (Winter 1954-1955), 65.

views on the role of the creative imagination and on the subjective nature of reality, as these appear in the novels; Andrew Wright calls one chapter of his book on Cary, "Theme: The Politics of Freedom"; and Ruth G. Van Horn combines both notions in her essay, "Freedom and Imagination in the Novels of Joyce Cary".[5] Such tabulations of Cary's philosophical position as it emerges in his fiction are useful, even if they do not account for the whole of a given novel's effect, or for the whole of Cary's thought. There is possible, however, a less literal and mechanical approach to Cary's nonfiction, an approach which can penetrate to the quality of mind lying back of both his specific ideas and his fiction, and which can help us toward an explanation of the nature, the achievement, and the limitation of his greatest work.

Such an examination would concern itself not with Cary's specific ideas and beliefs so much as with their mode, their common cast. Because his view of the world is, as he often maintains, coherent, it is also more coherent than he perhaps knows. There are striking family resemblances among his ideas, which, whether he is discussing politics, art, philosophy, or religion, reveal a governing habit of mind. His fiction is more profoundly affected by this habitual tendency than by any of the individual explicit ideas which have thus far supplied the substance of most Cary criticism. In particular, Cary's greatest work, the two trilogies consisting of *Herself Surprised* (1941), *To Be a Pilgrim* (1942), and *The Horse's Mouth* (1944), and, secondly, *Prisoner of Grace* (1952), *Except the Lord* (1953), and *Not Honour More* (1955), may be studied profitably in such a context. Cary's characteristic inclinations as a thinker make inevitable the first-person narrative method

---

[5] Walter Allen, *Joyce Cary* ("Writers and Their Work"; London: Longmans, Green, 1954); Andrew Wright, *Joyce Cary: A Preface to His Novels* (London: Chatto and Windus, 1958); Ruth G. Van Horn, "Freedom and Imagination in the Novels of Joyce Cary," *Midwest Journal*, V, No. 1 (Winter 1952-1953), 19-30. For similar studies, see [Julian Maclaren Ross], "Story of a Full Life," *Times Literary Supplement* (November 11, 1949), p. 732; Steinbrecher, *op. cit.*: and Carlyle King, "Joyce Cary and the Creative Imagination," *Tamarack Review* (Winter 1959), pp. 39-51.

utilized throughout the trilogies; they explain much of the success
of that method within the individual trilogy novels; and they
account, ultimately, for the moral and aesthetic limitations which
may, in the long run, keep the trilogies, the second especially,
from taking their place with the best fiction of their time.

Before we turn to the tenor of Cary's mind, we would do well to
pause over one of his central specific ideas, partly because he has
so often advanced it as the basis for all his fiction, and partly because it will prepare us to deal with the large controlling patterns
of his thought. In one of his most succinct formulations of this
idea, Cary says,

> The world loves its own creation, which is its life. Not
> merely the artist, but every man and woman, begins from
> childhood to create for himself a world to which, as creator,
> he is deeply attached. Each of these worlds is highly complex
> and extensive. One man, for instance, does not create for
> himself only a home, a business, a family, but a religion, a
> political idea, a nation, a world idea. He creates them in his
> imagination, and lives in them. Deprived of them, or even
> any large part of them, he would wither and die.[6]

Cary is not talking about an insurmountable metaphysical or epistemological isolation that cuts men off completely from one
another. "Men are together in feeling, in sympathy," he says,
"but alone in mind." Still, the isolation in mind is formidable and
quite irremediable: "We are alone in our own worlds. We can
sympathize with each other, be fond of each other, but we can
never completely understand each other. We are not only different in character and mind, we don't know how far the difference
goes."[7]

    [6] "The Way a Novel Gets Written," *Harper's*, CC (February 1950), 91. For
other formulations of this idea see "The Novelist at Work: A Conversation between
Joyce Cary and Lord David Cecil," *Adam International Review*, XVIII, Nos. 212-213
(November-December 1950), 19; and Joyce Cary, *Art and Reality* (Cambridge:
Cambridge University Press, 1958), pp. 72-74.
    [7] *First Trilogy* (New York: Harper, 1958), p. x.

We can readily trace, if we wish, this notion of the private world through most of the fiction that Cary has produced since 1932, along with the essentially objective or dramatic cast that it gives to his work. He has been content, in what has come to seem the best modern manner, to remove himself as author from his novels and stories and allow his characters to convey their own unique, individual worlds. His very first novel, *Aissa Saved,* involves Cary's remarkable entry into the mind and world of a primitive African girl who commingles missionary Christianity and pagan worship until they yield her a culminating apocalyptic vision. Of this novel Cary says that it "deals with individual religion, that is to say, the beliefs or unconscious assumptions which actually govern conduct. These assumptions are very different in every person. That is to say, everyone has his own faith. Of course each great religion does draw large numbers of people together in general rules of conduct, and general statements of belief. But each person makes a particular application of the rules drawn from all kinds of sources."[8] In *Aissa,* then, Cary's notion of a personal and private reality is dealt with primarily in religious terms. He continues to render the African religious sensibility and the world that it shapes brilliantly in *The African Witch* (1936), with its close scrutiny of juju. The other two African novels are similar achievements of empathic penetration. In *An American Visitor* (1933) Cary deals with the evolution of Marie Hasluck, an American visitor to Nigeria, from a vague, unrealistic liberalism to a genuine grasp of African life, a growth which is brought about chiefly by her increasing intimacy with Bewsher, a somewhat Africanized District Officer. Marie's world, in effect, undergoes correction and amplification under the tutelage of Bewsher and Africa. In *Mister Johnson* (1939) Cary deals once again with a native formulation of reality, this time the spontaneous, childlike world of a young African clerk who moves, during the course of the novel, from joyfulness and song to a touching death, as a result of his imperfect

[8] "My First Novel," *Listener* (April 16, 1953), p. 637.

assimilation of British culture and his unconquerable naïveté. His simple created world does not accord sufficiently with imperialistic complexities to see him through his life. In Cary's novels of childhood, *Charley Is My Darling* (1940) and *A House of Children* (1941), this same leading idea is in force. The first of these deals with a group of London children evacuated to rural England during the Second World War. It is concerned particularly with young Charley Brown's adolescent world and the place that delinquency and love have in it as it brushes against the harsh adult universe. *A House of Children* is an evocation of the childhood world of the novel's narrator, Evelyn Corner, set down with compelling tenderness and sensitivity. It is here that Cary introduces first-person narrative into the novels, although the autobiographical context—Cary's own childhood in Northern Ireland is the source of the book—makes the technique rather a different thing from his later use of it in the trilogies. The two women's novels, *The Moonlight* (1946) and *A Fearful Joy* (1949), are devoted to the same kind of exploration, this time of feminine worlds; and a number of Cary's best short stories are also grounded in the idea.[9]

It is in the trilogies, however, that the created worlds of individual human beings receive their fullest exposition. In order to exploit this concepion as fully as possible, Cary, not content with a mere Jamesian limited third-person objectivity, all but obliterates himself as author. He does so by creating six different authors, all of whom write their own novels in the first person. As a result, he is in a position to allow his narrators an unstinted autonomy in the projection of the worlds that they have shaped for themselves, as well as six different styles in which to do so. *Herself Surprised* is concerned with Sara Monday's domestic world and with the

[9] See, for example, "The Old Strife at Plant's," *Harper's*, CCI (August 1950), 80-96 [a discarded portion of *The Horse's Mouth*]; "A Special Occasion," *Harper's*, CCIII (September 1951), 97-98; "The Evangelist," *Harper's*, CCV (November 1952), 88-89; "Spring Song," *London Magazine*, I (March 1954), 29-31; "A Hot Day," *Time and Tide* (June 16, 1956), p. 710; and, for the most remarkable example, "The Breakout," *New Yorker* (February 2, 1957), pp. 28-36.

womanly force that sustains it. *To Be a Pilgrim* is Thomas Wilcher's account of politics, society, and family in the coherent world of Edwardian England, which is for him the only reasonable, sensible reality, and by which he gauges the decadence of the present. *The Horse's Mouth* is Gulley Jimson's testimony to the world of spirituality and art, threatened perpetually by stupidity, indifference, and hatred, preserved by an exertion of heroic, but almost inhuman, energy and dedication. His driving need to create new paintings, new forms, new modes is directly at variance with Wilcher's hostility to innovation; the private world which rests upon constant renewal clashes with the world of loving conservatism. In the second trilogy, Nina Latter reveals, in her narrative, *Prisoner of Grace,* her confused world of political expediencies, questionable loyalties, and burgeoning duplicity—all of it shaped during thirty years of marriage to Chester Nimmo. Chester advances his own surprising religious view of human affairs in *Except the Lord*. And Jim Latter presents his plea for his doomed world of honor and duty, along with his ranting hatred of Chester and political machination, in *Not Honour More*. Our examination of the trilogies—Cary's most significant and characteristic work— in the later chapters of this study will take us beyond Cary's freely proffered explanation of the private created world; but we should do him an injustice if we did not recognize it as the inspiration of these novels, of their conception, their substance, their technique, and of their miscarriage, as well.

The notion of a private universe which each man creates for himself, and without which he cannot continue to live, raises questions—even if, as Cary maintains, men are alone only in mind rather than feeling—about ultimate reality and truth. If each man construes experience subjectively, we may wish to know whether there is a verifiable external and objective reality, whether men have access to the true nature of things, or must rest content with narrow individual fantasies. Does one man's created world, we may ask, approximate such an objective reality more closely than another's? Can we, that is, refer to some criterion of adequacy by which to measure the scope and accuracy of a man's grasp of experience? On the whole, Cary does not occupy himself extensively, even in his nonfiction, with these questions. He is not directly or centrally concerned with this kind of judgment. As a result, the doctrine of private worlds becomes a way of avoiding real commitment to any particular private world. Cary tends to rest content with an account of the possibilities of diverse belief, so that his outlook is implicitly relativistic.

His own world, on the other hand, suffers from none of the narrowness that he assigns to other men. In both his speculative thought and the practice of his art, he is exempt from his own formula. The mere conception of a multiplicity of private worlds immediately frees Cary, in mind as well as feeling, from the confines of such a limited world. And his extraordinary skill at rendering, in novel after novel, the subjective worlds of African natives, children, women, and an array of men quite unlike himself—all unmistakably from within—bespeaks a transcendence, again both in mind and feeling, of his own doctrine. The trilogies alone shatter it at one blow. It is as though, in his own life, he was intent upon escaping the limitation that he found inherent in the human condition itself. Whether he was aware of such an intention or not, we can trace manifestations of it in the cast of his mind as he considered a variety of political, philosophical, and aesthetic problems. Out of a dissatisfaction with narrowness, he fashioned his own uncommonly spacious universe. He did so by fending off commitment, or by committing himself, in large measure, to a relativism founded on multiplicity, inclusiveness, and indeterminateness. Our purpose in the remainder of this chapter is to trace this process in order to measure its effects upon Cary's fiction in the chapters to come.

Cary's thinking teems with the multiplicity and variety of the world. When, in *Power in Men* (1939), he gives his fullest systematic account of his political theory, he inclines again and again toward an encompassing diversity. Liberty is for him not a negative idea denoting the absence of external restraint, but a positive, and ultimately irresistible, power of action and self-realization in men.[10] In the very nature of things, liberty, he maintains, tends inexorably to devolve upon larger numbers of men, new races, new classes, so that democracy, which is nothing more than government organized for the widespread distribution of power, is inevitable throughout the world. The centralized, monolithic state clashes with the nature of man and society. Cary projects, instead, a vision of turbulent thriving variety :

> It is because a modern democratic society possesses much liberty, and therefore much creative power, that it appears more unstable, more full of conflict and confusion than any yet seen.
> This tumult of life is the health of society. There is no more reason to be troubled by it than by the noise and inventiveness of a healthy child. It is not a sign of degeneration but of growing power. It does not argue for repression of liberty, but for its protection. . . .[11]

In yet another expression of the salutary effects of the distribution of power Cary says,

> Democracy has greater strength than any autarchy. It can stand much greater tension and disorder. It has astonishing power of recovery after defeats, which always destroy an autarchy. But it owes this power to a division of real government.

[10] *Power in Men* (London: Nicholson and Watson, 1939), pp. 2-7.

[11] *Ibid.*, p. 36. See also Cary's *The Case for African Freedom* (Searchlight Books; London: Secker and Warburg, 1941), p. 122, where he argues that even the most advanced states in the world waste nine-tenths of their potential by their inability to provide the particular education and job needed by each of their diverse members. "But," he maintains, "the ideal state, that which gives to all its members the best chance of happiness and realization, and makes the best use of their different powers, is obviously that with the greatest variety of social and economic organization."

> This division is itself the consequence of liberty and the means of progress. . . . The division of political power in the form of wealthy parties, trusts, unions, and associations is the means of political experiment and progress.[12]

The distribution of liberty is not merely a characteristic and inevitable tendency; it affords also the only objective standard of judgment by which to decide particular issues:

> Bentham's norm does not apply. But there is a norm which would, in the past, have applied to all three conflicts—for votes, for education, for economic power—a norm of liberty: the greatest liberty; that is, the greatest power of mind and body to the greatest number.
>
> Such a norm stands against the man so: How far has he realized his native powers? And against a state: How far has it enabled men to realize their powers?[13]

The rich diversity of interest which flourishes in a democratic state can be safeguarded best by the action of multiform pressure groups. These promote the devolution of power and afford each individual citizen a means of expressing his unique political and economic character, as the mere right to vote cannot hope to do:

> A man with a single vote in a constituency of thirty thousand has the choice of two or perhaps three members, each with a programme. The programmes differ, no doubt, in their main principles, but they are extremely vague in detail. A voter is lucky who finds any one of them completely in agreement with his own views; and even then he is only asked to decide general principles.
>
> But if the same man belongs, let us say, to a trade union, or trade association, a cyclists' or motorists' league, a benefit society, the Anglers' Association and the Footpath Society, he exerts through each a direct power upon government

[12] *Power in Men*, p. 143. Elsewhere Cary says, "The ideal state . . . is an abstract notion. It ignores the creative liberty of man which realizes the good, as well as evil, in an infinity of new forms," *ibid.*, p. 70.

[13] *Ibid.*, p. 76.

which exactly represents his will in each department of action.

For instance, as a miner he wants not only certain improvements in pay and hours, which belong to the general policy of his party, but he is interested in special safety regulations; in the operation of a steel cartel, as affecting prices of coal; in a thousand details of policy important only to miners. His trade union expresses his will in these details. But as a nonconformist he is interested in education. His party has a general programme for education, but he wants special consideration for his own schools. His church organization, through its paid secretaries and central officials, will express his will in these details. As a fisherman injured by the pollution of rivers he acts through the Anglers' Association with all the power belonging to millions of fishermen. . . .

Thus this man, apart from his political vote, is represented in actual politics by a group of active powers which taken together are exactly correspondent to his individual character. They are truly representative of that man and only of that man.[14]

Thus, to the formidable variety of unique voters, each bent on realizing his own powers and interests, Cary adds a swarm of clashing pressure groups, until his state becomes a vision of seething multiplicity. The state exists, in a measure, to preserve, realize and extend the multifarious interests of its people. Any view which tends to limit or confine so variegated a process is unacceptable to Cary. The Hegelian dialectic, for example, is far too simple-minded. "It does not square," Cary says, "with the facts of history or psychology. It has never succeeded in telling us, as it should, what is going to happen next in the process of history. It does not even reveal the process of thought. A man may think by jumping from an idea to the opposite, or he may not. He may fly off at a tangent."[15] So too, Cary feels, with Marx's meager class dichot-

---

[14] *Ibid.*, pp. 110-112. Cary's *Process of Real Freedom* (London: Michael Joseph, 1943), is largely devoted to an amplification of these views on the role of pressure groups.

[15] *Power in Men*, p. 45.

omy, which misrepresents the complexity of a nation's economic life:

> The class war as a war-cry of the continuous revolution is equally founded in abstraction. It neither exists in any real society nor can it be made to exist. The real conflict is between groups which form a cross section of classes. For instance there has always been conflict between producers and consumers; between the country workers who want good prices for their crops and town workers who need cheap food; miners producing coal or ore and steel workers using it. Moreover the finished product of one trade is the raw material of another. This conflict exists in every society, whether democratic or communist.[16]

Attempts to minimize conflict within a society by standardizing education, so that men will share the same dogma and the same desires, strike Cary as quite misguided. Where such programs have been practiced, among primitive African tribes or in countries under priestly or caste rule, he maintains that two kinds of effects follow. If a high degree of uniformity is achieved, stagnation and political weakness result; with the destruction of its initiative, a great race can become the easy prey of foreign conquerors. Secondly, when such a system breaks down—it is constantly resisted by all men's inherent desire for liberty—those who have lived under it are powerless to judge for themselves and can be exploited by any demogogic spellbinder who comes along.[17] Beyond this, Cary insists that on the whole it is futile for any society to try to eliminate the natural diversity and uniqueness which must always characterize its members:

> Schemes to avoid the conflict of ideas by teaching all children the same things are based on a fallacy.... For each child inherits different powers and acquires by a different total experience. Among a hundred children given the same standard scheme, each will form a different personal idea.

[16] *Ibid.*, p. 138.
[17] *Ibid.*, pp. 22-23.

Countries with absolute education show precisely the same diversity of morals, manners, bitterness, spite, and moral degeneracy as democracies, as well as cynicism, hypocrisy and despair peculiar to themselves. Even in politics and religion they cannot secure uniformity. This fact is obscured by the necessary hypocrisy of an absolute police state, but it is seen at once when the absolute authority breaks down.

Education, therefore, gains nothing by denying the fact of a child's unique quality. It must treat each child as a free and distinct person, who cannot be deprived of his own private idea of the world.[18]

Thus the state's business is to secure for its members the liberty to fulfil their dissimilar natures, for it is substantially powerless, in the long run, to do anything else. Cary's political theory, then, whatever its validity, is of interest to us here for its advocacy of a multiformity in government capable of coping with the multiformity of society.

This vision of political multiplicity rests on Cary's view of the immeasurable multiplicity of reality at large. Speaking of people who try to live by simple precepts, copybook maxims, and slogans, whether political, artistic, or religious, he says,

They are the idealogues who force all history to fit some preconceived dialectic or blueprint, who see religion as a trick to keep the poor quiet, or alternatively, accept the miseries of poverty as ordained by God. They are people who have lost all contact with reality, who live in a fantastic world, and sooner or later they run headfirst into reality and it breaks them.

The reality which smashes every idealogue and his system is human nature, incessantly striving towards a personal achievement in a world which is essentially free and personal. For the actual world does not show the consistency of a machine, which is a repetition; on the contrary, nothing in the world of actual forms is ever repeated, not even the shape of a tree. Every event, like every individual, is unique, so that

[18] *Ibid.*, pp. 215-216.

the persistence of nature, as a whole, is not that of a mechanism, but of a living character, whose real existence is the only limitation on its freedom. To exist, at all, requires a personal elemental force [*sic*], but within this form there is an infinite variety of particular variation. A beech can take any shape so long as it remains a beech.[19]

This inexhaustible variety of the objective world is enhanced to infinity by human emotion and historical process:

The emotions are subject to neither analysis, division or measurement. So they can exist in an endless variety of qualities and intensities, both for the artist who expresses them and for those who receive his meaning, in an infinity of creation like that of history which never repeats itself, and for ever produces novel and unexpected events with the same constants of human and material nature. That is to say, history, and the arts which are so closely woven into the fabric of historical process, display an infinite variety and novelty of actual consequences.[20]

So manifold is reality, as Cary has it in a characteristic phrase, that "no dogmatic schema, however elaborate, can begin to classify the exuberance of actual events for a standard evaluation."[21] And this exuberance is further compounded by the creative imagination:

The same creative imagination which is necessary to every human being to decide the simplest problem of conduct, to answer such questions as "What exactly in this situation is important for me, and what is not?" "What will be the effect of my doing so-and-so?" also perpetually invents new arts, new political ideas, new religions, new machines, new fashions, new swindles. The world is changing while I write and rather faster than an hour ago when I began.[22]

[19] *Art and Reality* (Cambridge: Cambridge University Press, 1958), pp. 155-156.
[20] *Ibid.*, p. 142.
[21] *Ibid.*, p. 153.
[22] *First Trilogy,* p. xi.

In effect, Cary has it that the world is infinitely various and tends inevitably to become more so.

Art, which attempts to deal in a coherent way with the "exuberance of actual events," gets caught up in multiplicity too, as Cary reflects on its nature. Since it is subject to the continuous revolution worked by the creative imagination, changes in style follow one another ceaselessly. "The symbol, the symbolic system," says Cary, "is not only arbitrary, it is highly fragile. It is always dying. Fashions in art, in literature, are little more enduring than those of dress."[23] And the multiplicity and exuberance of events cannot be neglected by art without great loss. Allegory, for Cary, is an ineffectual and misguided mode because it belies the complexity of reality:

> Allegory gives a clear, a definite meaning; not to the soul, but to the conceptual judgment, and in a form of dry precept whose falsity is at once detected by the soul. For that soul does not live in a world of pedagogues laying down general laws, but in the free world of persons whose feelings are individual and whose actions are always particular. . . . Allegory is false because it lays down categorical imperatives for conduct in a world of particular and unique events. It treats the world as a mechanism whereas it is a world of free souls.[24]

Cary's suspicion of abstractions and moral absolutes can be detected here as well; we shall need to consider it further on in our discussion. But Cary is far from suggesting that art fall victim to the multiplicity of life. Its function, he maintains, is rather to uncover for our contemplation the beauty and order which are potential in the multiform possibilities of the universe:

> When we recognize beauty in any ordered form of art, we are actually discovering new formal relations in a reality

[23] *Art and Reality*, p. 71.
[24] *Ibid.*, p. 163.

3

which is permanent and objective to ourselves, which is part of that real that includes both human nature and its reactions to colour, line, mass and sound, and the material consistencies which sustain them. That is, we are recognising aesthetic meaning in the character of the universe. . . .

When the Impressionists devised their new technique to express and reveal their new intuition, they gave us a revelation of a beauty no one had seen before. But it had always been potential in the actual nature of the world of colour, light, paint and human sensibilities. They revealed a truth as a scientist reveals a new element. Such an element is true in the deepest sense. It is a part of the universal order of things.[25]

Such revelations by artists entail a difficult compromise between the multifariousness of life and the order of art. "The great problem before a writer," Cary asserts, "is to convey, in one work of art, one formal conception, a significance which is simple enough for immediate apprehension by the feelings of a reader, and yet not false to the immense complication of actual life . . . which in itself, of course, has no meaning, or such a confusion of meanings that it adds up to nonsense."[26] So crucial, for literature, is a writer's ability to confront "the immense complication of actual life," that out of the confrontation Cary shapes a definition of literary greatness. He is thinking, characteristically, of greatness as richness in scope:

> A great writer, in this sense, whether poet, historian or novelist, is one whose world of organized experience harmonizes into one coherent impression the largest area of actual confusion. Tolstoi's "War and Peace" is a deliberate attempt to make sense, both to mind and feeling, of the whole realm of human action and inhuman fate.[27]

The multitudinous world does more than afford a standard of

[25] *Ibid.*, pp. 138-139.
[26] "The Way a Novel Gets Written," p. 89.
[27] "On the Function of the Novelist," New York *Times* Book Review (October 30, 1949), p. 1.

greatness for Cary; it induces religious belief as well. In a B.B.C. interview conducted in 1957, the year of his death, Cary told Jack Morpurgo,

> I can't make sense of the world, myself, without religious faith. . . . [It] is essential to anybody who believes in creative freedom. The moment you believe in creative freedom you have to have some sense of unity because the world splits up into complete individuals. Each individual is separate, but we know directly that the world is full of things that unify it also. Therefore you must have some kind of religious idea to explain that sense of unity, to explain, for instance, how love is born throughout the world and goes on being born in every generation.

As we shall see, however, the "things that unify" Cary's world are continually giving way to the things that break it up. In the novels religion itself helps to fragment reality, because faith is treated as a private psychological, rather than a unifying metaphysical, phenomenon.

It becomes clear, then, that regardless of the subject engaging Cary, and quite apart from the specific problem which he is considering, his mind tends naturally to respond to the multiplicity of things. Some of the good consequences, for the trilogies, of this susceptibility are obvious enough. The rich profusion and interaction of attitudes, personalities, things, historical periods, ideas, social stations—the whole extraordinary range and diversity that distinguish the novels—have their source in this tendency. But less fortunate consequences occur as well. In order to define them, we shall need to examine the implications of Cary's multiplicity as it leads to other habitual modes of thinking.

We have seen how Cary's reluctance to be confined by his own schema of the private world gives him a taste for multiplicity. The same kind of reluctance takes him from multiplicity to a desire to incorporate into his thinking a number of dualities and antitheses.

Being so sensitive to the manifold possibilities of reality, he is loath
to choose among them. We can trace some of this characteristic
inclusiveness, once again, regardless of the specific matter in hand.
Politically, for example, Cary's positive definition of liberty as the
power to realize oneself and one's desires is aimed, largely, at his
wish to reconcile freedom with government intervention. In this
perspective, the English factory acts and the increasing state regu-
lation of the Liberal government of 1902-1914 do not so much
represent restraints on the liberty of employers as they do a significant increase in the real liberty of the British population at
large.[28] Just as his thinking comprehends both liberty and regula-
tion, it is prepared to deal with another of the everlasting political
contrarieties. "Competition and co-operation," he says, "are both
instinctive to man, they are both rooted in the nature of his liberty
and freedom, and they are both essential means of his realization
and his progress."[29] Cary's more general conceptions are equally
inclusive. Within the first seven pages of *Art and Reality* he touches
on the existence in the universe of both chaos and law, matter and
spirit, a subjective and an objective reality, and—rejecting Croce's
aesthetic—intuition and expression. The world, furthermore, is for
Cary both determined and free: "Although all events are determined, those that are ideas for action formed in some mind are
partly self-determined and unpredictable. This brings uncertainty
into every chain of causation where one link is the human will."[30]
Elsewhere, in a paragraph full of the dynamic eloquence that
dualism lends to his thought, Cary insists on preserving both mind
and body:

> This gap [between the sensuous impression and the purely
> reflective and critical act] is simply another representative of
> the mind-body gap, which all idealist philosophers and
> mechanists are so eager to get rid of: the first by abolishing

[28] *Power in Men*, pp. 30-31.
[29] *Ibid.*, p. 128.
[30] *Art and Reality*, p. 8.

the body and the second by abolishing the mind. Unfortunately, though they can contrive this abolition easily enough in words, it remains very definite to our experience. All of us are aware every day of the conflict between our will and bodily machine; no amount of willing, no amount of thinking can compel the body to be completely subservient. On the other hand, we are equally aware of their interdependence; mind needs body to exist and body needs mind for any purposeful activity; that is to say, this gap of which we are so acutely aware occurs within a unity. If we could imagine a motor-car complaining of the gap in its spark-plugs, we should hasten to explain that the gap, though certainly existing, is not only an essential part of its construction as a complete unity, but that without this gap it could not work.[31]

Very little of the created universe works either, for Cary, without some such gap between polarities. In an attempt to preserve the poles of both good and evil, he first dismisses as rather inadequate the traditional justification of evil. While it is said that men cannot be good unless they have the power to be evil, this explanation, Cary maintains, makes God responsible for evil. "But," he continues, "would we admire a nurse who took away the nursery fire-guard to please herself with the idea of the children's prudence in not being burnt alive?" Having now to defend the reality of evil on some other basis in order to preserve his duality, Cary proceeds to a remarkable alternative which joins man and God in an exciting finite enterprise:

It would be easier to believe what we see every day, that God's will is limited by obstacles which arise naturally, that evil exists because creative liberty is real, and because God really exists. Real existence in space-time involves limitation. That is, God could not abolish the evil that men do without abolishing man's liberty; but that is to abolish his own creative power. If liberty, the power of the cells, is necessary to the

[31] *Ibid.*, p. 28.

existence of man, the liberty of all nature is necessary to the real existence of God.

God in that case would not be responsible for the evil of the real world.[32] He would struggle with it as a man struggles to realize his own good will against limitations which are in his own real being. That struggle would then be the proof of God's real existence.[33]

Once again, the idea of God derives from the comprehensive design of Cary's universe. Yet theism is by no means the only possibility. "Thus those who believe," Cary says in his very next sentence, "in the personal God and those who believe in impersonal process can each be right. . . ." His desire to have things both ways extends to his speculations on art as well. We have noted already his insistence on both intuition and expression in *Art and Reality*. He is also concerned in that book to claim for the artistic process not only the intuition, which is the source of art, but the conceptual and rational powers of the mind, which organize and articulate perceptions; so that, in effect, a rigorous formal education will help rather than destroy a gifted writer. Cary believes, too, that art begins with the artist's intuitional discovery of something new about the world, that is, a real insight into the objective nature of things. Yet, because life is chaotic, the writer needs to impose on it a moral order "that does not present itself" in life itself.[34] Hence, Cary combines a fidelity to objective reality with a reliance on a devised order somewhat foreign to that reality. Being fully aware, also, of attempts by aestheticians and critics to merge form and content, Cary wishes still to preserve what he takes to be one of the inherent antagonisms of literary art:

> We are always told that [form and content] are inseparable, but this is true only in the art of philosophy. For the writer the situation is very much more complex. He has to

---

[32] "Omnipotence in theology means 'power to do all that is possible,' not 'power to do everything.' " [Cary's note.]

[33] *Power in Men*, pp. 263-264.

[34] *Art and Reality*, p. 164.

deal with language which consists, it is true, of forms which are also contents. That is to say, they are meanings. On the other hand he has his intuition, the emotional experience that he wishes to convey in all its original force. This is to be the content of his book, but when he gets to work he has to ask himself how the manipulation of words, themselves already charged with meaning, will convey this other larger meaning which is to be his content. And when he has put them together in scenes conceptually devised to convey this content, he has to ask himself if they do so; that is to say, he has, on the one hand, a set of forms, and on the other hand, the content which he wishes to convey. He is of course actually comparing two contents, that of the forms he has on the page and that of the content he has in his imagination. But in this comparison, the first set of forms, the symbols on the page, have a double aspect: that of their content, as symbols, sentence by sentence and page by page, and that of their total effect.[35]

The statement is shot through with a sense of the antipodal pull which it is the writer's business to incorporate and overcome. The old and the new provide yet another divergence which Cary wants to cure by inclusion. Referring to the debate in the press about whether the new Coventry Cathedral was to be a modern or traditional building, he makes a forceful statement of each point of view—a characteristic gift of his—and then proceeds to his own conclusion:

> Both sides, in short, had very good reasons, but what was really wanted at Coventry was what the church has had so often before, a new style, which refers to and recalls the old, as Early English referred to Norman and Perpendicular referred to Decorated, and yet had all the novelty, the excitement of the new creation.[36]

For Cary, art is primarily a mode of inclusion and works by means of the symbol, which is, he says, the only means "by which one

[35] *Ibid.*, pp. 96-97.
[36] *Ibid.*, p. 60.

individual mind can express itself in material form and so communicate with another. For the writer, this form is language."[37]
Out of the symbol's very defects, he adds, comes its extraordinary
joining power:

> As we have seen, [the symbol's] weakness is in its failure to
> be exact either as label, as concept—because it carries in-
> variably association of feeling—or as a consistent vehicle of
> emotion—because it is always sinking back into a mere sign.
> But since, however unstable, it combines both elements, it is
> the only means by which it is possible to achieve any unity
> between the knowledge of fact and the feeling about the fact,
> the machine and the soul, the universal consistencies and the
> individual character, so that they can be joined together in
> an ordered experience of the real which, we must suppose,
> includes them both in one total personal character of
> existence.[38]

And, in the eloquent concluding words of *Art and Reality*, Cary
pays tribute to the inclusive synthesizing power of great art, with
its unique and triumphant preservation of the rich dualism of
experience:

> It is only in great art and the logic of the subconscious
> where judgement has become a part of the individual emo-
> tional character that we move freely in a world which is at
> once concept and feeling, rational order and common emo-
> tion, in a dream which is truer than actual life and a reality
> which is only there made actual, complete and purposeful
> to our experience.[39]

As we move, in Cary's thought, from a sense of inexhaustible
variety, through a tendency to encompass antitheses, the next step
is inevitable. Inclusions are not likely to end in precise or specific
commitments. The mind which is scrupulous about not slighting
the multiplicity of reality is inclined to pull back from choice,

[37] *Ibid.,* pp. 57-58.
[38] *Ibid.,* p. 173.
[39] *Ibid.,* pp. 174-175.

which, by its very nature, limits and excludes possibilities. We can trace such a strain of indeterminateness in Cary's thinking, without, by any means, suggesting that it represents his whole intellectual life. That it exists at all as a tendency which we can begin to evaluate is sufficient for our purposes.

We have had occasion already to glance at Cary's sensitivity to historical change, to the "continuous revolution" which our creativeness imposes on us.[40] The idea is important enough in Cary's outlook to have served him centrally in three novels, *Castle Corner, To Be a Pilgrim,* and *A Fearful Joy,* all of which are concerned with the violation of the past by a continuing, irresistible present. In the context of commitment, the idea has additional implications. For example, speaking specifically about the succession of artistic styles and modes Cary says,

> A symbolic system of any kind quickly becomes ineffective, a bore. . . . The Symbol as thing, word, gesture, ballet-step, building, is a compound of concept and associations. A cathedral, a flag, like any other work of art is the product of conceptual thought designed to convey emotion by the associations attached to its form. But as a mere thing, it requires to have its associations renewed. It tends always to lose them and to sink into the empty object, the bare concept-label, the mechanical sign or gesture. The word becomes a word from a dictionary. The brush stroke, the style, of a painter becomes by repetition a term in his expression, analogous to a word. It is part of his language. He always makes that statement in that form. The new critics learn that language and teach it to the public. Pretty soon the public is seeing not a revelation of the real, but a fine example of So-and-so with all his characteristic tricks; and especially the new generation, taught the new language, see only the specimens, constructs in that language, and not the revelation. For the revelation has been made. The world has been illuminated for them.[41]

[40] *First Trilogy,* p. xi.
[41] *Art and Reality,* pp. 71-72.

Yet this unending sequence does not do away, in any final sense, with the symbolic system, or style, of a given period. For when sufficient time has passed, other associations begin to operate, renewing the force of a work of art. Thus, examining his newly discovered fondness for an old Victorian family painting that he had first seen and disliked in 1916, Cary says,

> From a contemporary portrait, or rather a portrait only a few years out-of-date, of two ladies and a child, the ladies in fashions which had just become ridiculous, in a room whose furniture had lately become demoded, the picture was changed into a period piece. Added to its effect was what had been felt and written about the Victorian age by historians, by novelists, in those forty years. Thus the whole mass of associations belonging to that picture and to the late Victorian style in which it was painted had become, not only enormously enlarged, but formalised within the idea of a period. This idea, the idea of a period and its character is, of course, also the creation of art. And as soon as it acquires a form and a meaning, it has a very powerful supercharge of value, not only aesthetic but general. It affects political and historical thought, the whole form of men's minds.[42]

In neither of these processes, the passing or the renewal of aesthetic modes, is Cary concerned with the fidelity of the art work to the reality of the period. Styles arrive and depart, but there appears to be no inherent truth in them, none of the intuition into the real nature of an actual world that Cary had spoken about earlier. Indeed, that historical actual world is reduced by Cary to "the idea of a period," a mere creation of art itself. Most of us, he suggests, are willing to rest content with such an approximation of historical truth. As a result, Cary tends to avoid individual valuations of periods and styles, preferring, instead, to point to an imaginative process. This indeterminate position is characteristic of a good deal of his thinking.

[42] *Ibid.*, pp. 80-81.

He is, for example, rather unreceptive to the idea of absolute truth. He says of his own philosophical views, "Perhaps I should repeat here that this picture of things, as I give it, is not intended for an absolute truth; no one can know what that is."[43] So too with the whole truth: "It is not valid to charge a writer with falsification because he emphasizes one truth rather than another. As for saying that he does not give the whole, that is absurd because the whole truth cannot be known."[44] Indeed, the philosophers who pretend to speak from such positions are merely artists presenting a personal view and substantiating it by contriving evidence. "The systematic philosopher, any philosopher," Cary says, "who attempts to convey any significant general idea about the world we know, the world we live in and suffer in, has like any other artist to select his facts to suit his idea. He has to devise a form to express and communicate his total meaning. And this form will dictate his valuation of details."[45] Plato is for Cary a great absolutist offender. "Plato's state," he says,

> is absolute, it is repressive, it imposes strict censorship on the arts, and its rulers judge what is good not by asking what is good for men, but simply, what is good. . . . Moreover, this good is imagined by Plato as a fixed and complete scheme. . . .
>
> Also, since he imagined the form or idea of the good as given immediately to his rulers by a kind of mystical insight, in practice he sought it in his own mind.
>
> The books of the *Republic* are full of discussion about the nature of government, of art, of education; in all of them we know that the conclusion is already formed. Plato is already convinced of the truth. He knows it in his mind, by insight. In the last resort, Plato's guardian philosophers are simply himself and the idea of the good is Plato's idea of the good. He belongs to the great class of religious and political theorists who have said in all ages, "I know inside me what is good for men, and they must do it."[46]

[43] *Ibid.*, p. 13.
[44] *Ibid.*, p. 115.
[45] *Ibid.*, p. 17.
[46] *Power in Men*, pp. 40-41.

In answer to the absolutist, who rushes toward commitment, Cary advances his own idea of toleration.

This idea, familiar enough in liberal thought, ought particularly to be seen in the context of the tendencies in Cary's thinking that we have been marking. It is one of the most direct consequences of his penchant for multiplicity and inclusiveness, and it points, like Cary's other indeterminate ideas, toward the conception underlying the trilogies. Here is Cary's formulation:

> A scientist who believes that the search for truth is the most important thing in the world does not need to quarrel with another who differs with him about the truth. One may think that the world is made of little bits of matter; the other that it is a system of waves or vibrations. Each has convincing proof. But both, if they are wise say, "Perhaps we are both wrong.". . .
>
> In the same way, an artist who believes that his own work is good and another's bad does not need to hate or murder the other artist. Art is purely ideal. It is not bound to any facts. Its variety and the conflict of tastes and fashions are therefore inevitable as long as artists are free to produce what they like.
>
> Thus the conflict of scientists does not belong to the nature of science, which is the search for truth, and the quarrels of artists do not belong to that of art, which is their creative liberty acting in its proper function. Conflict and quarrels arise only when scientists regard their facts and ideas as final and when artists regard art as complete.
>
> Toleration is essential to both because without toleration they contradict their own grounds of action, which are:
> Science is not yet complete. Art can never be complete.
>
> Thus all the ideal forms, so far as they are not false, have equal title to be respected.

That is to say, toleration belongs to the very idea of truth and the free mind seeking truth.[47]

It is, again, a commonplace of liberal thought, to which we all do formal obeisance, but Cary takes it a good deal more seriously than most of us. He gives to the tentativeness of scientific and artistic formulations and the elusiveness of truth rather an uncommon emphasis. And what is more remarkable still, he insists on the practice of intellectual toleration as well as the principle. For the teacher, he prescribes the following position: "Here are the facts as I know them and the ideas based on them, but both may be wrong."[48] And his own practice as a novelist is governed by similar considerations. Recalling the three years which he spent wrestling with the composition of his first novel, *Aissa Saved*, he indicates that a misguided eagerness to advance his own views caused much of the difficulty:

> When I had found answers to my own problems, I tried to put them in the book. Like anyone who has broken, with difficulty, out of a confused foggy disintegrated state of feeling and thought into moderately clear going, I wanted to tell everyone how to find the road. I did not realize that everyone has his own fog and therefore needs a special map; that most of those who wanted a way out had found it for themselves, and that the rest would rather stay where they were; that is, different people needed different kinds of faith; 'true' for them.[49]

Cary brings together here the antecedents from which his advocacy of toleration derives: the pathetic, hopeless, idiotic pride of the intellectual neophyte thinking to bring light to his brothers; the same young enthusiast's discovery that he has no brothers, really, for everyone has his own fog and needs his own map; and then his melancholy submission to isolation and separateness, which

[47] *Ibid.*, pp. 224-225.

[48] *Ibid.*, p. 230. By the time Cary came to write *Art and Reality*, he modified this position, though still acknowledging its desirability; see especially pp. 45-50.

[49] Preface to *Aissa Saved* (Carfax edition; London: Michael Joseph, 1952), p. 10.

annuls, in the name of toleration, his intellectual enterprise, assurance, and ambition. One submits, in this view, to the circle of oneself, yet mistrusts one's own formulations equally with those of other men; only demonstrable falseness limits the number of points of view turning in the air at any one moment. We can see toleration flirting with relativism in Cary's representation of human faith:

> [Ideas about ultimate reality] differ according to the temperament, education and characters of persons. For example, millions of men believe that:
> (1) God is a person who loves men and commands them to preach his message of love to the world, thus changing it from evil to good.
> (2) God is an impersonal order caring nothing for men, who can only acquire happiness by retiring from the world, which is unchangeably evil.
> (3) Universal war and competition are necessary functions of man, ordained by a higher power or process for his own pleasure or man's good.
> (4) Peace and universal cooperation are necessary states of mankind, ordained by a higher power or natural order for man's happiness.
> None of these ideas is grounded in facts demonstrably false. They arise from ideas which are either purely subjective and beyond test, or from scientific hypotheses based in some certain facts, like the evolutionary theory, the herd instinct; and children take to them readily according to their natural powers and their experience. The first is, of course, more common in northern Europe, where the family experience is of parents with Christian ideas; the second in the East. Children of a natural pugnacity or with a secret inferiority complex incline to the third. If it is represented to them they seize on it as natural to their powers. Children of a naturally affectionate nature or those who suffer from the neuroses classified under the general heading of escape incline to the fourth.[50]

Cary's toleration, as we might suspect, makes him an exacting and

[50] *Power in Men,* pp. 226-227.

skeptical critic of morality, which customarily requires specific, resolute commitments. In the course of his advocacy of the greatest liberty for the greatest number as a political criterion—a characteristically indeterminate standard—he adopts a severely critical tone toward the more traditional guide.

> Moral standards are the same everywhere. All people admire courage, generosity, unselfish devotion. But moral approval has been given to the Nazi revolution as well as the Spanish. It has been used to justify the shooting of Communists in Spain as well as Kulaks in Russia.
> Of course one can say, "The Russian revolution was justified and moral; the Nazi was immoral"; but if anyone asks why, the only answer is, "Because it is obvious, because every decent person must think so." These are different ways of saying, "Because I feel it so." . . .

> Though moral values are constant in the idea, they no more provide a true standard for specific action than the aesthetic values, colour, form, tone can give a permanent law by which critics can judge new works of art.[51]

Along with their vagueness, moral ideas appear impotent to Cary. While law among men is to some extent an expression of a common morality, it is ultimately police enforcement that keeps order and protects the peaceful majority. "Moral ideas," Cary says, "exist wherever men are, and there is more goodness and good nature in every community than strife; but one bully, one lunatic fool or drunken brute will abolish their effect."[52] Furthermore, moral problems occur in a bewildering variety of unique forms which must strain any rigid system. We live in a world, Cary insists, "in which every moral problem is itself unique, in which the law courts spend millions of money and years of time assessing separately each individual charge."[53] Sounding very Existentialist indeed, Cary speaks elsewhere of a world charged throughout

[51] *Ibid.*, pp. 69-70.
[52] *Ibid.*, p. 184.
[53] *Art and Reality*, p. 157.

with freedom and individuality, "where moral principles must be like those of an army on the march, inventive, flexible, forever balanced between the immediate circumstances (this man's nature, this crisis) and an ultimate end (the good, the true, etc.) and a final judgment is final only in the sense that it is the best (however bad) solution of an immediate problem."[54]

Judging by these observations, one might suppose that Cary has little, if any, use for morality. When a morality becomes sufficiently inventive and flexible, submitting eagerly to the shape and pressure of conditions and events instead of subjecting them to its own forms, it may well cease to be a morality at all. But, on the contrary, when he turns to consider fiction, Cary is careful to give morality even more than its traditional due. "All good novels," he says,

> are about morals. . . . A good novel is about what people do, and why they do it, and how it succeeds in making them happy, or otherwise; and these are moral questions. The idea that there is something aloof and dull about a novel that takes morals seriously is completely wrong: the truth is the other way round. . . . The novel reader may belong to Ethel M. Dell's public, or he may prefer Conrad, James, and Lawrence, but what he is interested in from first to last is conduct, that is, morals. The greatest writers of the world are just those who take the greatest interest in morals: it is because of that they are so exciting to read. Think of Dickens, Tolstoy, Hardy, and Conrad.[55]

And Cary unhesitatingly reinforces this view of morality as a criterion in *Art and Reality*: "We judge the value of the work finally by its revelation of a moral real. The power and quality of the artist's craft is in the force and authority of his revelation."[56] Beyond this, the writer imposes on the world which he creates in

---

[54] Preface to *Castle Corner* (Carfax edition; London: Michael Joseph, 1952), p. 6.
[55] "A Novelist and His Public," *Saturday Review* (November 27, 1954), p. 36.
[56] Page 150.

his fiction "a moral order that does not present itself in life. It is an ideal order which remains an object of attainment for that writer in the world as he knows it in fact."[57]

Yet, for all this, if we scrutinize Cary's notion of morality in fiction, it tends to resolve itself into a typically indeterminate dew. In connection with Tolstoy's *Kreutzer Sonata,* he says that we regularly distinguish between aesthetic and moral judgment, so that we might say of this story that it is a brilliant work but morally it is all wrong. "But," Cary continues,

> I suspect that our aesthetic judgment is still charged with a certain sensibility which we must call moral. We are struck, for instance, by a certain dignity and distinction in the handling of the story. With all its violence it has nothing exaggerated, nothing of what we call a false note, and these are moral attributes derived from a moral taste. If we compare *The Kreutzer Sonata* with some other tale of violence, let us say, *No Orchids for Miss Blandish,* we see at once a difference that is not purely aesthetic. You can say, if you like, that it resides in the mind of the writer, in his attitude towards violence, towards the whole story; but that is simply to say that moral sensibility is part of his genius. One cannot, in fact, split up the personality of a man—the sensible character of his being—into the aesthetic and the moral.[58]

Apart from the question of the inseparability of the moral and aesthetic sensibility—Cary's main concern here—we may consider his curious notion of the moral component itself as it informs the aesthetic. He speaks of "dignity and distinction in the handling of the story," of "nothing exaggerated" and no "false note," ideas, which, if they are perhaps peripherally moral, rather conspicuously avoid the central moral consideration, the judgment of conduct. So too, arguing for the moral preoccupation in Proust which helps to make him a great writer, Cary urges us to examine our reaction to Proust as we read: "You will find that all the time, at the very

[57] *Art and Reality,* p. 164.
[58] *Ibid.,* p. 136.

4

centre of your preoccupation, a moral judgment is at work, inquiring, comparing, discovering."[59] It is curious here too that
the moral judgment does not judge, but merely inquires, com-
pares, and discovers. When Cary descends to particular novels for
illustrations of the moral process in fiction, this evasive fuzziness is
even more marked: "Flaubert's angle towards bourgeois life is
particular and we need not accept it, but we accept the tragedy
of *Madame Bovary* as a powerful exposition of a moral truth,
that such a woman behaving in such a way ought to suffer that
fate."[60] But Cary fails to realize that unless we accept Flaubert's
attitude toward the bourgeois, that is, unless we can recognize
how genuinely oppressive Emma's narrow provincial middle-
class society is, we are hardly in a position to make any adequate
estimation of her experience, her tragedy, or her fate. Before we
can say that "such a woman behaving in such a way ought to
suffer that fate" is the "moral truth" of the novel, we should understand a good deal more about why she behaved as she did. Such
an understanding would qualify and complicate the moral truth
for the better. On *The Kreutzer Sonata,* Cary is even more characteristic, that is, more acute and more evasive. He says that
Tolstoy uses the story to advance a propagandistic view of women:
that they are "brought up for the marriage market, taught from
childhood to exploit their sex, that marriage itself is merely a sexual
conspiracy or a sexual battle, and that from these causes arise all
the evils of society." "But," Cary adds,

> because Tolstoy is a great artist, he has devised a form for
> his propaganda which makes it highly moving to us. He puts
> the message he wants to convey in the mouth of the pro-
> tagonist, the wife-murderer, and he makes us feel that this
> man's obsession is completely true to his nature and to life.
> We say, 'A man like that no doubt believes all this nonsense,
> and that is why he killed his wife,' or we may, more subtly,

[59] *Ibid.*, p. 150.
[60] *Ibid.*, p. 145.

reflect, 'All this nonsense is the excuse of a jealous man to explain why he killed his wife.' The book gives us a fine picture of that everlasting type, the neurotic, frustrated or merely selfish and stupid person, who puts upon society the reproach of his own failure. So at the very time we are saying 'What nonsense,' we are also saying, 'How true to the man— how true to the situation.'

*The Kreutzer Sonata* is completely successful as a work of art because, although it preaches, the message it is meant to give has been entirely assimilated into its form. The whole thing is an experience with the feeling appropriate to that form.[61]

This is all very well, but it raises some thorny problems. Cary is suggesting that Tolstoy has successfully dealt with a set of moral attitudes by undermining them utterly, that is, by assigning them to an obsessed man in whom we can discount them as mere nonsense. But this is rather absurd from an aesthetic as well as a moral standpoint; for if Tolstoy was chiefly concerned, as Cary maintains, with advancing these attitudes, his story must surely fail to realize his intention when it places them in the mouth of an obsessed protagonist. Nor does Cary argue for a subtler, noncommittal intention on Tolstoy's part. He speaks merely of the moral burden that the work of art is meant to convey being "entirely assimilated" into the form of the work. That the assimilation cancels the admitted intention by identifying it with a dubious protagonist seems not to trouble Cary. Moral indication and assertion concern him just as little, as we shall see, in his own fiction, even the best of it. Indeed, his remarks on Tolstoy's hero are quite pertinent to Cary's own wife-murderer, Jim Latter, of the second trilogy. Cary assigns Jim a set of values which are the source of Jim's conduct, but which the reader of the trilogy is hard put to judge. While we can say of them, "How true to Jim," we find it all but impossible to determine how true they are to Cary or to truth itself. The moral evasiveness and indifference of the trilogies

[61] *Ibid.*, pp. 109-110.

is related as much to Cary the reader as to Cary the novelist. Both as reader and writer, Cary is prepared to recognize the fictional character as a moral being, but not quite so ready to claim as much for the author. The latter, as we shall have occasion to see in Cary's fiction, tends to withdraw morally as well as technically when the novel moves from Victorian intrusion to modern objectivity.

Cary's fears for other readers of fiction and their capacities also tend toward moral neutrality. He feels that it will not do to state a case with all its necessary qualifications, in fiction, "because to do so is to appeal to the intelligence alone and to break the emotional continuity."[62] The great writers "do not preach," he says elsewhere. "If they did they would bore."[63] Indeed, Cary has it that the novelist must wheedle and bribe his reader in order to accomplish his real ends:

> The artist has no weapon that will penetrate the most delicate material carcass. He deals with the persons, with the souls, with the ghost in the machine. He must catch it when it is not aware of itself as a mind, a person, or character, when it has no practical aim or will, and when it has taken off the armour of its conceptual judgment, its conventional ideas, the tension of fear and hate, in order to relax. In this state it does not want to hear sermons; nine times in ten it does not want to learn anything at all, it wants only enjoyment, self-forgetfulness. And he must give it—the dream. He must transport this lounger into another existence, and make him know what he wants him to know, as an experience, as a realisation that simply happens to him. So when a passing headlight shows a landscape both unexpected and familiar, it is not for a long time that this glimpse reveals itself to him as an important event.[64]

Very little moral communication or commitment is likely to emerge from this combination of cajoling novelist and pleasure-

[62] Preface to *Castle Corner*, p. 5.
[63] "A Novelist and His Public," p. 36.
[64] *Art and Reality*, p. 169.

seeking reader. Such moral ideas as are transmitted through the dream must, Cary maintains, take the form of experience. That is, they must be embodied in an action in which the reader can share. He makes choices, then, along with the characters, guided by his own moral judgment. The novel exists to give him "a certain experience of moral beings in action."[65] This notion, however, is another of Cary's means of moral eschewal. It is certainly true that such participation and evaluation on the part of the reader are indispensable in fiction. It is true, as well, that the reader proceeds by comparing the fictional representation with his own sense of reality and conduct. Cary's formulation is quite accurate: "We can intuit the facts in the actuality of our daily life. We check our fiction by our own direct knowledge. That is to say, we can check the fundamental presentation of moral character. . . ."[66] However, the corroboration—which is the reader's only means of apprehending the moral purport of a novel when that purport is transmitted solely as "experience"—is not feasible in the context of Cary's thought. For the "actuality of our daily life" and "our own direct knowledge" are wide-ranging variables in Cary's private-world system, with its heavy emphasis on subjective value. While on occasion he does assert that "at a certain primitive level, all men agree,"[67] his case for the opposite view is a good deal more persuasive. Consequently, at this juncture at least, Cary's inclusiveness—his desire for both a private and a universal reality—cannot quite provide for an "experiential" novel's explicit moral communication. If the solution, then, must be that every reader makes his own personal moral estimates of the characters' circumstances and choices, without significant help, either direct or indirect, from the novelist, we have a fairly accurate anticipation of the conditions that obtain in the trilogies, and that begin to manifest themselves even in Cary's earliest novels.

[65] *Ibid.*, p. 151.
[66] *Ibid.*, p. 154.
[67] *Ibid.*, p. 153.

Novelists have traditionally afforded the reader a good deal more help than Cary suggests in these remarks on morality or, as we shall see, than he offers in the trilogies themselves. And Cary himself, as an astute student of the novel, recognizes elsewhere that the great writers of the past have never obscured their intention, the view of life which they sought to convey. Such clarity, Cary maintains, is necessary for the novel because of the chaotic nature of existence :

> Life, as it occurs, has no meaning. It is too full of chance, too stupid. We give it meaning by choosing from it significant patterns. I don't mean that we make those patterns, we find or think that we find them [a characteristic qualification] among the mass of nonsense as a man sees from a plane the track of a Roman road under crops and chicken runs; or a beach-comber goes out for drift wood to a certain bay at a certain hour of a certain month.[68]

Such a pattern, or theme, Cary says, is what the novelist endeavors, in the face of the apparent meaninglessness of life, to express in his work:

> Trollope found in life what we all find, a mass of detail without meaning, of useless cruelty, stupid evil, blind fate, fools doing accidental good and well-meaning saints doing immense evil; what he did was what every writer does, even those modest writers who frankly work for the pay: he created a work of art to give a certain kind of experience.
>
> He said in effect: "This is the shape of things under the confusion of appearance; these are the forces which really move people to action." His whole story, however complex, was designed to illustrate and develop a theme.[69]

Cary does not, typically, lay much stress here on moral value as a component of the novelist's theme, contenting himself instead with a conception of the novel as a revelation of underlying truth, the

[68] Preface to *Castle Corner*, p. 7.
[69] "On the Function of the Novelist," p. 1.

actual "shape of things." This emphasis on insight rather than judgment is a fairly persistent strain in his theory. But in another remark on thematic control, he makes the moral element a good deal more explicit:

> All writers have, and must have, to compose any kind of story, some picture of the world, *and of what is right and wrong in that world* [italics mine]. And the great writers are obsessed with their theme. They're sure they're right, and their message would save the world. This is as true of Lawrence as of Tolstoy, or Dante, or the monkish author of *Everyman*.[70]

And when Cary turns to what he takes to be the actual themes of a number of great novelists, as these are expressed in specific novels, the moral component is perfectly, if inadvertently, clear. "For Tolstoy," he observes, "Providence, in giving to man the power of love and response to love, had provided him with the only necessary clue to the good life. Any form of society not based on love was evil and also unnatural. Nature, in short, as Tolstoy conceived it, was the will of God. The artificial life of society as opposed to that of the countryman or the peasant was especially corrupt. In *Anna Karenina* he contrasted, therefore, what he considered the false and unnatural life of Anna and her friends with the natural and good life of Levin and Kitty."[71] As for Hardy, "his

[70] *Art and Reality*, p. 158.
[71] *Ibid.*, pp. 106-107. Elsewhere Cary speaks of Tolstoy's two themes and the great Russian's scrupulousness about committing himself only to one in a given book: "Tolstoy, as you know, had two answers. I mean he was awfully muddled in a way: on the one side he believed that Providence ran everything—and that belief impregnates *War and Peace*. Do you remember old Kutuzov, sitting down, and the Staff Officers come to him and say, 'What shall we do?' and the old gentleman's asleep, and doesn't care a damn, because he believes, do you see, that God will provide . . . That's one of the Tolstoys. On the other side is Tolstoy's terror of death; and also in *Anna Karenina*, his ethical judgment, which involves interference with the course of Providence . . . —he's not joined up; but he was such a great artist that he doesn't split up in any of the books. Each of his books belonged to one theory of life" ("The Novelist at Work: A Conversation between Joyce Cary and Lord David Cecil," *Adam International Review*, XVIII, Nos. 212-213 [1950], 24).

theme," Cary says, "was the injustice of life, the cruelty of blind
fate destroying innocent and guilty alike. . . . Tess's life is destroyed
not by any defect of her nature, not by any law of providence, but
by mere bad luck."[72] Flaubert, Cary asserts, achieves a
triumphant formal unity in *Madame Bovary*. "But that unity is
obtained by selection of facts, of characters, by special interpretation of events, which is partial and so far untrue. Country life is
not necessarily a bore, country doctors are not necessarily fools,
and their wives are often sensible, cheerful and even faithful."[73]
And Flaubert's criticism of provincial life is matched, in Cary's
view, by an equally strong and ultimately decisive commitment to
Emma herself: "What saves *Madame Bovary* from failing [as
imitations of it fail] is not the artifice, but something that apparently Flaubert did not mean to put into the book at all, his
romantic sympathy for the heroine."[74] Finally, in the course of an
astute account of Henry James's major theme, Cary brings his own
into illuminating contrast:

> The essential thing about James is that he came into a
> different, a highly organized, hieratic society and for him it
> was not only a very good and highly civilized society, but
> static. It was the best the world could do. But it was already
> subject to corruption. This was the centre of James' moral
> idea—that everything good was, for that reason, specially
> liable to corruption. Any kind of goodness, integrity of
> character, exposed that person to ruin. And the whole civili-
> zation, because it was real civilization, cultivated and sensi-
> tive, was fearfully exposed to frauds and go-getters, brutes
> and grabbers. This was his tragic theme. But my world is
> quite different—it is intensely dynamic, a world in creation.

Cary ignores the possibility of Tolstoy's having only one, rather ethical, view in
both novels. That is, that in *War and Peace*, Providence, to put it crudely, is on the
side of virtue. Certainly Napoleon and his career are morally distasteful to Tolstoy
in this novel.

[72] *Art and Reality*, pp. 107-108.
[73] *Ibid.*, p. 113.
[74] "The Way a Novel Gets Written," p. 91.

> In this world, politics is like navigation in a sea without charts
> and wise men live the life of pilgrims.[75]

In contrast to Tolstoy, Hardy, Flaubert, and James, whose themes,
by his own admission, consist of specific evaluative judgments to
which these writers are unmistakably committed, Cary's theme is
evasively vague and generalized. It is not a moral commitment at
all. Instead of composing "a picture of the world and of what is
right and wrong in that world," he is content to assert that it is
"intensely dynamic, a world in creation"; and he does not have
conviction enough even about this to express disapproval of the
characters in his novels, like Wilcher, who resist change. By offer-
ing us a world in which we navigate "in a sea without charts" he
delineates not the "shape of things under the confusion of appearance" so much as the underlying confusion of things, with which,
as human beings, we are presumably already too familiar. Cary's
greatest failing as a novelist—and his greatest strength as well—is
his submission to the variety and multiplicity of experience. In the
novels he is only too ready to abandon his own view and assert
merely that there are many views. Indeed, in the trilogies, where
this tendency has its culmination, each of the six novels is entirely
given over to the exposition and defense of a different view of life,
no one of them entirely congruent with Cary's own. As a result,
the kind of ordering which a novelist's particular and precise belief
can supply is largely absent in each trilogy as a whole. This, of
course, is not to say that Cary's broad sympathies, sensitivity to
multiformity, and remarkable objectivity are necessarily intellectual vices. On the contrary, they make him a refreshing and
significant, if somewhat reluctant, intelligence; and they offer us
the best means we have of taking hold of his novels, of understanding how they are made and what they are about. However, they
also create formidable problems of a moral and aesthetic nature,
which we shall be concerned with as well in the chapters that
follow.

[75]"An Interview with Joyce Cary," p. 71.

Cary himself is hardly unaware of the difficulty:

> I had tried to be objective; and this is not always very
> easy when one is entirely convinced that the world is such
> and such a kind of reality and not at all what some charac-
> ter believes it to be. One is always in danger of thinking, "But
> if I allow such things to be said, and to happen, the reader will
> suppose that they are true, that they ought to happen, and so
> make nonsense of the book."[76]

In general, Cary feels that it is only too easy for anyone, including
the author himself, to make nonsense of a book. Uncertainty about
the meaning of novels is yet another form that his indeterminate
impulse takes. Thus, speaking about the writer's need to assess his
own work as he writes, Cary says, "I am speaking as a professional
when I say that the great difficulty here is not only to see the objective clearly as it is, to value your achievement with an unpre-
judiced eye, but to know what it is all about. You are faced with
a mass of words, and a story like many other stories, your
characters and your general theme. But what is the meaning of it
all, the real meaning?"[77] In addition, Cary points out that the
novelist's original intuition and intention may undergo serious
alteration during the actual composition of a book, sometimes
quite uncontrollably. This, he says, happened to Dostoevsky when
he allowed Ivan Karamazov the more crushing arguments in the
Grand Inquisitor sequence of *The Brothers Karamazov,* though
the plan had been to allow orthodox dogma to triumph. "So that
[Dostoevsky's] scheme for that chapter," Cary maintains, "his
concept *a priori* of what the chapter would mean, was completely
ruined."[78] The elusiveness of meaning is at least equally troublesome for the audience, in Cary's opinion: "No two people can
possibly see the same picture in the same way, or read the same
book. In short, there are as many personal meanings in a work of

---

[76] "The Way a Novel Gets Written," p. 89.
[77] *Art and Reality*, p. 93.
[78] *Ibid.*, p. 85.

art as there are persons to appreciate, and each can find there his own truth."[79] And Cary is aware that this ordinary variation and uncertainty about a book's meaning becomes especially notable in a first-person narrative. Speaking about an experimental change from first to third person that he made during the composition of *Prisoner of Grace,* and about its effect on a particular episode, he says:

> The dialogue in the railway station scene was, of course, precisely the same, word for word. But it did not convince any more. For the reader is aware subconsciously that he is now dealing with a third-person narrative. And so he cannot give the same credence to the wife's descriptions of her own feelings. He knows that the author needs the woman's change of mind for his plot, and the author in a third-person narrative is always present at the back of a reader's mind. So the whole content, the meaning of the chapter was altered without the alteration of a single word in it.[80]

It follows, then, that the author tends not to be present at the back of the reader's mind, or in any really discernible place, in a first-person narrative. As a result, the writer's moral disposition, the whole force of his valuation of the action, is largely absent as well; and its absence augments the ubiquitous uncertainty of interpretation that Cary has already advanced for fiction in general. This account applies significantly to the trilogies. In the six first-person narratives of these works, we have an opportunity to measure the effects of such a relinquishment of authority. The second trilogy particularly, with its diametric and sustained conflict of value among the narrators and its issue in catastrophe, will warrant our closest attention.

While the indeterminateness that we have been tracing in Cary's thought, and the vice of objectivity that we shall be examining in the chapters that follow, do significant damage when they act

[79] *Ibid.,* p. 141.
[80] *Ibid.,* p. 98.

upon the trilogies as wholes, something rather different occurs in
the individual trilogy novels. In most of these, instead of an indiscriminate, irresolute permissiveness, we get a deeply committed
first-person narrator pronouncing on life, condemning and cherish-
ing values, trying to make sense of the world both to his own
sensibility and intelligence and his readers'. In writing each of
these novels, Cary qualified his general, encompassing ideas of
diversity and indeterminateness sufficiently to create six brilliant
narratives. But his suspension of generalized disbelief is only partially successful, because the shadow of his overarching noncommittal tendencies, and of the surrounding novels of the
trilogies as well, falls disturbingly on each of the component works.
Remarkable as they are, Sara's, Wilcher's, Gulley's, Nina's,
Chester's, and Jim's narratives are sustained by a factitious commitment—not Cary's own, but his exploitation of a possible,
hypothetical view—a view which is necessarily a mere pose. When
we compare their conviction to the earnest moral concern of
James, Conrad, Lawrence, or even the Joyce of the *Portrait*, we
must feel uneasy, as though, in the trilogies, we are in the hands
of an ultimately irresponsible intelligence, indifferently, yet be-
witchingly, contriving the whole standpoint of each novel. But
these are misgivings, fortunately, that come after our pleasure in
each individual book. Cary's failure on the level of the trilogies
cannot altogether do away with his achievement in each volume.
And, in the end, we could not have one without the other, for both
his achievement and his failure derive from the same persistent
strain of multiplicity, inclusiveness, and demurral that runs
through his thinking. It is an affinity that makes his greatest work
both feasible and vulnerable.

In the chapters that follow, we shall be examining the relation
between Cary's indeterminateness—his unshakable openness before
the possibilities and contradictions of life—and his fiction. As a
point of entry into the novels, this quality of Cary's mind offers us
a way of accounting for the most distinctive and significant aspects

of his work. With it, we can explore, from the first novels forward, his consistent exaltation of individual character and personality as the primary locus of reality and unity in the world—for Cary, the basis, at once, of all coherence and meaning and of all conflict as well. With it, too, we can explain much of the extraordinary vibrance, energy, and vitality of the novels, and of the people in them. We can also see how in Cary's hands, it becomes a method of conceiving and shaping fiction, the source of both theme and technique. On the less fortunate side, we can mark the limits of multiplicity and indeterminateness as a controlling attitude for a novelist. We can, that is, ascertain where and why such a habit of mind ceases to order both the substance and form of fiction meaningfully, so that the whole purport of a work may issue in ambiguity or confusion.

Since both the commendable and the dubious consequences of Cary's neutrality come to a head in the second trilogy, we shall deal with that remarkable work at considerable length in the concluding three chapters of this study. As the culmination of Cary's career as a novelist—these are the last three novels published during his lifetime—and the most ambitious of his attempts to bring the multiformity of reality under novelistic control, this trilogy will afford us an ideal text for defining and measuring his achievement. Before we enter upon that analysis, however, we shall want to prepare for it by tracing the gathering of the forces of indeterminateness through the whole range of Cary's fiction, from the first published novel, *Aissa Saved*, through the Sara Monday trilogy, to the posthumous and unfinished *The Captive and the Free* (1959). In the next chapter, we shall give our attention to this preliminary matter.

# II

## *The Uses of Irresolution: A Survey of the Fiction*

When he turned to writing novels, Cary almost immediately found a means of transferring his intellectual irresolution to fiction. From the outset, he embodied it in novel after novel by utilizing a race of self-absorbed men and women. Obsessed with their own pursuits, his figures are unwilling, and largely unable, to grasp the obsessions of their fellows. Cary, far from choosing among these pursuits and the conceptions which underlie them, ordinarily hovers modestly and anonymously in the rear, concerned only to secure for each of his characters an adequate, often irritatingly equitable, hearing. While he often employs a kind of omniscient narration in the novels preceding the trilogies, it is a thoroughly post-Jamesian variety, with Cary usually locking himself in the consciousness of a succession of characters. We do best to characterize this method, when Cary is most himself, as reticent omniscience; it has an air of "he could if he would." There is an unmistakable aspiration to the condition of drama in his books, but frequently without the ascertainable moral focus of a great play.

Essentially, Cary takes pains to deprive his novels of a moral center. We cannot locate it either in a given character or in a discernible authorial attitude. When the prose belittles or commends, it ordinarily does so on behalf of one of the figures. As readers of Cary we are always saddled with the responsibility of making judgments which he has himself been unwilling to make. Wherever we turn, we encounter his mystifying liberality. The novels, though, are able to live by letting live, for we almost never have the sense that a character is being deprived of his nature or his autonomy in order to serve thematic or structural ends. Having submitted himself to the indeterminate flavor of reality, Cary is in a position to profit from an attendant vitality.

Although this means of translating his habit of mind to the novel comes readily to Cary and persists through his whole career as a novelist, it undergoes a number of modifications. He by no means writes the same novel sixteen times simply by varying the cast of characters. The indeterminate world of his fiction is genuinely indeterminate: it has a variety of forms and the bases for it shift considerably. The novels are remarkably different from one another, and Cary certainly deserves Walter Allen's commendation for the protean facility he exhibits as he moves from one work to another.[1]

Still, groupings suggest themselves naturally enough, particularly where a common basis for indeterminateness serves several books. Cary's suspended, unresolved fictional world derives in large measure from a deft management of place and time. When he begins to write novels, he turns instinctively to a remote, unfamiliar setting—Africa. The four African novels, *Aissa Saved, An American Visitor, The African Witch,* and *Mister Johnson* owe much of their flavor to their location in a kind of indeterminate country. In *Charley Is My Darling* and *A House of Children,* on the other hand, Cary relies not on distance, but on the inaccessibility in time of childhood—a world more often than not quite closed to adults, where finality and accountability of perception and judgment are alike dispensable. In a third group, both space and time variegate the substance of the novels: *Castle Corner* deals with the British Empire in the first decade of the twentieth century as a multiplicity of things in space while *The Moonlight* and *A Fearful Joy* treat England proper as a multiplicity of things in time. The next group, the three novels of the first trilogy, *Herself Surprised, To Be a Pilgrim, and The Horse's*

[1] *Joyce Cary,* p. 5.

*Mouth,* employ the indeterminate first-person method that we have glanced at already, augmenting its effects with time and a decidedly picaresque use of space. At the close, there is Cary's posthumous novel, *The Captive and the Free.* This work abandons the first-person device in favor of what appears to be a species of Victorian narrative omniscience but is actually only another specimen of Cary's elusiveness. This arrangement, then, of the thirteen novels which precede—except for *The Captive and the Free*—the second trilogy will serve as our schematic basis for examining them in the remainder of this chapter.

*Aissa Saved* deals primarily with the imposition of Christianity on African pagans. In the strange, savage world of Nigeria, Cary sets an English missionary couple, the Carrs, and Aissa, a beautiful Nigerian girl who, as a result of their agency, undergoes a halting religious conversion and eventual martyrdom. Cary's primary contention about Aissa's Christianity is that it never succeeds in ridding itself of pagan elements and feeling. At the close of the novel, Aissa, incited by a circle of native converts to Christianity, relinquishes her lover, Gajere, and in an orgy of renunciation which is shot through with savage violence, wounds herself and offers up her infant son, Abba, as a blood sacrifice to Jesus. The novel culminates in Aissa's vision, as ants consume the remains of her ruined body, of her entry into an inextricably intertwined pagan-Christian paradise:

> Aissa grew weak; she could not remember where she was, the fire of the ants' tearing at her body did not scorch, it was like the warmth of flesh. Jesus had taken her, he was carrying her away in his arms, she was going to heaven at last to Abba and Gajere. Immediately the sky was rolled up like a door curtain and she saw before her the great hall of God with pillars of mud painted white and red. God, in a white riga and a new indigo turban, his hands heavy with thick silver rings, stood in the middle and beside him the spirit like a goat with white horns.[2]

[2] *Aissa Saved* (Carfax edition; London: Michael Joseph, 1952), p. 211.

The goat—reminiscent of the parrot at the conclusion of Flaubert's *A Simple Heart*—is Aissa's misconstruction of the Holy Ghost, i.e., "Holy Gote."

Cary's penetration of the native religious imagination—both Christian and pagan—is the highest achievement of the book, but he does not neglect the antithetical preoccupations of his white figures. Indeed, his treatment of the missionary religious intelligence in the Carrs, carefully attentive to Christian schisms between man and wife, and of the administrative-military intelligence in Bradgate, the district officer of Yanrin, yields Cary his characteristic interplay of forces and points of view. These issue in the impasse which we must learn to expect of a Cary novel.

For what we have in *Aissa Saved,* despite Cary's insight into all his figures, is an essential aloofness on his part from the tensions and issues that go forward. Bradgate's limitations—his obsession with bridgebuilding and his stout insistence on living an emotionally and intellectually unexamined life—are the most notable thing about him. Cary's sympathy with Bradgate in the latter's dealings with British officialdom is mingled with mild contempt for the district officer's lack of administrative ingenuity. Similarly, Cary is sensible of the Carrs' goodness, dedication, and piety, but skeptical about the validity and reality of their religion. Consequently, when we turn to the treatment of Christian belief among the Nigerians, we are two removes from religious reality, from a faith that is something more than mere energy, fervor, or psychological comfort. As we follow Aissa's religious evolution, with its exacerbations and remissions, her visions of the Holy Spirit, her gradual growth from girlish pride and irresponsibility to a willingness to surrender the earth and her child, and witness her fellow convert Ojo's final acceptance of her climactic sacrifice as Christian rather than pagan—then we see that Cary is having things both ways.

He does not for a moment accept Aissa's Christianity—nor Ojo's—yet he is suggesting that it becomes so real, so serious, so transcendent in her, even in its muddled form, that it passes beyond our capacity to gauge. The closing vision of paradise is a psychological fact, nothing more. Though this experience is brilliantly recorded, Cary is concerned only with its curiously confused quality. Not for a moment does he consider whether religious formulations correspond with anything real. He is committed only to the idea that energy, passion, and imaginative intensity exist and produce visions. The experience of vision, the emotion, the belief is real, is, indeed, life-giving. Aissa is saved by the power of her belief to inform her life with meaning. This treatment of religion as mental experience remains Cary's primary mode of dealing with it as he returns to it again and again in the later work.

In *An American Visitor,* Cary's emphasis shifts from Nigerian natives to their white rulers and the problems of empire. It is from the group consisting of District Officer Bewsher; Gore, his assistant; Marie Hasluck, an American anthropologist doing a series of newspaper articles on Africa; the Dobsons, a British missionary couple; and Frank Cottee, who heads a party of Englishmen seeking to make their fortune in Nigerian tin, that Cary fashions his final indeterminate stasis. Except for Marie, the American visitor of the title, they are all out of sympathy with one another's aims; and Marie's imperfect grasp of, and submission to, Bewsher's attitudes and the Christianity of the Dobsons precipitates the major disaster of the novel.

She begins as an anarchist and primitivist, ardently opposed to British rule in Nigeria and to all attempts to impose the alien, decadent forms of European civilization on the noble savagery of the Birri natives. This point of view brings her into sharp conflict with Cottee, who cares nothing for the noble Birri and their unspoiled primitive ways but everything for mining the rich tin fields in Birri territory so that he may become as wealthy as Africa can make him. She idealizes Bewsher, who is fond of his childlike Birri and enjoys his understanding of, and power over, them, but who is hardly the romantic absolutist and idealist that Marie is. He becomes for her one of the unshakable truths that she needs to prevent the universe from dissolving into chaos and flux:

> Marie was liable to these fits of doubt, and dreaded them.
> They had a physical effect upon her nerves. She felt some-
> times as if the actual ground had wavered and sunk beneath
> her. It was for a moment as if the most solid objects were
> illusory, as if there was nothing secure, nothing fixed, per-
> manent and trustworthy in the whole world; no peace, no
> refuge. . . . The cure was easy because in actual fact (she
> could tell herself) there were plenty of things in the world
> that you could be sure of. The difference between selfishness
> and unselfishness was a fact as obvious and much more solid
> than a rock; and so was the difference between Frank Cottee
> and Mr. Bewsher. For one was always thinking about himself
> and the other did not think about himself at all.[3]

After becoming Bewsher's wife, suffering over his narrow escapes from the increasingly hostile Birri tribesmen, and contracting tropical fever, Marie undergoes a brief but sweeping conversion to Christianity. Under the influence of this new absolute commit-ment to faith and love, she hides Bewsher's pistol when he asks for it in order to disperse a mob of Birri. As a result he is killed by the pagans whom he had hitherto always managed to control and subdue.

The debate between Marie and Cottee on imperial policy is a debate as well on the nature of culture and civilization, the whole life of man in society. It proceeds on a very respectable intellectual level indeed, complicated and subtilized even further by Cottee's bitterness at having lost Marie to Bewsher. It is joined reluctantly by Gore, whose main concern is to secure orderly, humane, and properly official rule in the district and, consequently, to temper, without violating administrative decorum at all, the more extreme figures. Bewsher's pagan affinities are not the least romantic—he merely humors Marie in her exaltation of uncorrupted Birri

[3] *An American Visitor* (Carfax edition; London: Michael Joseph, 1952), pp. 94-95.

virtue—but he is a crafty and effectual enemy of Cottee and the prospectors, and needs also to be reckoned with as a judge of the central problem of empire.

Once the dramatic embodiment of Marie's absolutist failure —Bewsher's death, almost at her hand—has played itself out, Cary has before him the task of making some final sense of the ideological conflict. If Marie's immature intellectual enthusiasms have proved inadequate, there is still the problem of imperialism, of history, and of society. But far from venturing on a resolution Cary writes a closing chapter in which he skilfully avoids all trace of one. He keeps the discordant attitudes in play to the very end, troubling only to complicate them further. The novel closes on a note of inconclusiveness passionately, painstakingly explored. Not only the African problem but the personal ones, too, remain at sixes and sevens.

After the military patrol which Bewsher had sought to avoid puts down the Birri uprising, the old patriarchal native government gives way and the Birri become a mob. Cottee, now on his way to becoming a wealthy man, contemplates the large issues and the figures who represent them in a brilliant, sustained meditation.[4] Bewsher and Gore seem to him foolish romantics for whom the world is on the verge of a new dark age. Bewsher's attempt to keep the Birri out of the general flux of civilization was, he feels, hopeless, for no single man could hope to resist the inevitability of such changes. People like Gore failed to understand that the world was forever in transition; that the roots of beauty "were as indestructible and as fertile as life itself; that although cruelty and lies might carry all before them for a time, they had never yet succeeded in abolishing the things of the spirit."

It is an eloquent piece of historical reflection and intuition, but it shortly dwindles into a shallow and offensive opportunism. "A period like this," he is soon thinking, "just because of its quackery, its confusion, its lack of standards, its cynicism and cowardice,

[4] *Ibid.*, pp. 234-236.

offered to a man intelligent and detached enough to seize them
extraordinary chances of amusement. There was scarcely any limit
to what he could do, given effrontery, money and the proper
jargon."[5] Cary is far from concluding the novel by turning it
into an essay on the thesis that the world is in perpetual revolution,
as Andrew Wright suggests.[6] Instead, he skilfully undermines
Cottee's ruminations on this theme—admittedly one of Cary's
own, widely expressed in the non-fiction—by linking them with a
crude desire for personal aggrandizement. Then, to ensure a closing
indeterminateness, Cary has Cottee respond reverentially to a
sobered, matured Marie. After hearing her speak of the meaning
and necessity of Bewsher's death, Cottee is transported

> to another state of being, where men and women were born
> to heroic destinies, and life was the magnificent stage of their
> glories and their sufferings; and it seemed to him, moreover,
> that the men and women who lived in this other romantic
> world, call them sentimentalists if you like, were the only
> ones who knew how to live at all. The rest were cowards,
> like himself, who were afraid to love, who were afraid of being
> laughed at. . . .[7]

But Cottee's commitment is not allowed to stand. A moment later,
after he has a closer glimpse of Marie, it is toppled over. "But
no," Cary says, recording Cottee's shift, "the fancy dissolved like
a transformation scene. This ugly little woman a tragic queen,
Monkey Bewsher a hero, it was absurd."[8] In the next instant, lest
we dismiss Marie too facilely, Cary has her, kneeling at Bewsher's
grave and irritating Cottee, speak the very last words of the novel.

[5] *Ibid.*, p. 236.

[6] *Joyce Cary*, pp. 93-94.

[7] *An American Visitor*, p. 238.

[8] *Ibid.* Warren G. French, in his capable "Joyce Cary's American Rover Girl,"
*Texas Studies in Language and Literature*, II (Autumn 1960), 281-291, emphasizes
what he takes to be Cary's unceasing distaste for Marie *qua* idealist. In doing so,
however, French tends to lose sight of her geniune intellectual growth; and, in any
event, he does not claim that the novel makes a very conclusive statement on the
problem of Africa itself.

They are at once true to her customary enthusiasm and, yet, perhaps, true as well to the character of Bewsher's life and its meaning. The point is that after witnessing Cottee turn and turn again,
and entering into his thoughts and feelings only to have them torn
out from under us, we are not quite in a position to know. "I'm
not praying," Marie says, "but where Monkey is, the ground feels
kind of different."

Deliberately and skilfully Cary has employed a series of persuasive shifts of feeling in Cottee to keep the personal differences
which have determined the whole plan of the novel alive. To a
large extent these differences take their insolubility from the
mystery of Africa itself and the whole tangled dilemma of
colonialism. In *An American Visitor* we are allowed some awareness of the inadequacy of extreme attitudes, Marie's early primi-
tivism, for instance, but by the close we are hard put, once again,
to move from the personal construction to any form of objective
truth. Thinking has once again made all things so.

*The African Witch* is Cary's largest, most comprehensive
African novel. He catches up, in a wide-ranging panorama, diverse
specimens of both native and British life, in an effort to give the
inconclusiveness of *An American Visitor* a less personal basis. "My
book," he says in his preface to the novel, "was meant to show
certain men and their problems in the tragic background of a continent still little advanced from the Stone Age, and therefore
exposed like no other, to the impact of modern turmoil. An over-
crowded raft manned by children who had never seen the sea
would have a better chance in a typhoon."[9] It is very much a
novel about an intractable continent, whose multiform problems
are quite beyond the poor powers of its British managers and of
its British-educated leaders like the young Rimi prince, Louis
Aladai. Cary's panoramic ease of movement and range serve his
purposes remarkably well. And the ambiguity of the swarming continent, the inaccessibility of saving truths, the scarceness

[9] *The African Witch* (Carfax edition; London: Michael Joseph, 1951), p. 12.

of effectual sympathy inherent in Cary's subject make that subject an ideal one for his indeterminate vision. At the close, Africa sinks back unavoidably into its savage juju practices, every noble European aspiration having quite flickered out.

There is a considerable range of British inadequacy. The Resident, Burwash, is a bumbling, imperceptive official, terrified of taking a false administrative step or employing an unfortunate phrase in reports to his superiors. Much of the finest energy and passion of the Britishers goes into their games, polo and bagatelle, sometimes played, symbolically enough, when things to which they are oblivious are about to descend upon them. The stupid arrogance and racial bigotry of such younger Englishmen as Prince and Honeywood are repulsive, and, at the very least, tactically impossible for colonials. A streak of vicious racial hatred turns up, surprisingly, in one of the more sympathetically treated Britishers, Captain Rackham, though it has a sexual basis which is perhaps responsible for its intensity. In love with Judy Coote, a former don who is Louis Aladai's old friend from Oxford days, but finding himself more and more drawn to Honeywood's athletic and beautiful sister, Dryas, Rackham is in something of a personal turmoil. When he learns that the Anglophile Louis has been isolated in the bush overnight with Dryas and that they have been seen dancing, he attacks the young Rimi prince with his fists, thereby making necessary his own resignation from the colonial service. Judy Coote, for all of her learning, wisdom, and good will, is as little able to manage her relationship with Rackham as she is to realize her prescriptions for Aladai and the Rimi. Most regrettable of all is Dryas Honeywood's disastrously well-bred conscience. Her physical aversion to the Negro Aladai, because she is ashamed of it, compels her to be unnaturally kind to him. This strange debt to her dislike of Aladai misleads him where he is blindest—in his adoration of British goodness and graciousness—and precipitates his encounter with Rackham.

The Africans are certainly no better. Elizabeth, Louis Aladai's sister, for whom the book is named, is an imposing juju priestess who prevails against all her enemies and shows some signs of rather mystifying supernatural powers. But she is a figure of darkness and murderous ignorance. Aladai himself is a gifted young idealist eager to bring the blessings of European learning and art to his enslaved people; but he is a divided and ineffectual figure, torn this way and that by hybrid loyalties to England and Rimi. After Rackham beats him, all his intellectual and emotional refinement dissolves, and he sinks into the most brutal savagery under the influence of Coker, a native rabble-rousing preacher obsessed with blood and human sacrifice. Eventually, Aladai is willing to believe only in British betrayal. The other Africans are largely dominated by Elizabeth's juju, which, though a formidable force, destroys more easily than it either heals or creates.

Cary's effort to portray the chaos of African administration, the discrepancy between vast problems and infinitesimal human capacities, is notably successful. Africa is too much for everyone in the novel to grasp or control. In a world where confusion constantly proliferates and people, no matter how dedicated, or gifted, or assertive, constantly fail to master more than a few rudimentary subjective ideas, Cary is on his home grounds. Commitment would be out of place for him, the point of the novel being that commitments do not work in Rimi. There is not even any reason to believe that any figure in the novel knows very much about what has happened or about its implications.

In his preface to the Carfax edition of *Mister Johnson,* Cary explains why he chose to write this novel in the present tense. The conventional past tense, he says, places the reader in the past, where his experience, even of a novel, is partially historical, deriving much of its quality from a contemplation of general causes, from reflection, comparison, and judgment. But, Cary continues, with a story in the present tense, when the reader too is in the present, he is carried unreflecting on the stream of events; his mood is not contemplative but agitated.

This makes the present tense unsuitable for large pictures . . . ; it illuminates only a very narrow scene with a moving ray not much more comprehensive than a hand-torch. It can give to a reader that sudden feeling of insecurity (as if the very ground were made only of a deeper kind of darkness) which comes to a traveller who is bushed in unmapped country, when he feels all at once that not only has he utterly lost his way, but also his own identity. His is, as they say, no longer sure of himself, or what he is good for; he is all adrift like sailors from some wreck, who go mad, not because of the privations inside, but outside, because they have nothing firm to rest their minds on, because everything round them is in everlasting motion.

This restless movement irritates many readers with the same feeling, that events are rushing them along before they have time to examine them, to judge them, and to find their own place among them. But as Johnson does not judge, so I did not want the reader to judge. And as Johnson swims gaily on the surface of life, so I wanted the reader to swim, as all of us swim, with more or less courage and skill, for our lives.[10]

The power which Cary ascribes here to an eccentric technical device is enormous. He maintains that merely by writing in the present tense a writer can restrict his field of vision, make his world uncertain and indeterminate, and eliminate judgment. Whatever value these remarks have as theory, they have, curiously enough, only a meager application to *Mister Johnson*. The unadorned tale of the African clerk, Johnson, who reveres the ways of his British masters, marries a beautiful young native girl, sings and dances with spontaneous verve, inspires native road builders to unusual exertion, and finally dies for having murdered a white man, is certainly done on a far smaller scale than the three preceding African novels. However, the novel, with its point of view largely restricted to the naïve clerk's conception of things, is considerably

[10] *Mister Johnson* (Carfax edition; London: Michael Joseph, 1954), pp. 9-10.

less indeterminate than its predecessors. And in its climactic section, as Johnson awaits punishment for his crime at the hands of District Officer Rudbeck, whom he worships for having once or twice complimented him on a neat piece of work, the novel takes on a touching import which makes judgment not only desirable but inescapable.

This crime is as unthinking and inevitable an act as most of those that compose the exuberant young clerk's life. After successfully robbing the till of Sergeant Gollub's store several times, Johnson is surprised in the act by the Sergeant carrying a gun, and stabs the white man in a panic in order to avoid being shot. Rudbeck, who takes Johnson into custody, is at this time disgusted over a reprimand that he has received from his superiors in connection with crime in his district. An obsessive road builder, Rudbeck frequently neglects what he takes to be lesser considerations. Cary, far from sharing with Rudbeck an underlying, invidious colonial paternalism, as Arnold Kettle maintains,[11] or conceiving the District Officer, with Andrew Wright, as an African Captain Vere,[12] takes rather a skeptical view of him. In his gloomy interrogation of Johnson, Rudbeck is clearly still more concerned with his own administrative problems than with the clerk's plight. He has always been rather oblivious to Johnson and to Johnson's admiration and affection. When his request for reprieve is refused by the legal authorities, Rudbeck, now more disgusted than ever, begins makeshift preparations for having the clerk hanged. His exasperation with his superiors is still his dominant feeling. The Johnson matter is merely another occasion for it. When he is prodded to perform the execution he thinks, "They've asked for it." It is only very gradually, as Johnson repeatedly requests that his friend Rudbeck himself perform the execution and that he be shot rather than hanged, that Rudbeck emerges from his stolid

---

[11] *An Introduction to the English Novel*, II (Hutchinson's University Library; London: Hutchinson House, 1953), 183.

[12] *Joyce Cary*, p. 86.

self-absorption. He receives Johnson's blessing and reassurance:

> "That report of mine [Rudbeck says]—I don't know if I was quite fair to you."
>
> "Oh yes, sah." Johnson shakes his head while he quickly seeks a means of restoring Rudbeck's opinion of himself, and also, of course, his own idea of Rudbeck. "Oh, no, sah—I much more bad dan ever you tink . . . I damn bad low trash, good for damn nutting tall."[13]

After these exchanges, the muddle, the unfortunate intractability of things, make themselves felt in Rudbeck. With touching, generous concern, Johnson, on the verge of execution, reaches out to console and encourage his friend:

> Rudbeck sits hunched in his chair. He is still dissatisfied, not with Johnson's explanation, for he knows that Johnson is actually a thief and a murderer, but with everything. He feels more and more disgusted and oppressed, like a man who finds himself walking down a narrow dark channel in unknown country, which goes on getting darker and narrower; while he cannot decide whether he is on the right road or not.
>
> Johnson, seeing his gloom and depression, exerts himself. "Don' you mind, sah, about dis hanging. I don' care for it one lil bit. Why"—he laughs with an air of surprise and discovery—"I no fit know nutting about it—he too quick. . . ."[14]

Rudbeck's gloom is undergoing a subtle shift. Without really being aware, he is responding with an augmented disgust to Johnson's situation and extraordinary kindness and concern. The generalized, vague nature of the officer's oppression is the token of his unconsciousness of its new occasion, his slight emergence from his own self-absorption. A few moments later he shoots Johnson in the back of the head, before the young Negro quite knows what has happened. It is a generous and insubordinate act—he is

[13] *Mister Johnson*, p. 223.
[14] *Ibid.*, p. 224.

under strict orders to have his prisoner hanged—in which he acquiesces to Johnson's wish almost without having thought about what he is doing. When it is over, he "goes toward the office with his usual rolling gait. He is insisting with the whole force of his obstinate nature that he has done nothing unusual, that he has taken the obvious, reasonable course."[15] When his wife, who knows nothing of what has occurred, asks him what is going to be done with Johnson, Rudbeck rouses himself from his stolid trance and responds with a glimmering recognition:

> Rudbeck's forehead wrinkles. He looks, as usual when he reflects on any serious matter, perplexed and troubled.
> Suddenly and unexpectedly to himself, he tells her the story. She looks at him for a moment with the same face as the clerk's, astonished and horrified as if at a murderer. Her lips move as if she is going to cry.
> But Rudbeck, growing ever more free in the inspiration which seems already his own idea, answers obstinately, "I couldn't let anyone else do it, could I?"[16]

With these words, the novel ends. In them, Rudbeck expresses a fellow feeling, a sense of genuinely human responsibility which he has been acting out without quite realizing the source of his impulses. The idea "seems already his own" because, in truth, it is largely Johnson's legacy to him. The clerk's heroic kindliness and selflessness have drawn Rudbeck, willy-nilly, into a genuine moral and emotional relationship. The recognition breaks in upon his inert consciousness in a way that must leave it forever altered.

The all but unconscious quality of this development in Rudbeck, which Cary handles with extraordinary dexterity and restraint, suggests a certain indeterminateness. Rudbeck's sympathies are, in a sense, both there and not there. We have a mere flicker of fellow feeling in a man who can barely explain himself without causing us to smile at his insensitivity. Yet, the gesture of human

[15] *Ibid.*, p. 226.
[16] *Ibid.*, p. 227.

community and involvement has been performed unhesitatingly. Africa, its inaccessibility and its customarily nonhuman juxtapositions of white men and black, has been triumphed over. The painful disjunctions of the first three novels yield here to a furtive, but significant, exchange of affection and consideration. One of the least promising of Cary's colonial officers has been forced by Negro love, naïveté, and distress to an act of unpremeditated tenderness and regard. It is purely personal and fleeting—none of the larger issues raised in the previous wide-ranging novels have been resolved. But Cary's moving expression of Rudbeck's determinate regard constitutes a fitting beginning with which to bring the African group to an end.

The novels of childhood, though considerable achievements, need not detain us long. The principle of their tentative, indefinite quality is implicit in their subject matter. Childhood is, almost by definition, the time of groping, incomplete perceptions, of puzzlement and uncertainty. It is not difficult to understand Cary's attraction to the child's world and its benighted pain and joy. Instead of comprising the "last refuge of human worth" in our time, as Mark Spilka suggests that childhood does for Dickens, Dostoevsky, and Kafka,[17] for Cary it makes available in heightened form the discontinuities and enigmas of adult life.

In the preface to *Charley Is My Darling*, Cary speaks at length of the child's submersion, frequently, in a morally indeterminable world:

> The world that stands to be explored by the child is also a moral structure which, simply because it is one of related ideas, is much harder for him to grasp. He perceives that it is there, he feels its importance to his comfort and security every moment of the day, but it is not present to his eyes and ears; he cannot see and touch it. He is not equipped with the experience and judgment necessary to put it together for

[17] "Kafka's Sources for 'The Metamorphosis'," *Comparative Literature*, XI, No. 4 (1959), 307.

> himself. For this purpose nature has provided him (and many
> other small mammals which grow slowly in understanding)
> with parents. And if they refuse the duty of making the situa-
> tion clear to him he will suffer. . . . A good deal of what is
> called neurosis and frustration among young children is due
> to nothing but the failure of parents and teachers (often the
> most conscientious) to do so, that is, to give a clear picture
> without uncertainties. Without such a picture, children don't
> know where they are, and they do all kinds of evil (because it
> is just this sphere of good and evil which is puzzling them)
> to find out.[18]

This clear picture is at something of a premium in Cary's own
view of the world, but his adult characters, as we have seen in at
least the first three African novels, have an abundant stock.

The novel proper deals with a young war evacuee, Charley
Brown, sent in 1939 from a London slum to the west country of
England. His head is shaved when it is discovered to be lousy, and
he starts, consequently, at a considerable disadvantage with the
other evacuees, who make the most of this anomaly. His daring
and imaginativeness, however, much of it in the nature of moral
inquiry and experiment, soon elevate him to leadership. As leader,
he performs his crowning piece of audacity—the almost orgiastic
irrational destruction of the interior of a neighborhood home.

When he is apprehended for this crime and it is discovered in
addition that Lizzie, a deaf country girl with whom Charley has
fallen deeply and innocently in love, is going to have a baby by
him, the climactic conception of the novel takes shape. Childhood,
Cary suggests, is not merely formidable for children, but unintel-
ligible to most adults. In a touching scene with Lina Allchin, the
thirty-year-old, well-bred billeting officer of the district who has
befriended Charley, Cary projects for us, in the immediacy of the
present tense, the pain and hopelessness of this mutual miscom-
prehension. Lina is upbraiding Charley for having got Lizzie,
whose real name is Bessie, with child:

[18] *Charley Is My Darling* (Carfax edition; London: Michael Joseph, 1956), p. 9.

"I can't understand it," Lina says, but obviously she is sure that in this situation at least, she can't be wrong. "I didn't think you were like that."

"Like what?" Charley thought. "What am I like?"

"It's so cruel and mean—and you don't seem to care a bit."

Charley is struggling against the woman's mysterious purpose, which he feels to be dangerous. He feels as if she is trying to push him into a dark place from which he will never escape. He has no words to describe a sense of guilt, a conviction of sin, but he feels by nervous imagination what they are.

"Aren't you ashamed of yourself, Charley—not even a little ashamed?"

A huge blackness rises upon Charley and he makes a desperate leap to escape from it. He reclaims: "But Liz didn't say nothing—"

"Bessie has tried to excuse you from the beginning, but that doesn't make it any better, does it? Charley, if you try to wriggle out of this, I don't think I'll be able to forgive you."

The young woman's voice trembles with disgust and anger, which works upon the boy with all the nervous force of its sincerity. He feels the pressure and fights more desperately against it.

"But I didn't—I didn't—it ain't like that—" He wants to explain that neither he nor Lizzie are guilty of anything; that the same thing has happened to them both. But the idea is beyond him. The very feeling of it is already disappearing from his attempt to grasp it. He says desperately: "But me and Liz—"

"Think what you have done to her—she will have to be sent away from home—her own mother and father are ashamed of her—and you only think of excusing yourself. I wonder do you realise, Charley, how disappointed I am in you. I think I never want to speak to you again. A boy that treats a girl like that—a girl like poor Bessie, and then tries to justify himself."

At these words, poor Bessie, so skilfully chosen, the black wave rises again and this time Charley's overwhelmed. He burst into tears. Lina Allchin says in a new voice, full of relief and happiness: "Thank God, Charley. You have got some decent feelings after all—I wasn't mistaken in you."

"Yes, Miss, I'm sorry—I been bad—to everybody." Charley repents violently between sobs.

Lina, too, is tearful. She congratulates the boy on his repentance: "Now I do hope for you, Charley; and you know I will always be your friend."

She goes away happy and leaves him remorseful, still more confused than before: "But she wouldn't listen—it wasn't like that."

His violent emotion, which was remorse, now becomes anger. "Why did she go on at me? She didn't even listen. It wasn't like that."

He is enraged with Lina, not only on his own account, but because he feels that Liz, too, is involved. "It wasn't like that—she isn't poor Liz—and wot was wrong with it?"

But he feels also unsafe. For now he can't think of Lizzie and himself together without hearing Lina's judgment and catching her contemptuous feeling. All his love-making with Lizzie, which an hour before had the beauty of its happiness, now suddenly takes ugly and squalid shapes.

He is angry, ashamed, bitter, and, above all, confused. He says to himself, arguing when argument itself is an expression of doubt: "It isn't like that—she don't understand. Lizzie and me—"[19]

We have here a dramatization of the distance between child and adult moral comprehension. Charley is helplessly incapable of communicating his sense of the unimpeachability of his love for Lizzie and hers for him. As he makes halting attempts to form his conception in words, his inarticulateness leaves him vulnerable to Lina's fluency. Lina, full of unhesitating adult moral certitude, can only soil and degrade Charley's essentially innocent childlike feeling. She overwhelms him with the utterly foreign construction which she wishes to place on his experience and is finally delighted that Charley appears willing to share her sordid view. She leaves happy in the belief that she has extended the domain of adult

[19] *Ibid.*, pp. 323-325.

moral definition, but we know from the anguish of Charley's re-
iterated "It wasn't like that," that he is far from relinquishing his
own hold on what has happened to him and Lizzie. It is not for
adults to know, Cary is suggesting, how it was really. Indeed, in
the formal hearings which follow this, we encounter adults whose
penetration is even shallower than the determinedly kind Miss
Allchin's. Lizzie sums up the whole failure of her elders to ascribe
a genuine emotional life to the young in words laden with Carian
metaphysical import: "They didden know about us—how could
they if they wurn't us?"[20]

As the two young people are led away by the police authorities
at the close, they enter upon a genuine adulthood of feeling, tenderness, and mutual concern. As they kiss—for the first time—
they appear to be children still to the sergeant in charge. But they
are at this moment neither children nor grownups. They are larval
forms who have been forced to shed some of the beneficent moral
vagueness of childhood and hover now on the threshold of the
summary moral precision of adulthood.

*A House of Children,* on the other hand, is devoted to an extensive exploration of the child's world itself. Cary's skilful use of an
adult first-person narrator, looking back over a summer spent in
Ireland when he was eight years old, introduces a dual perspective.
The narrator has a sympathetic, perceptive sensibility, capable of
grasping the quality of childhood emotion and infusing it, to some
degree, with adult coherence as well. This retrospective insight
constitutes the prevailing medium of the book, and in it Cary
triumphs, almost in his own person—the novel, cast as a memoir,
is largely autobiographical—over the incommunicability that
forms the basis of *Charley Is My Darling.*

At times the narrator's command of childhood and maturity
takes the form of unabashed generalized disquisitions:

> The only certain distinction I can find between childhood
> and maturity is that children grow in experience and look

[20] *Ibid.,* p. 341.

6

forward to novelty; that old people tend to be set. This does not mean even that children enjoy life more keenly than grown-ups, they are only more eager for experience. Grown-ups live and love, they suffer and enjoy far more intensely than children; but for the most part on a narrower front. For the average man or woman of forty, however successful, has been so battered and crippled by various accidents that he has gradually been restricted to a small compass of enterprise. Above all, he is perplexed. He has found out numerous holes and inconsistencies in his plan of life and yet he has no time to begin the vast work of making a new one. He is a traveller who, when he has reached the most dangerous part of his journey among deep swamps and unknown savages, discovers all at once that his map is wrong, his compass broken, his ammunition damp, his rifle crooked, and his supplies running short. He must push on at high speed, blindly, or fail altogether and fail his companions. I think that is the reason for the special sadness of nearly all grown-up faces, certainly of all those which you respect; you read in their lines of repose, the sense that there is no time to begin again, to get things right. The greater a grown man's power of enjoyment, the stronger his faith, the deeper and more continuous his feeling of the waste of life, of happiness, of youth and love, of himself.

But for children life seems endless, and they do not know a grief that has no cure.[21]

These sentiments are unmistakably Cary's own—the conception of adult perplexity, of the map that is all wrong and the compass that cannot give direction, are the staple images of his indeterminate vision. To the extent that he speaks, as narrator, in his own voice, the first-person method of *A House of Children* is distinctly different from the great dramatic utilization of the form in the trilogies. He exhibits a willingness to pronounce here that is unusual for him; but the pronouncement is characteristically diffuse. Life, it says, is too vast, too multiform for even the most decent

[21] *A House of Children* (Carfax edition; London: Michael Joseph, 1955), pp. 66-67.

adults to order, to master. Cary's primary concern in *A House of Children,* however, does not involve him even in this much commitment. His main effort—and it is memorably realized—is to set down the feelings and sensations of childhood, for it is in these that, for him, childhood chiefly lives. The memoir—it is hardly a novel at all—cast in Cary's most beautiful and lyric prose, consists largely of experience recollected in sensation. It recovers the world that was lost to the adults of *Charley Is My Darling;* but it is a strangely remote, irrelevant country where feelings exist in forms no longer particularly meaningful, except as curios of development, to an adult intelligence. The condition of childhood is not made to matter for maturity, as it is made to matter in a work like *The Prelude.* Hence, while Cary penetrates deeply into the life of the children that he deals with, he cuts himself off from the fold of adult readers in the process. The penetration, the recovery, is often charming:

> It is hard for anyone to grow tired of lying in a summer meadow, even though he does not move at all, or barely feels, if the stars appear early, the slow roll of the planet under him; but in an ass cart there is plenty of movement and noise. Its jogs are sudden because of its narrow axle; and its rattle quick. It has also a peculiar swaying motion from side to side because of the movement of the ass, carefully picking its way among holes, and shifting the weight from one foot to another. These movements can give the sense of travel, to add to the other pleasures of lying under the sky, with infinite time at disposal; provided that it is accepted as an additional pleasure and not demanded as a necessary foundation of the whole. It was pleasant to think, now and then, we are moving; whereas it would have been maddening to expect a destination. I had long learnt not to expect it, and so, far from impatience, I felt a keen lazy pleasure in the slowness of our motion, because as I thought, it will last a long time. Ass cart travelling is pure life in the present.[22]

[22] *Ibid.,* pp. 210-211.

So, too, is childhood pure life in the present; but it is the past and the future as well that plague us as grown men and that demand our best energy and highest wisdom. The retrospective idyll, even when it is perfect, amounts to little more than a superior form of play.

The novels of the next group, *Castle Corner, The Moonlight,* and *A Fearful Joy,* have met with a good deal of disparagement, even at the hands of so stout an admirer of Cary as Andrew Wright. Much of this belittlement and dissatisfaction arises from a failure to see how close they come in conception to the essential shape of Cary's mind and intuition. To admire Cary is, to some degree at least, to consent to what he is doing in these books.

In his discussion of *Castle Corner,* Wright puts his objections succinctly:

> *Castle Corner* has no central focus. Of the ninety-three characters who appear in the book, none dominates the story, nor is there a sense that the generations of the Corner family impinge upon one another enough to provide continuity in this way. Also, the construction of the book is too often haphazard, as though Cary has more material than he can control. . . . Finally, Castle Corner itself does not constitute a symbol of sufficient strength to dominate the whole: Africa and England are geographically of nearly equal importance to Ireland in the novel. In short, there is such a richness of characterization, story and setting in *Castle Corner* that the book fails on account of its very diffuseness to achieve the unity which is necessary in the construction of any novel.[23]

All these objections grow out of a fundamental misinterpretation of the novel. It appears to have no central focus because Cary is devoting all his powers to achieving a spacious, multiform, inclusive vision, and he has deliberately avoided the kind of personal focus that Wright appears to miss. Cary's actual subject is the

[23] *Joyce Cary,* pp. 66-67.

Empire in the early years of the twentieth century. As a result, his setting is necessarily far-flung—the shifts from Ireland to England to Africa are not signs of Cary's failure to recognize that he is writing an Irish novel, but of his central imperial theme. That theme is the decline—all but unmarked by the figures in the novel —of the Empire. We measure the falling off of its vigor, purposefulness, effectiveness, ideals and grace in the generation growing into power as the book closes. No single character dominates the story, to return to Wright's objections, because Cary wants us to have the sense of individual powerlessness to turn back the general course of decline. His figures are either overcome by change, or, if they keep pace with it, out of touch with the confident idealism of the Empire under Victoria. The failure of generations to impinge on one another so as to provide continuity is, similarly, an integral part of Cary's conception rather than a fault. The novel is concerned not with continuity but with discontinuity, with the attenuation and fragmentation of political and economic energy. By the same token, Castle Corner ought not to dominate the whole; the point is that in passing into the hands of lesser men, the old family seat loses its centralizing, unifying power. Finally, the sense of an excess of material, of richness, and of diffuseness is precisely the atmosphere that Cary needs in a work dealing with the Empire as it enters upon the perils, setbacks, and confusions of its life in the twentieth century.

The novel opens with old John Corner in his castle, God in His Heaven, and all right with the Empire:

> For old John, at eighty-three, brought up in the eighteen twenties, God the Father was the ruling conception of life. God was Father of creation, the King was father of his people, and he, John, was father of his tenants, both English and Irish, especially the Irish here at Castle Corner. He found them helpless and foolish children.[24]

But this firm Anglo-Irish grasp of hierarchy, station, and imperial

---

[24] *Castle Corner* (Carfax edition; London: Michael Joseph, 1952), p. 9.

paternalism fades with the old man's death. The estate passes into the hands of one of his sons, John Chass Corner, and most of the fortune into those of his other son, Felix. John Chass, whose achievement is gracious living and hospitality, is hardly equipped or inclined to keep pace with shifting economic, political, and social conditions in Ireland. A product of the geniality and ease of a bygone time, he has no effective means of perpetuating the old familial order and control. After suffering an unexpected defeat in a local election and getting into financial straits, he is forced to surrender Castle Corner. His sickly, beautifully mannered son, Shon, dies as a mere boy—a sprig of doomed gentility: "A few minutes later he had another fit of coughing; blood flowed from his mouth, he was dying. He could not speak, but when his mother stooped to kiss him he pursed up his lips dutifully like one saying good-bye and thank you after a party."[25]

Felix, on the other hand, is incapable of continuing the family obligations and role for different reasons. A speculative man, formidable and impressive in appearance, he suffers from an intellectual aimlessness which keeps him from ever effectually focusing his life and energies. At the most, he is capable only of an African financial fiasco, reminiscent of the descents into the dark continent in Conrad. Stranded with his native paramour, Dinah, in rather depraved company at his African business outpost, he sinks pitifully, albeit intellectually, into a vitiating drunken apathy:

> Dinah, encouraged by Felix' genial smiles and conversation, got up and gingerly sat on his knee. He put his arm round her and continued to explain his system for the regeneration of the world by a rational system of education in those ideals of happiness compatible with each other's existence; the education he was giving to his son.
>
> But though he continued to speak about Cleeve's education for a long time, he had more and more difficulty in remembering whether he had actually given Cleeve an education,

[25] *Ibid.*, p. 214.

or whether he intended to do so. He could see also that Hatto and Jarvis were now drawing maps together and this caused him a vague uneasiness. He felt that he must take some decisive step to prevent something or other.[26]

But decisiveness is rather alien to Felix. He passes on to his son Cleeve not so much a good education as a vaguely inquiring intelligence which is forever opening out onto improbabilities.

Indeed, the generation which succeeds that of John Chass and Felix is even less capable than their own of steering the course of Empire. Cleeve, after attending Oxford and pursuing a number of youthful enthusiasms, eventually has an affair with a kitchen maid, Bridget, who as his wife, we are led to believe, will inherit Castle Corner. Shon, John Chass's son, has died. Philip, the son of the deeply religious and philosophical rector Feenix, becomes a futile alcoholic, never realizing any of his promise and eventually taking his own life. All the energy and ambition of Philip's uncle, James Slatter, who has long entertained the idea of buying Castle Corner for his nephew, also comes to nothing in the boy. There is a similar falling off between generations as Cary supersedes the upper-middle-class English liberal, Adam Chorley, widely cultivated and deeply immersed in Liberal politics, with his detached, decadent young aesthete of a son, Cobden.

The class which shows signs of vigor can hardly bear comparison with old John Corner. Benskin is an emerging entrepreneur, not untouched by a desire to serve and extend the Empire, but hardly embodying the noble aristocratic virtues which presided over it in the preceding century. Indeed, his wife, Helen Pynsant, though one of Cary's most charming and adept women, has an aura of thoroughgoing disreputability and decadence about her. Her affair with the Beardsley-like Cobden is the new age in little. And there is the financier, Nussbaum, of whom Cary says: "He did not believe in the Empire any more or less than he believed in God, but he considered that both de-

[26] *Ibid.*, p. 168.

served the support of intelligent men; like the police force and the gold standard."[27]

One lone figure seems to carry on the old traditions with some verve, but he does so with a considerable difference. Harry Jarvis, a young relative of the Corners' who has entered upon a military career, perceives and regrets the decline that we have been observing:

> It seemed that he was obliged to stand helpless and watch the ruin of everything he loved.
> Harry Jarvis had a strong sense of the past. His romantic feelings had been turned into the idea of antiquity, and anything old was beautiful to him. To see an old custom die was for him like seeing an old and glorious hero leave the world; and to feel deprived of that glory. He had suffered as much for the end of the prayers as for the death of old John.[28]

Cary's tone here is far from uncritical. Though he is writing about change and decline as they affect a vast portion of the Empire, he does not for a moment share Jarvis's indiscriminate, romantic, antiquarian love of the past. Nor does he share with Jarvis the sources of the young soldier's dedication and exertion, though these offer an alternative, rather widely embraced at the time, to much of the aimlessness and futility that Cary has been tracing. Jarvis derives his purpose from a ruling conviction of the period:

> Below this [imperial idea of national glory] was the master faith of the age; the idea of the struggle for existence; the survival of the fittest; the idea that some power in nature itself, a scientific providence discovered and proved by Darwin, had ordained progress by universal war. The imperialist god of Darwin, the faith of war and competition, pervaded all books, newspapers; speeches, board meetings; all the million schools of the new educational systems where science was thought of as truth; even the very missionary meetings

[27] *Ibid.*, p. 371.
[28] *Ibid.*, p. 93.

which assumed the white man's right to Christianize the world. It gave to the hunt for markets and the wars of the stock exchange the dignity of moral virtue. . . . It was so strong that it ruled even statesmen who had been brought up to believe in another one, in a quite different providence which was supposed to have designed all things for brotherhood instead of competition.[29]

Eventually this master faith leads young Jarvis to a preposterous African triumph which illustrates the pointlessness inhering even in the energetic scions of Empire. Responding to the promptings of his own obsessed imperial heart, Jarvis, in a harebrained, audacious expedition, leads a handful of unwilling men to the conquest of the Daji emirate. But his is an ambiguous triumph, ignored by his newly subjected people and the Empire alike:

> The people paid no attention to Jarvis and neither did the Government. His dispatches announcing the treaty of peace with Daji and his intention to remain in possession of the emirate until further notice were not acknowledged. The Government was in the same difficulty that offsets all imperial governments in such a crisis. They could not disown Jarvis without danger of trouble at home; or support him without danger of trouble abroad. So they did nothing and waited to see if France would take the first step, which, under the circumstances, was almost bound to be a false one, because the position itself was false in its very basis.[30]

The declining imperial world of *Castle Corner* cannot easily accommodate such pure, atavistic expressions of colonizing energy as Jarvis's. It is already too far-flung to remain intact for long.

And yet, to the extent that the idea of decline loses itself in the idea of inevitable change, an important element in the conception of *Castle Corner* is indeterminate. Cary is not unreservedly insisting on the coming doom of the Empire. To some extent he is also

[29] *Ibid.*, p. 161.
[30] *Ibid.*, p. 334.

marking a realignment of energies and purposes which gives
promise of a not altogether inglorious future. Cleeve's seriousness
and intelligence seem more likely to find a proper, if less imperial,
object than his father Felix's. Benskin's middle-class idealism is a
more vital force, after all, than John Chass's gentle hospitality.
And Bridget, who feels an indefinable power of fate directing her
toward a permanent union with Cleeve, is not without her own
peasant springs of energy and endurance. She does not for a
moment deserve to be linked, as a symbol of a new depraved epoch,
with such a figure as Yeats's insolent fiend, Robert Artisson,
lurching past a wasted landscape after the wind has dropped and
the dust settled. She simply brings  tidings of a new, less determinable, order.

*The Moonlight* makes far less use of space than *Castle Corner*,
and more of time, to achieve its uncertainties. In this respect it is
quite typical of the major portion of Cary's work, which is occupied again and again with the relation between time and value.
In *A Fearful Joy* and *Herself Surprised* we shall see Cary dealing
with this problem by chronicling an individual life which spans
the critical period from about 1880 to 1940. In *The Moonlight,*
however, and in *To Be a Pilgrim,* his procedure is to juxtapose
Victorian and modern generations by means of dextrously managed associational flashbacks, occurring in the consciousness of an
elderly character who lives on into the turmoil of the contemporary world. Miss Ella Venn, contemplating the nineteenth-century
part of herself and of her sister Rose, is Cary's elderly figure in
*The Moonlight,* while Ella's daughter, Amanda, is the center of
the troubled present.

Andrew Wright perceives some of the inherent indeterminateness that arises from Cary's particular management of this juxtaposition in *The Moonlight*:

> The excellence of [*The Moonlight*] lies in the sympathy
> which is evoked not for one generation against the other, but
> for both generations in conflict and in creation. . . .

While it is a measure of Cary's sympathy as well as of his understanding that this is not a book which extols "modern" values by pillorying the Victorian, neither does *The Moonlight* nostalgically try to rebuild the Victorian edifice. There is a real question whether the young Amanda's neat, cold town life, whether Robin's [Amanda's second cousin and ineffectual lover] modern, perceptive bitterness, represent an advance on Rose's Victorian system of love by guilt. But as it is impossible not to sympathize with Rose—Cary as usual dares us to do so when, for instance, he shows her conveying her father's corpse to Florence Villa so that he can be said to have died at home rather than at his mistress's lodgings; and the reader must accept his dare—so it is impossible not to sympathize with Amanda, experimenting coolly if not always collectedly with her own nature, unable to be unselfconscious, even in the act of love.[31]

Yet in his very next sentence, Wright refuses to see that the bountiful, undecided sympathy which he has just described must be reflected in the design of the novel—that the division is integral to the whole: "But," he says, "like *Castle Corner, The Moonlight* fails on account of a division of interest. The book has no sustained 'commanding centre' . . ."[32] Because he looks for such a center in a particular character, Wright fails to see that for both novels it exists, rather, in the subject itself.

The subject of *The Moonlight* is not the whole of the conflict between generations that we have already remarked, but the particular form that this conflict takes when it is centered about the idea of womanhood. Cary recognizes that this idea has a dual aspect: an unchanging, almost Platonic, essence and the shifting formulations of each age. Of Rose, Ella, and Amanda he says in his preface, "Each belongs at once to her sex with its nature and relations, and to a period, with its temporary answer to that everlasting problem."[33] In the novel, this means that we are given

[31] *Joyce Cary*, pp. 67-68.
[32] *Ibid.*, pp. 68-69.
[33] *The Moonlight* (Carfax edition; London: Michael Joseph, 1952), p. 5.

Rose's Victorian dutifulness and purposeful self-denial side by side
with Amanda's intellectual and sexual emancipation. The former
holds an orphaned family together, though in return for her courageous willingness to accept responsibility and authority, Rose
earns only enmity; and the latter issues, for the most part, in
Amanda's twentieth-century aimlessness and unrealization.

As a modern young woman, Amanda, a specialist in historical
research living in the English countryside with her mother, moves
through a series of unfulfillments, beginning with an affair with
a neighboring farmer, Harry Dawbarn. Harry, who is a Lawren-
tian figure with a difference—a kind of Oliver Mellors worried
about home economics and animal husbandry—eventually se-
duces Amanda at the local fair in the timeless manner of the
laborer and wench. The scene is permeated with Lawrence's
sexual excitement and inevitability, but the rush of feeling and
intoxication fails to blot out, even at the sexual climax, Amanda's
consciousness of her own unsuitability for the role. As Harry performs, with some finesse, the ritualistic preparations, Amanda
must force herself to comply, not out of desire but out of a duty to
her own supposed womanhood. "I must simply do," she thinks,
"what has to be done."[34] And, unable to escape the pronouncements of her almost neuter emancipated intelligence, she continues to reflect detachedly during the entire sexual event:

> "Well, really, is this the way one comes to the crisis of one's
> life. How simple. But, oh dear, I wish I wasn't quite so tired.
> I'm really too tired—even to—take notice, to get *any* profit.
> But I suppose that's all part of the system, too. The Fair,
> the Noah's Ark, the dragons, the cider, the lights, the dancing,
> the music, what a complicated way to make wives and
> mothers and husbands and children, and good wives, tender
> mothers. At least, I hope so. . . ."
>
> She saw Harry's cap against the sky, he had not troubled
> to take it off. She reflected, "Isn't he even going to kiss me

[34] *Ibid.*, p. 216.

first—but no, he isn't very religious. Or, perhaps, it's because—he is so religious, yes, medieval—they used to dance
and juggle in church. Oh God, I am so tired, I could scream,
scream."[35]

There is in Amanda a distressing exhaustion of female vitality.
Unlike Constance Chatterley, who moves from sterile and meaningless idleness into a liberated and exuberant sexuality, Amanda's
intellectual pursuits and crippling uncertainty about the course
that her life should take deplete her beyond the power of animal
sexuality to rejuvenate. For Harry is hardly a compatible man
for her. Unfortunately, neither is her second cousin Robin,
a futile, cynical young man of Amanda's age who has a depressing,
halting, lacerating relationship with her. At the close of the novel,
having refused both as husbands, and carrying Harry's child, she
takes up her residence in London where she can support herself
through scholarly research and have her baby. In the last glimpse
of her that the novel gives us, Cary suggests, tentatively and barely,
that her weariness and emptiness may yet be assuaged by the
miracle of a new-born absorption in her child. It is as though she is
prepared to surrender all claims to sexual fulfillment in her own
person and take up, instead, those of motherhood. She looks forward, all but hopelessly, to being reborn as a woman, ready to
meet, with unquestioning dutifulness, the new complex demands
that her responsibilities make on her:

> She sat down, meaning to smoke a cigarette, but remem-
> bered that she had foresworn smoking till her baby was born.
> So she remained with bent head, not reflecting, but allowing
> the sense of time to fall upon her, existing in a feeling that
> seemed not her own, since it was without will or desire. And
> this feeling was one of pity and emptiness; not self-pity, but
> a universal pity as for all the loss, the frustration, the waste,
> in the world, and the emptiness was the shell of this pity. It

[35] *Ibid.*, p. 217.

> lodged in a vacuum, without object, without will or hope or
> love. It was merely a vast still grief.
>
> At last Amanda lifted her hands and put them on her
> waist. She was growing big. She said to herself. "But do
> miracles happen? It will be interesting to see."[36]

Cary, however, is not content to work with the simple contrast
between generations—the idea of the historical "period, with its
temporary answer" to the everlasting problem. Rose, forbidding,
imperious, self-sacrificing, is by no means the only representative
of Victorian womanhood. Amanda's mother Ella, full of warm
and loving impulses, unruly in a way utterly foreign to her sister
Rose, and Bessie, the third Venn sister, sloppy, lively, and
matronly, who marries the man that Rose gives up because of
family duty—these enrich and complicate Victorian possibility.
So too, for the twentieth century, do such spawn of the first wave
of the feminist movement as Bessie's children, Iris and Dorothy,
who have been stripped of every vestige of feminine feeling and
character. They have been unsexed, though Dorothy is technically
a wife and mother, in a way that Amanda, despite all her distress,
has not been.

On the whole, the unchanging character of womanhood remains ambiguous and inaccessible in the novel. Some of the
definition of the contrast between generations is lost because of the
variety of women dealt with in each period—Rose has some of the
masculinity of an Iris, for example, and Amanda is not utterly
without some of the instinctive feminine predispositions of her
mother, shriveled and starved though they are. Beyond this, it is
difficult to gauge the extent to which either age approximates
"some fundamental and eternal character of being"[37]—that is,
the unchanging nature of women—because that eternal character
does not define itself clearly in the novel. It is quite like Cary, in
his penetrating preface to *The Moonlight*, to speak, on the one

[36] *Ibid.*, p. 315.
[37] *Ibid.*, p. 6.

hand, of the greatness and dignity of the Victorian conception: "Woman's chastity and refinement of sentiment are so precious to civilization, and to her own responsibility as wife, as mother, that they must be guarded from every contamination";[38] and on the other hand, of the modern young woman, who "has almost complete sexual freedom, but, with it (or so I think, but I am, of course, too near the facts to be very sure of their relative significance), a sense of responsibility and integrity which, in this completely different situation, has value and distinction possibly greater than the other."[39] We can glimpse, through his hedging, Cary's willingness to shift his criteria so as to be able to hail value wherever it survives. He is—and this will become clearer as we deal with the remaining novels—often ambivalent about the passing of old orders. Not all of his moral fluidity can keep him from coming to grief, or at least from losing his way, as he repeatedly makes the circuit from 1880 to the eve of the Second World War. His desire to have the best of both worlds, however, even though this desire is informed by his awareness that the best cannot endure in the old forms, becomes the basis of some of the most successful—though frequently equivocal—representations of historical change that we have in modern fiction.

There is a considerable unanimity of opinion among critics about the plenitude of event, time, and milieu in *A Fearful Joy*. John McCormick speaks of its "furious pace";[40] Andrew Wright sees it as "a film run too fast, a double-feature run through the projector at twice the ordinary speed";[41] and Mark Schorer says that it "is packed with a miscellany of events that begins in the heart of the Victorian age and ends in Socialist England."[42]

---

[38] *Ibid.*
[39] *Ibid.*, p. 7.
[40] *Catastrophe and Imagination* (London: Longmans, Green, 1957), p. 151.
[41] *Joyce Cary*, p. 69.
[42] "The 'Socially Extensive' Novel," *Adam International Review*, XVIII, Nos. 212-213 (1950), 32.

Schorer, indeed, cites the book as a prime specimen of the
"socially extensive" tradition of English fiction, as opposed to the
"morally intensive" one that Dr. Leavis has celebrated. To these
observations, and, in some degree, to the disapproval implicit in
them, most readers of the novel must consent.

Yet we need, also, to grasp Cary's motive for undertaking to
treat a sixty-year period crowded with social, political, and intellectual change. He moves us not merely through the time span
from the eighteen eighties to the nineteen forties, but through the
centers of activity: the aestheticism and decadence of the nineties;
the Boer War; mechanical developments, like the automobile and
aeroplane; feminism; the political and economic aspects of mobilization and war production during the First World War; the de-
mobilization and depression of the twenties; the rise of Hitler;
the thirties; the Second World War and its aftermath; and the
election of the Labor government—all with due attention to the
social, political, and intellectual tone of these episodes. He is concerned obviously with change and with social history. But he is
deeply concerned, too, with the central figure of the novel, Tabitha
Baskett, and with her responses to the life that fills the long interval
of time which she moves through. Using a third-person mode
largely limited to Tabitha's consciousness, and casting the whole
narrative in the present tense, with its aura of immediacy, even
urgency, Cary sees to it that the novel has a center in his heroine
as well as in the relentless historical change. Indeed, we come at
the change through Tabitha's experience of it. And in doing so,
we grasp the underlying conception of the book: Tabitha's remarkable, heroic ability to absorb change, respond to it, shape her
life anew again and again under the stresses and deprivations that
time brings. She does so with the help of Dick Bonser, a roguish,
rakish man who begins his relationship with Tabitha by eloping
with her because he thinks her an heiress, and who descends upon
her periodically, through almost sixty years, bringing with him,
unfailingly, a revitalizing, redeeming joy. Though irresponsible,

almost childishly self-indulgent, and only questionably fond of
Tabitha, he communicates to her what she forgets and must repeatedly learn again when next he appears: that life can be
exuberant and glorious when it is confronted, embraced, and enhanced by the imagination of joy—and when one allows oneself
to love someone as unreliable and unpromising as Bonser, with no
eye to the consequences. Even when they are both old, Bonser,
who is now wasted with dissipation, works the same spell in her:

> She is softened with laughter, and she cannot quarrel with
> his lies. The very warmth of the big hand covering half her
> thin chest penetrates her with the kindness of the flesh. It
> remembers her happiness with the man. She says, "You
> always made a fool of me, Dick." But as he compliments,
> fondles her, she is moved by a feeling that expands as if by
> itself, as if old dry roots were swelling in the flesh that laughter
> has softened, quickened, with a pressure, with keen sudden
> pangs that cause her at last, do what she will, to burst into
> tears. She does not want to cry; she hates this pain of love
> which is so despicable, which has no grain of respect, but
> yet she rests her aching head against the man's chest. She
> sighs, "We were happy, Dick you did make me happy, fear-
> fully happy. I know I had no right, I behaved badly to every-
> body."
> "Don't you believe it, Pops." He kisses her, and though
> she can't see his face she knows he is grinning with enormous
> self-satisfaction, the joy of the amorist, the conqueror, the
> beguiler, the salesman; the look she has seen on his face a
> thousand times while he has flirted with some woman. "Don't
> you believe a word of it, honey. You were a sweet little dear;
> and so you are now, every little bit of you. . . ."[43]

Soon after, she is deprived of the agency of Bonser through his
death. But in a remarkably poignant passage, Cary has her respond, irresistibly, involuntarily, to the invitation of life through
the agency of being itself. She is forcibly compelled to a continued

---

[43] *A Fearful Joy* (Carfax edition; London: Michael Joseph, 1955), p. 351.

7

participation in existence. Convalescing from a serious illness, only recently deserted by her one surviving relative, her ganddaughter Nancy, desolate and exhausted—"Living is not worth while any more," she thinks, "it is nonsense"—Tabitha finds herself watching children play in Kensington Gardens on a fine, sunny afternoon:

Some mysterious warmth rises in Tabitha to meet the warmth of the sun. It is like a sap, which diffuses through her nerves a sensitivity, so that they respond not only to the sun warmth, but to all the life about in its complex of feeling; to the middle-aged leaves, still strong under sentence of death; the parched grass; the flowers in the beds, watered that morning, but already running to seed and soon for the rubbish heap; the children in their absorbed animal existence, their passionate ambitions and fears, their brutal angers, only not dangerous because of their weakness; and she tries to protest, "No, no, I'm too old, too lonely." She is frightened by this agitation of sympathy. She turns to go home; seeking the peace of despair.

But right in her path there stands a small square girl, a child so square that Tabitha's eyes are instantly caught by the spectacles. She is very fair, and her hair, clipped round, makes square edges upon her projecting scarlet ears. Her body is square, her arms are square, her plump hands are square, her thick, absurdly short legs are two oblongs, her freckled eyebrowless face, with its insignificant nose and two large dirty tears hung mysteriously upon its square brick-red cheeks, is completely square, and she has in the middle of it a square hole, astonishingly large and square, for a mouth. And now from this whole issues a tremendous ear-splitting yell of misery and protest against the whole world, the very universe; a yell so powerful that it causes the child itself to reel sideways, in one block.

Tabitha is seized with laughter. She can't help laughing, an irresistible passion of laughter shakes her whole body, and at once a tearing pain shoots through to her heart. She thinks, "Stop—stop—it's killing me—I'm dying," and sinks breathless upon a seat.

She is protesting with all her might against this laughter, this life which has taken hold of her, which is threatening to kill her, but still she is full of laughter. Her very agony is amused at itself. She presses her hand to her heart as if to grasp that frightful pain in her fingers and squeeze it back, crush it out of existence. She is terrified that it will kill her, and never has she wished so ardently to live. Her whole being prays to be reprieved this once—for a month, a week, till that letter comes from Nancy.

And the prayer that is torn from her is not to the father or the son or the spirit. It is the primitive cry of the living soul to the master of life, the creator, the eternal. "Oh, God," her blue lips murmur, "not quite now."

Gradually the pain becomes less, the terror falls before the longing, the prayer. She perceives that she is not going to die that afternoon. And, as cautiously straightening her back, she looks again at the sky, the trees, the noisy quarrelling children, at a world remade, she gives a long deep sigh of gratitude, of happiness.[44]

Here, in some of his most adroit language and most delicately managed feeling, Cary communicates the presiding motif of the novel and one of his most persistent intuitions into human existence. Tabitha, exhausted by time, experience, loss, and illness, begins by turning away in fear from the faint revival of life and sympathy in her; she cannot bear to be exposed again to the pain of living. But in the square child—an almost perfect Carian intuition—she reads the startling, resurrecting comic joy of life, and the absurdity of her own despair and relinquishment. The child's "yell of misery and protest against the whole world, the very universe" is Tabitha's surrender writ ludicrous; she grasps the preposterous self-importance and groundlessness of all deep protests against, and alienations from, the universe and from the springs of joy in life itself. At the moment when she is won back—by this random human encounter—to a Carian celebration of life, she is threatened by death, and her fear inverts itself. She does not

[44] *Ibid.*, pp. 387-388.

dread living at this point, but dying. Her prayer is addressed not to any formal institutional deity, but to Cary's own god of life. When it is answered, she contemplates a "world remade"—that is, revived to her imagination and, consequently, made viable to her mind and heart.

The novel is "packed with a miscellany of events" because they serve to excite, then weary, then reanimate Tabitha; because, like the absurd, life-giving square child, they sustain Cary's irrepressible affirmation of—his essential reverence for—existence. We master change and loss and old age by preserving our emotional and imaginative power to be reborn, as events and fashions are reborn, or, at least, give way to one another. The clutter and crowding and furious pacing push this cherished human resource to its uttermost in Tabitha, and make its ultimate triumph the more moving as a consequence.

The plethora, however, of episodes, settings, and considerations in *A Fearful Joy* suggests, unmistakably, that the human response, as we see it in Tabitha, must necessarily be rather indiscriminate. Life is vast and life is multifarious, says the novel. Part of the arduousness of Tabitha's imaginative rekindling of her own responsiveness and concern arises from the sheer bulk of experience to be acted upon; the imagination's success is the sign, once again, of Cary's assent to undifferentiated life, to life on any terms. There has, perhaps, never been a writer in whom existence so passionately and resolutely precedes essence. This assent to the whole range of life's possibility is what explains some of the extraordinary energy in Cary's major figures. In order to deal with experience in carloads and to utter Carian benedictions on it in this inclusive form, his people need heroic powers. Still, regardless of how imposing her affirmations make Tabitha Baskett, the swarming, unevaluated life that fills *A Fearful Joy* requires more ordering than mere chronology and consent can confer on it. Mark Schorer sums up the inconclusiveness in words which, if they ignore Tabitha, reflect the impact of the book as a whole. "The lesson would seem to be that here is a hundred years of uneven history, and that trusting to our instincts, we may certainly expect to endure a hundred more. Such a lesson does not suggest a great or even a thoughtful novel, in Dr. Leavis's sense."[45] Nor will it, for that matter, even in a sense less morally intensive.

It is in the first trilogy, consisting of *Herself Surprised, To Be a Pilgrim,* and *The Horse's Mouth,* that Cary discovers what Andrew Wright has called his "inevitable style."[46] Wright has in mind, primarily, Cary's devotion to the idea of a subjectively imagined and created reality. If we add to this Cary's vision of reality as essentially indeterminate, we see at once the need for this private world—in order to live, people must put their own construction on the unordered turmoil around them—and the even greater inevitability of the trilogy and its technique. In these three novels, Cary adds to his other devices an adroitly indeterminate narrative method, which becomes his most characteristic and significant contribution to the art of fiction.

In his preface to the first trilogy, Cary explains the connection between his philosophical formulation and the first-person technique of the novels:

> What I set out to do was to show three people, living each in his own world by his own ideas, and relating his life and struggles, his triumphs and miseries in that world. . . .
>
> Their situation, in short, was to be that of everyone who is doomed or blessed to be a free soul in the free world and solve his own problems as he goes through it. . . .
>
> Each of us is obliged to construct his own idea, his own map of things by which he is going to find his way, so far as he can, through life. He must decide what he wants and how he shall achieve himself. . . .
>
> The ruling idea is all important. A Hindu pilgrim without any possessions in the world save a rag round his loins and his staff may well be happier than a Texas millionaire. But

45 "The 'Socially Extensive' Novel," p. 32.
46 *Joyce Cary,* p. 107.

the millionaire will not be able to enter into the pilgrim's world any more than the pilgrim could live comfortably as a millionaire. Their reactions to life, their feelings about the world, their valuation of achievement would be completely beyond each other's understanding. And this is the case, to a more or less degree, with all of us. We are alone in our own worlds.

We can sympathize with each other, be fond of each other, but we can never completely understand each other. We are not only different in character and mind, we don't know how far the difference goes.

That's why each of my three chief characters had to write in the first person and reveal his own world in his own style.[47]

We have recourse, then, in the trilogy, only to the three private worlds presented in the three novels; when one narrator's account clashes with the others, the truth lies nowhere, or, what amounts to the same thing, everywhere:

> Sara regards herself as a tenderhearted creature whose troubles are due to her good nature. This estimate is true. Wilcher sees in her an easygoing mistress who will cherish him in his decrepitude. He is quite right. Gulley calls her a man grabber, and he is also right. All the ideas of the three about each other are right from their own point of view.[48]

As for Cary's point of view, or the reader's, we need, in this perspective, give them no special consideration. The theory would make them as partial as those of the narrators. Cary has now devised an indeterminate form by means of which he can explore an indeterminate world.

Sara Monday's narrative, *Herself Surprised,* covers much the same period of time as *A Fearful Joy,* in something of the same way. Sara's is the presiding consciousness, as Tabitha's was, but the first-person method makes Sara even a more absolute center. The history of her life begins in 1880 and continues to about 1940.

[47] *First Trilogy* (New York: Harper, 1958), pp. ix-x.
[48] *Ibid.*, p. xiv.

It is organized, appropriately enough for so womanly a woman, around her domestic preoccupations and the three men with whom she is primarily concerned, her first husband, Matthew Monday; the painter, Gulley Jimson; and the old lawyer, Thomas Wilcher. She comes as a blooming country girl to the Monday home to take a position as cook. Matthew, a timid, aging bachelor dominated by the women in his family, falls in love with Sara and marries her, despite a considerable social disparity. Sara makes something of a man of Matthew, giving him confidence and a measure of masculinity; but he is hardly man enough. During her long marriage she has a brief affair with Hickson, a millionaire friend of Matthew's; she also begins a relationship with the indomitable Gulley Jimson, who appropriately enough, destroys Matthew's new conceit of himself by means of a penetrating satiric portrait, unhappily commissioned by Sara. Sara takes up with Gulley after Matthew's death, thinking that they are to be married. When she learns that he already has a wife, she lives with him still, drawn equally by what she takes to be his need of her domestic ministrations and his exuberance and courage. When he leaves her, after beating her a number of times, because he cannot tolerate what he takes to be her insistence on organizing his life along her own domestic lines, she goes to work as a cook for Thomas Wilcher at his family estate, Tolbrook. Wilcher, who is far more willing to be domesticated than Gulley, soon makes Sara his mistress. Before they can be married, however, Sara is caught stealing from Wilcher by a troublesome niece—Sara has previously been in financial difficulties with the authorities—and enters, at the close, on an eighteen-month prison term. It is in prison that she writes her story—the narrative of *Herself Surprised*—for the newspapers, in order to earn money so that she can meet more of the domestic responsibilities that she has been accumulating for almost sixty years.

The novel is drenched in the womanhood of Sara. Her language, with its kitchen similes, its overbearing solicitude for her "poor mannies," and its lurking sensuality, represents Cary's rather successful attempt to set down the archetypal feminine principle. The old Eve is distinctly visible in Sara. Yet when we consider this part of her in conjunction with the genuine good will, generosity, even sacrifice that leads Caroline Gordon to regard her as a saint,[49] we come to see that we cannot place Sara, with any real assurance, as a moral being. Our constant attempt to do so as we read her narrative constitutes one of the major attractions of the book.

Sara's conception of herself is curiously indeterminate. She never ceases to surprise herself with what she is capable of. As readers, we are usually at a loss to decide when she is a genuine mystery to herself, impelled by deep, unsearchable springs of female energy and instinct, and when she is simply exploiting this mystery so as to excuse some rather questionable behavior. The comedy of the book resides, largely, in this second possibility. Her sexual generosity is as casuistic as it is bountiful, yet it has a distressingly plausible unavoidability about it as well. When, as Matthew's wife, she allows Hickson to have his way with her, she casts her submission in these terms:

> But since Mr. Hickson had flirted so with me once, touching me, he had to do it again. And this is the great difficulty for a woman. How to put an uppish kind of man into his place, without hurting him more than he deserves. For after all, it was no great crime in Mr. Hickson, to be a man and like me as a woman. Or if it was so, then Providence must answer for our shapes.[50]

Later, while waiting to marry Gulley, she explains in comparably kindly terms her acquiescence to him on a beach, and the even kindlier aftermath:

> I love the heat and lying in the sun and I know it makes

[49] *How to Read a Novel* (New York: Viking, 1957), p. 99.
[50] *Herself Surprised* in *First Trilogy*, p. 26.

me lazy and careless so I don't care what happens. So that
my mind was laughing at little Jimson when he held my
hand and told me he could make me so rich and give me furs
and jewels; yet my flesh delighted in his kindly thoughts. So
it grew sleepy and I forgot myself and he had his way, yet
not in luxury, but kindness, and God forgive me, it was only
when I came to myself, cooling in the shadow that I asked
what I had done. . . .

Though I jumped out of bed the next night when he came
in to me, I thought it was not worth while to keep what little
decency was left me, and to deny him what he thought so
much of. So I got back again to him, as sad and mild as any
poor girl that has no right to her own flesh and let him do
as he pleased.

So it was every night. I even made it seem welcome to
please the man, for I thought, if I must give him his pleasure,
it was a waste not to give him all that I could.[51]

Later still she becomes Wilcher's mistress, partly out of concern
for his lumbago—he makes late visits on chill evenings to another
woman—and partly to preserve her comfort at the Wilcher town
house:

Now I have to confess that I was quite confused between
my conscience and my duties, and indeed I prayed one night,
and cried over the whole thing, since I thought that even if
Mother could have been alive, she wouldn't have been able
to guide me, yet all the time, I knew I would give way. For I
liked my happiness in Craven Gardens and my comforts and
my peace and my dear Mr. W. himself far too well to do anything to lose them, or do them any injury.[52]

All three passages are remarkable for their moral inventiveness.
In the first two, Cary's and Sara's tongues are in their cheeks,
as the rationalizations proliferate. In the third there is more frank-
ness. Ambiguity, though, plays over all of them. We have the
sense that the deepest motives are unexpressed or inexpressible,

[51] *Ibid.*, p. 110.
[52] *Ibid.*, p. 214.

yet not altogether unrelated to some of the touching improvized reasons Sara gives. Even her excuses and self-deceptions originate in the best part of her—her flesh. If flesh could speak, she makes us think, it would do so in her very accents, and with something of her fuzziness.

In addition to commanding too many motives, Sara, on occasion, cannot tell why she has acted. The indeterminate motive is a remarkably serviceable enigma in her hands, her chief means of hiding her looser nature from herself, of surprising herself. After posing nude for Gulley the first time, while still Matthew's wife, she says, "It seemed to me then that I had been a fool to be so prim before and yet I wondered at myself. I could not tell whether I had done a religious thing or a bad one."[53] After taking up with Wilcher she says, "It was from this time that I began to pay Gulley installments every week, but whether to keep him in some comfort and please my conscience, or only to keep him away and please my flesh, I never could tell."[54] The fact of pleasure is, in either case, of course, unambiguous enough. Speaking of Gulley's and her mutual friend, Rozzie, now dead, Sara observes, "For his idea was that I had been jealous of Rozzie. And perhaps I had been. For God knows I never knew myself."[55] And as she looks back on the money that she has stolen from Wilcher, she says, "But as for my robberies, that was another thing and I still wonder at myself. For at this very time, when I was helping Mr. W. to economize, and cutting down even his own dinners, I was cheating him. How I came into this double way of life, I cannot tell. . . ."[56]

Sara is, in sum, a moral virtuoso. She can elaborate moral justifications when such a course seems expedient, or plead a lack of self-knowledge when explanations would be damning. Much of this protection, ironically enough, is unnecessary because her sub-

[53] *Ibid.*, p. 67.
[54] *Ibid.*, p. 208.
[55] *Ibid.*, p. 255.
[56] *Ibid.*, p. 225.

terranean objects are largely unexceptional—they consist for the most part in seeing to it that people whom she can construe as family are decently provided for, and that her own days are spent among things that are clean, fit, sparkling, and tidy. Even her bad checks and her thefts from Wilcher are the result of commendable impulses—at the close she needs money in order to keep Gulley and Rozzie's son, Tom, at a decent school. It is true that she can throw up formidable moral smoke screens. Here, for instance, is a brilliant piece of obfuscation on upper-middle-class values, touched off by Sara's hope that Clarissa, a friend of the family, will intervene to secure for Bobby Brown, Wilcher's nephew, the Tolbrook estate:

> She was clever and besides, she was a lady and understood the minds of that class, as I never could. For one minute you would think it was all religion with them, and money nothing; in the next, money was all and religion nothing. But, of course, money for them often comes out as duty, and so religion, while for the poor, money is always money only, because there is not enough of it to be duty. So Bobby agreed that if he had the property, he would be Wilcher Brown, and yet, as I said, it was not against his religion, because the property was so big that it was his duty to get it and improve it.[57]

And we might set alongside this intricately naïve casuistry Sara's culinary formulation of Cary's own moral fluidity:[58]

> [Bobby] was at the age when boys begin to read and think they know everything because the books make it seem easy. I suppose they must, like a cookery book, for how could they put the hard parts, like real life, which are different every time; your cream all turned that morning, or a hole in the stockpot; or the kitchen boiler to be cleaned.[59]

[57] *Ibid.*, p. 221.
[58] See pp. 29-30 above.
[59] *Herself Surprised*, p. 187.

But on the whole, her deepest impulses, though Cary often keeps them from her own view as well as the reader's, are sound enough. Unlike Nina Latter's moral confusions in *Prisoner of Grace,* they do not issue in ominous anarchic recklessness. Sara's flesh may be trusted to do the human, maternal, wifely, life-giving—if officious—thing. The equivocal, mystifying part of her becomes, in the end, what we must know her by.

Like Sara in her novel, Thomas Wilcher in his, *To Be a Pilgrim,* is an indeterminate figure within the larger indeterminate design of the trilogy itself. Born in 1868 and writing in 1939, he is centrally concerned in his narrative, which is written as a journal at Tolbrook after Sara has been sent off to prison, with the problem of time—that is, with the contrast between life in Victorian England and life on the eve of the Second World War. Cary juxtaposes past and present by means of flashbacks, as we have seen him do in *The Moonlight;* but in extending Wilcher's control over all the material of the book by means of the first-person journal narrative, Cary has provided himself with even richer possibilities of inconclusiveness.

In a sensitive study of *To Be a Pilgrim,* Barbara Hardy has observed that Wilcher's life is the life he has lived rather than the life he is living at Tolbrook under the eye of his niece Ann. He participates in the past, Miss Hardy says, but merely looks on in the present.[60] Speaking of Wilcher's juxtapositions of past and present whenever recurring events—births, marriages, financial dealings, deaths—take him back to what has happened forty, fifty, even sixty years ago, Miss Hardy observes, "The counterpoint makes the criticism. The presence of the ghosts defines the living. . . . The real action is the oblique criticism of the present by the past. What the present lacks, vitality, passion, grace, the past is shown to possess."[61]

By and large, this oblique criticism and its formal embodiment

[60] "Form in Joyce Cary's Novels," *Essays in Criticism,* IV (April 1954), 193.
[61] *Ibid.,* p. 186.

in flashbacked juxtapositions gives the book its shape. But Cary has not allowed Wilcher to stand as simply an old crank alienated from the present. Instead, Wilcher emerges as an endlessly divided figure, more notable for his tergiversation than for his allegiance. It is true that he has a profound attachment to the life that he knew as a child and young man. Standing in his mother's room at Tolbrook, which has been left untouched since her death, he says:

> To me it is a holy place. In this cold morning light I look at its faded hangings, its worn carpet with the sense which only the old can know, of a debt which was never acknowledged and can never be paid, not only to my mother, but to a whole generation. Of storied richness which can return to the spirit only in the form of the things it touched and loved.[62]

It is true, as well, that he is revolted by modernity—here is his estimate of one of the young ladies pursuing his nephew John in the years following the First World War:

> Once or twice a young woman had called for him at the office, a creature whom, at a first meeting, I took for a young prostitute from the cheaper streets. Her figure was slim and flat, her face disproportionately large and round. In repose, with its small features, large blue eyes, and brassy hair, it reminded one of those dummies put in hairdressers' windows. But it was seldom in repose. Gladys was always jerking her head, twitching her little mouth, rolling her eyes, and bumping her shoulders. In conversation she would wriggle her behind as if it itched and frequently she plunged her hand into her breast or down her back in order to scratch herself. Her voice was the chatter of a colobus monkey; her laugh the shriek of a cockatoo. She was daubed like one of Edward's [Wilcher's brother] pictures; and her nails were always dirty.[63]

[62] *To Be a Pilgrim* in *First Trilogy*, p. 24.
[63] *Ibid.*, pp. 261-262.

And his horror of his niece Ann's godless psychologizing and impotent cynicism, especially in her recent marriage to her cousin
Robert—the Bobby Brown of *Herself Surprised*—pervades all of
his dealings with her, until she too comes under the influence of the
past. Wilcher is busy, as well, trying to frustrate Robert's attempts to modernize and mechanize agriculture on the Tolbrook
estate.

But this acceptance of the past and repudiation of the present
undergoes extensive and tortuous modification in Wilcher. He is
a learned, even a wise man, who, unlike the largely unthinking
Sara, has brooded deeply and deliberately over the process of historical change. He knows that life must go on by taking new forms
and that an unyielding attachment to the past, especially to such
material embodiments of the past as Tolbrook, can be life-defeat-
ing. Pondering Robert's sojourn in Canada as a farmer, Wilcher
writes:

> The English summer weighs upon me with its richness. I
> know why Robert ran away from so much history to the
> new lands where the weather is as stupid as the trees, chance
> dropped, are meaningless. Where earth is only new dirt, and
> corn, food for animals, two- and four-footed. I must go too,
> for life's sake. This place is so doused in memory that only to
> breathe makes me dream like an opium eater. Like one who
> has taken a narcotic, I have lived among fantastic loves and
> purposes. The shape of a field, the turn of a lane have had
> the power to move me as if they were my children and I have
> made them. I have wished immortal life for them, though
> they were even more transient appearances than human
> beings.[64]

This is no mere gesture made with the rationalizing part of
Wilcher's mind, but one of his insistent intuitions. Very early in
the novel, he endorses fervently the figures who have disowned
possessions and moved through life with a sense of it as a temporary passage, a pilgrimage: his sister Lucy who gave up her

[64] *Ibid.*, p. 130.

class and her home at Tolbrook and, in a dazzling act of faith, married an evangelical Benjamite preacher, Matthias Brown; his father, an old soldier who spoke of Tolbrook as "Not a bad billet" or "Not a bad camp"; and Sara who viewed life as "places" and "situations," who put no roots in the ground because her "goods and possessions were all in her own heart and mind, her skill and courage."[65] We get the impression repeatedly that Wilcher's narrative aspires, unsuccessfully, to the condition of the picaresque. The title of the novel itself derives from a hymn of Bunyan's which expresses this view of life for Wilcher and which identifies it for him with the tradition of English Protestantism. When he does obeisance to the idea of existence as a pilgrimage untrammelled by the past, Wilcher formulates what he takes to be the quintessence of English faith. As a young man, he has heard the hymn sung by Brown at a Benjamite meeting:

> No foe shall stay his might
>     Though he with giants fight
> He will make good his right
> To be a pilgrim. . . .

Brown had no arguments that did not fill me with contempt. But when he sang these verses from Bunyan . . . then something swelled in my heart as if it would choke me unless I, too, opened my mouth and sang. I might have been a bell tuned to that note, and perhaps I was. For the Wilchers are as deep English as Bunyan himself. A Protestant people, with the revolution in their bones. . . . Our grandfather was a Plymouth Brother; he was converted by one of the Wallops, and there are Quakers, Shakers, fifth-monarchy men, even Anabaptists, on the maternal side.[66]

The fact that Wilcher's advocacy of a nontraditional confrontation of the present takes the trouble to trace its own tradition is a token of the irreparable cleavage in him. The whole weight and structure of the book exalts the Victorian experience; the contrasts

[65] *Ibid.*, p. 8.
[66] *Ibid.*, p. 13.

almost always imply a regrettable falling off in the present. Yet the past is found wanting as well. There is, first, Wilcher's liberal sprinkling of his brother Edward's morose satirical couplets over the pages devoted to this same past :

> Mad Englishmen. Why not? Whose Sunday bells
> Ring in raw beef and fifteen different hells.[67]
>
> Let tyrannies all to free republics pass
> The one by coppers ruled; the other, brass.[68]
>
> Government rascals! so cries honest Hob.
> True, God made rascals; each man for his job.[69]

There is the failure of faith in Edward himself, a brilliant Cabinet minister who unaccountably withdraws from political life at a critical time, and in his mistress, Julie, a gifted actress who allows herself to languish into desuetude. Of them, Wilcher says, "They were faithful to friendship, to kindness, to beauty; never to faith. They could not make the final sacrifice. They took a holiday at the wrong time. . . . They would rather die in peace than live in pain."[70] And there is Wilcher's own failure as well. He has an abiding reverence for the true pilgrims of the novel, Lucy and Brown:

> They were both people of power; life ran in them with a primitive force and innocence. They were close to its springs as children are close, so that its experience, its loves, its wonders, its furies, its mysterious altruism, came to them as to children, like mysteries, and gave them neither peace nor time to fall into sloth and decadence.[71]

But Wilcher is quite aware, for all of his affirmations of faith, his plans to flee Tolbrook and set up house in a cottage with Sara, his understanding of his enslavement to the past, that he has never

[67] *Ibid.*, p. 15.
[68] *Ibid.*, p. 149.
[69] *Ibid.*, p. 171.
[70] *Ibid.*, p. 202.
[71] *Ibid.*, p. 93.

been one of the "people of power." He can recall how, when he was a young man at a moment of critical choice, one part of himself cried out, "Foolish and wicked boy, you are destroying the peace of your home and your heart," and another urged, "Be reckless, have faith—take no thought for the morrow—cast your bread upon the waters."[72] But his whole life has consisted of taking thought, and as an old man he confesses, "The truth is, I have always been a lover rather than a doer; I have lived in dreams rather than acts; and like all lovers, I have lived in terror of change to what I love."[73] More than this he is aware that as he once, as a boy, regained, on his mother's breast, "the power to live" after a terrifying experience, taking this power from "that warmth, that life that had given me life already," so he had always taken from the "people of power," some "direct communication of their energy, their confidence." Far from having himself lived in the past, he has only observed the life there, too, or taken strength enough to sustain his life from those who had strength to give. Wilcher falls between two worlds and is in the strange position of advocating a life and faith to his niece Ann that he has himself never been capable of living. Characteristically enough, when he finally consents to the improvements that Robert wants to make at Tolbrook, Wilcher sees Tolbrook going forward and backward at once:

> Robert does not destroy Tolbrook, he takes it back into history, which changed it once before from priory into farm, from farm into manor, from manor, the workshop and court of a feudal dictator, into a country house where young ladies danced and hunting men played billiards; where, at last, a new-rich gentleman spent his week ends from his office. And after that I suppose it was to have been a country hotel, where typists on holiday gaze at the trees, the crops, and the farmer's men with mutual astonishment and dislike. Robert has brought it back into the English stream and he himself

[72] *Ibid.*, p. 72.
[73] *Ibid.*, p. 333.

8

has come with it; to the soft corn, good for homemade
bread; the mixed farm, so good for men; the old church
religion which is so twined with English life that the very
prayers seem to breathe of fields after rain and skies whose
light is falling between clouds.[74]

Wilcher, like Cary, can have it both ways. The vision here is of
the pastness of the present, the presentness of the past. It is the
vision of indeterminate time entertained, at the last, by a figure
whose life has been plagued by time and his sense of powerlessness
before it. When we add to the oscillations that we have been tracing, the possibility that Wilcher is not entirely sane—Ann is a physician who has him under observation during the entire time that
the journal, or novel, is being written at Tolbrook—we see that
there is almost no end to the ambiguity that Cary has lodged in this
second volume of his trilogy. The triumph of *To Be a Pilgrim* is
that it holds its polarities together in the imposing, tormented
figure of its narrator. It is Cary's most sustained exploration of his
divided and, now, barely distinguishable worlds.

Cary, it should be clear by now, organizes his novels by means of
central conflicts which frequently are not resolved. In *Herself
Surprised* we witness the spectacle of Sara rather comically
divided against herself, and in *To Be a Pilgrim*, the almost tragic
situation of Wilcher, who is torn ceaselessly by the pulls of past
and present. The major conflict in *The Horse's Mouth* exists between the aging painter, Gulley Jimson, who narrates the novel,
and the entire society in which he lives, and with which, in the
manner of the *picaro,* he has extensive dealings. The novel is
organized to show that none of these dealings, which range from
the almost inhuman hostility of the town council which knocks a
wall out from under Gulley at the close, to the charity and solicitude of the barmaid, Coker, ever involves the least understanding
of what Gulley is about in his painting—even in his heroic desire
to paint. The book is, in a sense, a memorial to that militant and

[74] *Ibid.,* p. 328.

obsessive inner vision which has, in large measure, defined the artist since the nineteenth century, as he has been driven more and more to justify, preserve, and expound his function. As a result, Gulley emerges as one of the most formidably isolated and misunderstood figures in contemporary fiction.

Yet this presiding conflict is treated comically in the novel. Cary, in his preface to the Carfax edition of the book, explains the reason for Gulley's facetiousness by using a military analogy:

> Anyone who has served in a war knows the man who is suddenly full of jokes on the night before an attack, even just before going over the top.
>
> Jimson, as an original artist, is always going over the top into No Man's Land, and knows that he will probably get nothing for his pains and enterprise but a bee-swarm of bullets, death in frustration, and an unmarked grave. He makes a joke of life because he dare not take it seriously. He is afraid that if he does not laugh he will lose either his nerves or his temper, that he will want to run away from his duty, or demand with rage 'what is the sense of anything in a world at war,' and either shoot the nearest officer or himself.[75]

Cary conceives of the novel as fundamentally serious, then, and of Gulley's plight as essentially tragic. But the comic device with which Gulley arms himself in order to stave off madness and despair, by tending to fix our attention more and more on itself, threatens at last to stave off all seriousness as well. It is difficult to preserve any idea of Gulley as a spiritual descendant of William Blake, creating, in an ineffably new visionary and symbolic style, works of the highest imaginative and spiritual grandeur, as we behold him plaguing his former patron Hickson in a hilarious threatening phone call,[76] or spend, in what is perhaps the funniest scene in the fiction of the present century, an afternoon and evening with him at the home of the millionaire Beeders.[77] The

---

[75] *The Horse's Mouth* (Carfax edition; London: Michael Joseph, 1956), p. 7.
[76] *The Horse's Mouth* in *First Trilogy*, pp. 6-8.
[77] *Ibid.*, pp. 141-149.

comedy in these scenes, and in any number of others, is too fundamental, too intrinsic a part of Gulley to be a mere tactic. It defines
him and his relationships more surely and more memorably than
anything else about him. If he is at war with the massive indifference and antipathy that surrounds him and his work, we remember the outrageous gusto with which he does battle more than the
complex of exalted causes which he does battle for.

The style that Cary has devised for Gulley is largely responsible
for his comic force. Unlike Wilcher, who is never funny, and Sara,
who is unwittingly funny, Gulley is a great and deliberate
comedian, exulting in his capacity for reducing his enemies to a
fantastic, almost metaphysical, ridicule. It scarcely matters during his tirades that he overshoots the mark, that what he says may
correspond only at points with the reality under consideration;
for these speeches exist, like the art of Oscar Wilde, for their own
sake. The exuberance that goes into them is the most genuine
evidence of Gulley's creative power that the novel is able to communicate. Here, for instance, is Gulley's survey of the elegant
collection of paintings at the Beeder apartment :

> Usual modern collection. Wilson Steer, water in water-
> colour, Matthew Smith, victim of the crime in slaughter-
> colour; Utrillo whitewashed wall in mortarcolour; Matisse,
> odalisque in scortacolour; Picasso, spatchcock horse in torta-
> colour; Gilbert Spencer, cocks and pigs in thoughtacolour;
> Stanley Spencer, cottage garden in hortacolour; Braque, half
> a bottle of half and half in portercolour; William Roberts,
> pipe dream in snortercolour; Wadsworth, rockses, blockses,
> and fishy boxes all done by self in nautacolour; Duncan
> Grant, landscape in strawtacolour; Frances Hodgkin, cows
> and wows and frows and sows in chortacolour; Rouault,
> perishing Saint in fortacolour; Epstein, Leah waiting for
> Jacob in squawtacolour.[78]

And here is the prodigious rant which Gulley looses on his self-

[78] *Ibid.*, pp. 137-138.

appointed disciple, Nosy Barbon, and a busload of innocent Britishers. It keeps gathering momentum from its own delight in what it has invented, rather than from any real intuition into, or even concern with, the nature of governments:

"What is a government, Nosy? It's a committee of committees and a committee hasn't even got trousers. It's only got a typist, and she's thinking of her young man and next Saturday afternoon at the pictures. If you gave a government imagination, it wouldn't know where to put it. It would pass it on to the cat or leave it out for the charwoman to be taken away with the tea leaves. The only good government," I said, "is a bad one in the hell of a fright; yes, what you want to do with government is to put a bomb under it every ten minutes and blow its whiskers off—I mean its subcommittees. And it doesn't matter if a few of its legs and arms go too, and it gets blown out of the window. Not that I've personally got a bad opinion of governments, as governments. A government is a government, that's all. You don't expect it to have the virtues of a gorilla because it doesn't belong to the same class. It's not a higher anthropoid. It has too many legs and hands. But if you blow off some of the old limbs, well, imagine. There you have a piece of government lying in the middle of Whitehall, and it says to itself, 'This is most unusual. I distinctly heard a bang. I must inquire at once—yes, immediately—I must appoint a commission.' So then it opens its eyes and looks at the crowd and says, 'My God, what has happened, what are those creatures?' And the people say, 'We're the people, you're the government, hurry up and do something for us.' And the government says, 'I'll have a committee on it at once.' And the people say, 'You haven't got any committees—they're all dead—you're the government.' And the government says, 'Haven't I got a secretary?' And the people shout, 'No, we've just chopped her up with a rusty axe.' 'Or an office boy?' 'No, we've pushed him down a drain.'
" 'But I can't be a government all by myself.'
" 'Yes you are, and you've got to do something.'
" 'But one man can't be a government, it isn't democratic.'

" 'Yes it is,' the people say. 'We've sent for another bomb. But you've got ten minutes still, so you'd better do something.

"So then the government looks round and thinks. It uses its imagination because it hasn't got any committee and because it hasn't got a secretary. It gets an idea all by itself, and it says, 'Jimini Christie, look at all these people. Look at their trousers and their gamps. What squalor. It seems that they aren't in the government.' And then it makes a law that everyone is to get a steel-stick umbrella and a trouser-press free. And all the old clubmen who used to be in government say, 'It's impossible, it can't be done. The people won't stand it.' But it is done, it is possible, and the people not only stand it, they ask for trousers as well, to put in the presses. And then the old clubmen themselves ask for new trousers and take it all as a matter of course. And then the bomb comes and the people blow that government into cottage pie and start again with committees. For the people is just as big a danger as the government. I mean, if you let it get on your mind. Because there's more of it. More and worse and bigger and emptier and stupider. One man is a living soul, but two men are an indiarubber milking machine for a beer engine, and three men are noises off and four men are an asylum for cretins and five men are a committee and twenty-five are a meeting, and after that you get to the mummy-house at the British Museum, and the Sovereign People and Common Humanity and the Average and the Public and the Majority and the Life Force and Statistics and the Economic Man brainless, eyeless, wicked spawn of the universal toad sitting in the black bloody ditch of eternal night and croaking for its mate which is the spectre of Hell."[79]

It is difficult indeed for Cary to move from this kind of unfettered language and emotion to that solemn portrait of the artist which seems also, in some measure, to be his concern in *The Horse's Mouth*. He has himself spoken of the book as "a very heavy piece of metaphysical writing . . . a study of the creative imagination working in symbols."[80] That he is, to some degree,

[79] *Ibid.*, pp. 209-210.
[80] "An Interview with Joyce Cary," *Paris Review*, p. 76.

successful with this aspect of the novel, we can gather from Pamela Hansford Johnson's deliberately unqualified remark that *The Horse's Mouth* "is the most piercing study of the artist's mind in the whole of English literature."[81] Certainly Cary's use of motifs from Blake's poetry, and of the figure of Blake himself as the type of the symbolic artist at war with his time, is wonderfully appropriate. Both Gulley and Blake live in creation in a way that society does not and cannot afford to; it seeks always to institutionalize and preserve while they want only to overturn, to give new forms to ultimate spiritual realities. Gulley's Blakean visions, as he contemplates the massive biblical paintings which occupy him during the course of the novel—"The Fall," "The Raising of Lazarus," and "The Creation"—are a commendable attempt on Cary's part to convey the quality of a genuinely symbolic imagination engaged in the fusion of spiritual intuition and plastic forms. The interior monologues which Cary employs for this purpose achieve a remarkable wedding of the contemplative, the poetic, and the visual; they constitute one of his most considerable attainments as a writer of prose. Yet, as Barbara Hardy has pointed out, far from existing as mere patches of virtuosity, these renditions of Gulley's interior life go forward in the midst of the indifferent, debilitating surroundings in which he is compelled to live, so that the visions serve at once to define him and his difference.[82] One of these moments comes at Hickson's home, where the millionaire patron and Coker are haggling over the rights to some of Gulley's earlier work. Gulley abstracts himself from the quarrel, as he must in order to proceeed with his plans for "The Fall," and turns his gaze inward:

> There was a visitor's book, nicely bound in morocco, lying on a buhl desk with pens and inks. I took a few blank pages out of the end and carried them over to one of the little tables where the light was good. And began to scrawl some figures

[81] "Joyce Cary," in *Little Reviews Anthology*, 1949, ed. Denys Val Baker (London: Methuen, 1949), pp. 205-206.

[82] "Form in Joyce Cary's Novels," p. 188.

that had come into my head. Eve under the willows. And the
everlasting maiden. Oothoon. The eternal innocence that
thinks no evil. Yes, I thought, there's Billy again. Handing me
the truth. Even when I wouldn't take it. That's what he was
saying all his life. A tear is an intellectual thing. And a joy.
It's wisdom in vision. It's the prophetic eye in the loins. The
passion of intelligence. Yes, by Gee and Jay, I thought. The
everlasting creation of delight. The joy that is always new
and fresh because it is created. The revelation ever renewed,
in every fall.

> Oothoon wandered in woe
> Along the vales of Leutha seeking flowers to comfort her;
> And thus she spoke to the bright Marigold of Leutha's
>       vale:
> 'Art thou a flower? art thou a nymph? I see thee now a
>       flower,
> Now a nymph. I dare not pluck thee from thy dewy bed!'

Leutha's vale being the valley of desire and the marigold
her own virginity.
   I took another sheet and let my hand run over it. But I
couldn't make out why I gave poor Eve-Oothoon a head as
big as her body, and little fat legs, and why she had her hands
over her ears. Unless she was trying not to hear Hickson and
Coker who were getting quite excited over the papers. . . .
   And the night took a shape in my eye like a map of
Australia. Inside this dark shape Oothoon and her gorilla,
that is Eve and Adam, were fitted together in a nice compact mass while the tree of knowledge in red ink with blue
leaves was throwing down a shower of tears and little red
apples over them. I didn't know why I wanted the tears till I
remembered the fish. I suppose, I said to myself, I need a
small regular pattern somewhere to give mass to the big
forms.[83]

And the weight of these meditations is supplemented by seriousness of other kinds. There is the fine contrapuntal conversation

---

[83] *The Horse's Mouth* in *First Trilogy*, pp. 95-97.

between Captain Jones, Coker, and Gulley where no one is really listening to anyone else except Gulley who, before our eyes, transmutes the touching tale of the Captain's deaf daughter into an idea for a symbolic canvas. There is the whole relationship with Coker, full, equally, of humanity and misunderstanding. There is Plant, the shoemaker, pathetic in his aspirations, his tragedy, and his consolations. There is Snow, the white cat at Alfred's bar, who, deaf and castrated, becomes the emblem for Gulley of the insurmountably isolated essence of any existent being, artists especially. And there is the distilled tragic wisdom of Gulley and Blake which lurks everywhere in the novel, not as despair, but as a kind of terrible affirmation: Go and love without the help of anything on earth.

But the major problem in *The Horse's Mouth* is whether the novel can hold its seriousness and its comedy together. The Blakean meditation that we have examined is followed hard on the heels by Gulley's theft of some *objets d'art* from the Hickson living room and his outrageous scramble from the police. And the novel, as a whole, is constantly mingling the exalted with the hilarious. This mixture is very much a part of Cary's design for the book—as it is very much a part of his encompassing vision of human life—but the question is whether the exalted is not finally and rather irreparably impaired as a result. Shakespearian admixtures of tragedy and comedy do not, ordinarily, involve the tragic protagonist, unless he is so elusive a figure as Hamlet, or so mad a one as Lear. It is true that our age, as R. W. B. Lewis's *The Picaresque Saint* suggests, is more open before such possibilities; but the irrepressible comedy of *The Horse's Mouth* tends, at the last, to leave Gulley more clown than either saint or symbolist. It is his comic vitality—the mere protective device with which Cary fitted him out—which usurps the rest of him and becomes almost the exclusive source of our interest in him. The *picaro* in Gulley overmasters the representative symbolic artist. We remember him not so much as a desperate clown, a tragic clown, or a Blakean clown, who embodies the predicament of original art in a petrified, unimaginative world, but simply as a clown—inspired, if you will, but by a satirical and comic impetus. We must love him in the end for his sheer comic exuberance and energy. He is very much in the line of those other incarnations of pure and indiscriminate vitality that we have met in Cary's fiction—Aissa, Mister Johnson, Charley Brown, Sara, and Lucy—and that culminate in the head-long, unexamined, ominous energy of Chester Nimmo in the second trilogy. Gulley's speculations on Blake and on the in-herently unjust design of the universe do not serve, any more than Sara's moralizing, to make him a coherent, assessable figure. He can, in his own phrase, "keep on keeping on"; but Cary never asks, as we may be inclined to, where he is going.

The major elusiveness of the first trilogy, however, is not in its individual narrators but in its total design. We have looked, al-ready, at Cary's formulation of his intention for the whole of the trilogy—an attempt to project, by means of a dramatic use of the first-person mode, three personal worlds in three personal styles. These worlds were to clash—Wilcher's attachment to the past and its institutions is at odds with Gulley's flight from the tradi-tional—but they were to have, nonetheless, a validity for the people who shaped them. Similar clashes among the narrators' estimates of one another were to occur and be resolved similarly.[84] This is as far as Cary's devotion to subjectivity will allow him to go. Ultimate reality is for him largely a private affair. Andrew Wright, however, thinks more in terms of finality as he contemplates the trilogies. He sees them as triads of novels which, after counter-point, interplay, and cancellation, precipitate an ascertainable reality. Speaking of the world which each of the trilogy novels portrays, he says, "That these worlds constitute different aspects of a single world, and that this world has a 'final' shape is a fact clearly to be drawn from a consideration of each of the trilogies as

[84] See Hazard Adams, "The Three Speakers of Joyce Cary," *Modern Fiction Studies*, V (Summer 1959), 108-120, for an exhaustive treatment of this matter.

a whole."[85] The truth is, however, that Cary is a good deal less final, less determinable than this. The final shape of the first trilogy, like the final shape of the second, where the implication becomes portentous indeed, suggests only that there is an infinity of possible shapes, each final for the particular imagination which has shaped it. Upon this floating, indeterminate rock, Cary builds his major fiction.[86]

[85] *Joyce Cary*, p. 109.

[86] Cary's last, and posthumously, published novel, *The Captive and the Free* (London: Michael Joseph, 1959), is particularly interesting in this connection. Because it was incomplete when he died, not having undergone the extensive final revision to which all his novels were subjected, it would not be quite fair to deduce too much from the version that we have. Yet that version is a rather tempting illustration of the persistent indeterminateness that we have been examining—perhaps all the more illuminating because Cary did not have time to cover his traces. Dealing centrally with religion, the novel makes a brilliant linkage between spiritual and sexual energies and the mass media—newspapers especially—which have become, in our time, a major means of propagating them. Since it is a book which occupied Cary during the last months of his life, which he wanted desperately to finish before he died, and which treats matters of the highest importance to him, it would seem that in it he was at last ready to make the kind of assessment of the experience of his characters which he had, in one way or another, been avoiding for almost thirty years. The narrative method—a surprising return to third-person omniscience, complete with virtually Victorian authorial intrusions—seems, likewise, to be designed to allow Cary to speak out, here at the end, in his own voice. But, instead, the work issues in ambiguity. Its protagonist, Preedy the faith healer, is as indeterminate and enigmatic a figure as Cary ever set down. The validity of his faith, even of his procedures, remains in question throughout the narrative. He is the last of those feverishly energetic figures, beginning with Aissa, who will and blaze their way through the pages of Cary's novels. Whether he is "captive" to the young women from whom he draws spiritual sustenance, or "free" because his faith has made him so, or both at once, remains unclear. In the end, *The Captive and the Free*, like *Aissa Saved*, testifies only to the psychological reality of faith. Religion, in its pages—and sex too, for that matter—emerges as a major source of the energy which presides over human life when it is most attractive to Cary. Whether it is real religion—whether such a religion is possible in a metaphysical rather than a psychological sense—is neither affirmed nor denied. Perhaps, in the end, only energy and intensity are real for Cary.

# III

## Prisoner of Grace:
### *The Morality of Perplexity*

Joyce Cary's treatises, *Power in Men* (1939), *The Case for African Freedom* (1941), *The Process of Real Freedom* (1943), and *Britain and West Africa* (1946), are evidence of a serious interest in politics which was bound to express itself, eventually, like all his other interests, in fictional form. His experience as a soldier and colonial officer from 1912 to 1920 acquainted him directly with British governmental and administrative procedures and afforded him a rich supply of quasi-political material which he began to utilize in his earliest novels. The four African novels which he published in the thirties, along with *Castle Corner* of 1938, are all at least peripherally political. By 1942, Cary was apparently far enough along in his speculations to have one of his characters, Edward Wilcher in *To Be a Pilgrim,* make some suggestive exploratory remarks on the centrally political novel. These have an interesting bearing on Cary's second, or Nimmo, trilogy, consisting of *Prisoner of Grace* (1952), *Except the Lord* (1953), and *Not Honour More* (1955):

No one [Edward says] has written a real political novel—giving

the real feel of politics. The French try to be funny or clever, and the English are too moral and abstract. You don't get the sense of real politics, of people feeling their way; of moles digging frantically about to dodge some unknown noise overhead; of worms all driving down simultaneously because of some change in the weather, or rising gaily up again because some scientific gardener has spread the right poison mixture.

You don't get the sense of limitation and confusion, of walking on a slack wire over an unseen gulf by a succession of
lightning flashes. . . . I should like to do for politics what
Tolstoy has done for war—show what a muddle and confusion it is, and that it must always be a muddle and confusion where good men are wasted and destroyed simply by
luck as by a chance bullet.[1]

This "sense of limitation and confusion," is certainly one of the
impressions that emerge from Cary's second trilogy. If he intended,
in this work, to convey the real nature of politics, he took up what
for him is an unusually objective and, in Edward Wilcher's view
at least, determinate and accessible idea. But in the light of such an
intention, the form which Cary chose is puzzling. Each of the
novels in the trilogy is narrated by a character holding a view of
political life quite incompatible with the views of his fellow narrators. Thus, to the muddle and confusion which inhere in democratic politics as a subject, Cary adds the technical and philosophical confusion that arises from three clashing first-person accounts
of that subject. In a sense, this is a consistent and coherent position.
Cary, for instance, would maintain that the one confusion grows
out of the other, that political life is muddled because the people
engaged in it seek their own subjective ends guided only by their
own subjective values.

If we hope for a more conclusive, a less confusing, exploration
of politics, the trilogy as a whole, by progressively canceling its
own positions, is likely to disappoint us. If we come to it with less
tolerance and acceptance than Cary, it assuredly will. But, oddly
enough, if we bring more precise moral discriminations to bear on
the individual novels than Cary has permitted in the trilogy as a
whole, they become very rewarding books indeed. They escape,
that is, momentarily from the chaotic fluidity of Cary's universe
and allow us to experience their action within the context of a
single, ascertainable personality. In the narrators and their indivi-

[1] *To Be a Pilgrim* in *First Trilogy,* pp. 266-267.

dual accounts we must find as much peace and significance as the trilogy ever allows us.

*Prisoner of Grace,* the first novel of the second trilogy to be published, appears to be essentially a study of the corruptive and disruptive effects of political life on a fundamentally non-political personality, Nina Latter, the novel's narrator. In order to trace this process, we shall want first to deal with Nina autonomously, as though she, rather than Cary, has written *Prisoner of Grace*— an illusion quite in keeping with Cary's plan. Her earliest sentences sound the defensive accents of a woman who, though she began life as quite a different creature, now reflects the consequences of thirty years of immersion in English political life, beginning at about the turn of the present century:

> I am writing this book because I understand that "revela-
> tions" are soon to appear about that great man who was
> once my husband, attacking his character, and my own. And
> I am afraid that they will be believed simply because now-
> adays everyone believes the worst of a famous man.[2]

The great man, once Nina's husband, is Chester Nimmo, the major embodiment of political life in the novel and in the trilogy. His career, with its humble beginnings, its closeness to evangelical and radical Christianity, its constant advocacy of high moral and religious principle, its expedient twistings and turnings, its ecstatic intensities and energies, its demagogic marshaling of political emo-tion, its culmination in a British Cabinet post during the First World War, and its decline in the postwar reaction—all this supplies the novel with its political substance and Nina with her political experience. But the book is, in a sense, less about Nimmo himself—he has his own narrative piece to speak in *Except the Lord,* the second volume of the trilogy—than about Nina's com-

---

[2] *Prisoner of Grace* (Carfax edition; London: Michael Joseph, 1954), p. 9. All subsequent page references to the novel are to this edition and will be cited parenthetically in the text. I have followed the original, somewhat erratic, style of punctuation throughout.

plicated reactions to him and to the political milieu which he creates for her. These reactions, and the first-person mode in which they are communicated, give us Nina's world and her habitual inability to manage it; they suggest to us both the baffling, overwhelming experience of politics and Nina's gradual submission to a moral climate which as a young woman at the opening of the book she misunderstands and repudiates. During the course of the novel, the more she understands, the more she consents to.

Cary, then, communicates in this first novel some of the "sense of real politics" by placing the narrative in the hands of an almost disinterested political observer. It is true that fairly early in her married life, Nina has become a prisoner to the greatness that she recognizes in Nimmo and to her own peculiar sense of guilt and obligation toward him; she never departs completely from her intention to defend him as well as herself. Yet she is frank enough and sufficiently fascinated by what has happened to her to be capable of tracing her own moral and political evolution with some fidelity. Cary is at pains throughout the novel to provide her with a note of urgent honesty, for as he puts the matter in his preface to the Carfax edition, "She had to be trustworthy in herself or the book became an essay in the cynical and told nothing true of the political experience" (p. 7). As a result of this trustworthiness, and of her having at no point a political direction or program of her own, she becomes for us a fairly reliable witness to the quality of political life, though she falls well within the limits of subjectivity and partial knowledge that Cary ascribes to all humanity. But it is part of the technical dialectic of the novel that she also becomes far more than a mere observation post. She emerges ultimately as a register of the ravages that politics works on human life.

Nina begins her narrative with an account of the events which lead to her marriage with Chester Nimmo. As an orphan with aristocratic connections on her mother's side, she is raised during the eighties and nineties of the last century by her Aunt Latter at

Palm Cottage, near an English town called Tarbiton, in rather unusual intimacy with her dashing young cousin, Jim Latter. At seventeen, Nina, pregnant with Jim's child, is forced to marry her Aunt's protegé, Chester, then an ambitious clerk in a Tarbiton real-estate office, already active in local religious and political affairs, and only too pleased to begin a political career with Nina's dowry. Thus Nina begins thirty years of a marriage which has its own complicated political dimension: Nina, by reason of her humanity and desire for happiness, tries constantly not to despise her gifted lower-class mate; he, in turn, confronts her tirelessly with his own social unworthiness, her condescension to him, thus involving her repeatedly in attempts to prove, out of her own graciousness, that the class difference between them is not significant. This strategy is Chester's first hold on Nina, his first means of binding her to him as a prisoner.

Chester's political ambitions, for instance, soon involve him in radical attacks on the landed interest in the Tarbiton area and the town council. When Nina objects to the distortions and lies—she cannot for a moment believe that it is the policy of the council to "keep the poor poor"—Chester answers that of course her "sympathies are all the other way":

> "You don't know what class is," he said (and I saw him shaking with excitement). You don't know how different you are. Why you would have more in common with a negro— I mean a negro gentleman—than with Bill Code" (Bill was our gardener for one day a week). "You think me a cad" (and he made a face as if he were going to burst into tears). "No, no, that's not fair—not true" (he put out his hand and just touched me on the breast, as if to say, "Forgive me") "You *feel* me a cad" (p. 33).

Nina learns, soon enough, that she cannot argue with Chester about his class obsession; his tactic is to apologize for nagging her about the matter, then begin to do so again the very same day. After a time, she begins, out of a sense of guilt which his accusations arouse, to help him with his campaign for a seat on the town council. Her participation draws her closer to Chester—she thinks for one curious reason or another that she is beginning to love him. Yet she is surprised again and again by his utterly incalculable behavior, such as his indignant denial of all knowledge of their son's illegitimacy, or his abrupt transitions from quarreling to love-making to prayer.

During these early stages of their life together Nina's response to Chester is characteristically ambivalent. "It seemed," she says, "that I was two women, one of them quite furious still and watchful of every move by this cunning enemy, and one of them so close and sympathetic to him that she felt all his feeling like her own" (p. 44). And the oscillation is conveyed vividly by the confessional immediacy of the narrative mode. On the whole, in this early period, her moral reservations about Chester's political maneuvering persist, and they afford the chief basis for marital difficulty. Inevitably, though, the demands of a strenuous political campaign exact more sympathy than watchfulness from Nina, and on the occasion of the Lilmouth riot, in which both she and Chester are almost injured after Chester makes an impassioned pacifist attack on British militarism in behalf of the pro-Boer movement, she expresses, in one of the key passages of the entire novel, her new knowledge of political affairs and of her own unavoidable political involvement. Nina is commenting on the self-satisfied feelings shared by Chester, his close friend Goold, and his supporters generally following the riot:

> I don't say that they said openly what a good thing it was for them to provoke violence and get people killed. In fact I don't believe for a moment that they even thought it. It was at this time I began to feel among "political" people the strange and horrible feeling which afterwards became so familiar to me (but not less horrible), of living in a world without any solid objects at all, of floating day and night through clouds of words and schemes and hopes and ambitions and calculations where you could not say that this idea

was obviously selfish and dangerous and that one quite false and wicked because all of them were relative to something else. The lies were mixed up with some truth (like Chester's belief in a class plot), and the selfish calculations (like Goold's planning to make trouble at Lilmouth) melted at the edges into all kinds of "noble" ideals (like Chester's passion for freedom of speech).

So that even when I heard the "belles assemblies" [Aunt Latter's name for the gatherings of Chester's supporters] denouncing the "jingoes" for provoking riots I dared not think, "Good heavens, what cant!" And when I felt their triumphant joy after a riot (because they felt that it would lose the government some more votes) I knew it wouldn't be fair to say that they were simply hypocrites who thought they had hit on the right way (as indeed they had) to get back into power.

And now it was harder for me to "live my own life", because since the Lilmouth "outrage" (it was no good telling them I had done nothing but disobey Chester's orders) [to stay away from the Lilmouth meeting] I was looked upon as a "heroine of the cause" and I was received with bouquets and cheers when I went out with Chester (pp. 59-60).

Although Nina's characteristic attempt at honesty is still operating here, notably, as always, in the parenthetical interjections which aim at preserving whole rather than interested truths, she has at this point evolved to a difficult new position, which is full of significant moral implications for the entire novel. On the one hand, she discovers, and continues to discover more deeply later on, the inability of conventional morality to deal with political complexities, to make clean separations between right and wrong —we can catch the Existential note in this passage. As a result of this discovery, moral rigor appears impossible and even moral definition becomes somehow unfeasible. Yet, on the other hand, Nina's desire to be moral, more adequately and subtly moral, remains. Inevitably, though, despite this desire, she begins to suffer, from this point forward, from the debilitating moral uncertainty and hesitation, brought about, distressingly enough, by an increasing knowledge of what she takes to be political reality. Her earlier power to condemn reprehensible calculation and motive never again recovers from this accession of political and moral insight. As a result, she begins to assume her most important function as the novel's first-person narrator, a function which brings us close to the center of the novel.

The suggestion of moral undependability in a first-person narrator is assuredly not new in the English novel. In the eighteenth century Defoe set up a curious contrast between pious impulse and squalid behavior in Moll Flanders. In our own time, these modest beginnings have had interesting fulfilments in James's *The Sacred Fount,* where the narrator's obsessive speculative intelligence fashions an irresponsible morbid phantasmagoria of adulterous relations, and in Ford's *The Good Soldier,* where an apparently decent, patient, and forbearing narrator, because of the ambiguity of narrative tone and perspective, can be construed by a reader like Mark Schorer as a man suffering "from the madness of moral inertia." Cary himself, as we are aware, exploits similar possibilities in the first trilogy. Sara has an utterly charming moral obtuseness which makes her at once better and worse than she knows; Wilcher is, for all his piety, half-mad and given to indecent sexual exposure; and Gulley never thinks twice before stealing or duping others, despite his exalted dedication to the aesthetic life. In *Prisoner of Grace,* though, we shall see moral unreliability reach a new intensity. Rarely before in the first-person novel have the issues been so momentous and the narrator's moral inadequacy—taking the form of confusion and perplexity—so central to the conception of the subject.

The relationship between Nina and Chester, which we have been tracing, proceeds on the same discordant basis which their marriage itself has established at the outset. Although Nina has acquired a good deal of ethical flexibility, she manages still to offer sufficient opposition to Chester throughout their married life to unsettle their relations continually. Throughout the novel

one source of disagreement and exacerbation after another offers
itself. Nina's resumption of sexual relations with Jim Latter leads
to the key railroad scene where Chester prevents her from leaving
him by ringing changes on the idea that Nina stooped to him in
marriage. Chester's secretary Bootham, installed after the Latter
affair, distresses Nina by spying on her. Aunt Latter constantly
generates friction between Chester and herself as well as between
Chester and Nina. Chester's powerful effect on Nina's young son
Tom provokes her to insist that Tom be sent to the Latter family
boarding school, fashionable and traditional Eastborough;
Chester, politically committed to the underprivileged, fights violently against the snobbishness of the plan. Indeed, the novel·is
packed with occasions which supply points of difference and an
opportunity for Chester to manipulate Nina with consummate
political skill. Through all this altercation, Nina is undermined by
a growing moral liberality which eventually ushers in the note of
unabashed relativism:

> [Chester] had, I saw, taken firm hold of his principles,
> and they were quite good principles. From his political point
> of view he *was* right. But so (I thought) was I. Of course it
> is quite common for people who are both right to quarrel.
> One of my cousins married a Latter who drank and treated
> her badly, and, besides, they had no children and she longed
> for children. So she ran away with another man. But her
> husband would not divorce her, and her children were illegit-
> imate, and the new lover's family tried to make him leave
> her, and they were both very unhappy. But no one could
> say that anyone was in the wrong. They just had different
> principles (pp. 165-166).

The moral capitulation that we have here prepares us for the disintegration to come. In order to gauge both, we need, as readers,
steadfastly to refuse to identify Cary with Nina and to allow ourselves to be lulled by any of her assorted ethical lullabies. We must
also be prepared to recognize an obliquity in Nina which flourishes

not only beneath her professions of truth and integrity, but also in spite of her unceasing endeavor to live honorably.

Though the first half of the novel focuses most of its attention on the political aspects of Nimmo family life, Chester's public career has all the while been going forward rapidly. From the Tarbiton town council he has moved on to Parliament, and in the Liberal landslide of 1905, he is offered the place of Undersecretary for Mines. By the midpoint of the novel, then, Chester enters into national political life, and the controversies in which he is caught up have a new scope and weightiness. These require, accordingly, more rigorous and acute moral discriminations of Nina, but she fails repeatedly to make them. Or, if we take another and more distressing view, she makes them too readily and too glibly.

The "Marconi Case" is the first of these crises. Knowing that a radio firm, Western Development, is about to receive a large contract for equipment and that this would boom Banks Rams, Western's electrical equipment supplier, Chester invests heavily in Banks Rams. Nina's cousin Wilfred hears of a Conservative move to inquire into the transaction and warns Chester in time for him to dispose of his shares and make a statement to the House in which he maintains that he has bought no new shares in Western Development, and that his holdings in the electrical industry are actually smaller than in any previous year. Nina defends this act vehemently on questionable grounds, engaging in a number of special pleas:

> But owing to the very special conditions of politics . . . it would have been *quite misleading* for Chester to have told the whole story of Banks Rams. It might have produced a *great injustice*, that is, the ruin of Chester's career. I know it is a very difficult question, what you can tell the public—it depends on the public mind at the time (and I often think, after my experience as a Minister's wife, that ten per cent of

the public mind is just plainly and simply lunatic and, of course, being lunatic, makes nearly all the noise and *seems* to have all the influence); but anyone knows that the noblest men have thought it right to be careful of how much they tell (p. 214).

And reflecting on a "clever young woman from Oxford" who has interviewed her about the contract scandal, Nina adds:

> I was so angry with her that I would have accused her of being shallow and cheap, if I had not realized that in other respects she was a very warm-hearted and honest creature, and only silly (like so many others—clever or not) about "politicians"; as if they were naturally wicked because they have to "manage" people. But I'd like to know what would happen if nobody tried to manage people, if mothers always told the facts to children (saying to the stupid ones that they were stupid) and never took any consideration for their nerves and their fits of temper and frights and silliness (p. 215).

In moments like these Nina's justifications proceed on the assumption that England is composed of a child, or a partially lunatic, electorate—an assumption quite at variance with the theory of democratic government to which, presumably, both she and Chester subscribe. Her impatience with the vagaries of the population is not, however, a symptom of fascist inclinations but part of a philosophical position on human reason and imagination which emerges obliquely at this point in the narrative through a skilful juxtaposition of public and private experience.

Nina breaks off her discussion of the contract scandal suddenly and turns to Chester's friend Goold and his wife Daisy. She describes the way in which Daisy, quite unconsciously, went about getting a new carriage from an unwilling Goold. Time and again, driving about in her old trap, Daisy would get soaked through her best dresses, even managing to tear them, and the trap itself began to suffer extraordinary accidents. Without any calculation on her part, Daisy would drive it about "with such a despairing expectation of misfortune" that accidents inevitably occurred. In the end Goold bought a carriage, his reason being that the trap was worn out and the carriage "offered itself" as a bargain. Nina offers no comment on this episode, but the design and purport of this crucial section of the novel become clear after another striking juxtaposition.

Only a few pages later Nina deals with another of Chester's political crises. He decides in 1913 to take a pacifist line and marshal the antiwar sentiment in England. As Nina reflects on the move and on the charges of Machiavellism and hypocrisy which were made against Chester at the time, she writes, "I think hypocrisy is a very rare vice. Tartuffe and Pecksniff always seemed to me very hollow characters—quite untrue to life. People don't need to be hypocrites. They can so easily 'make' themselves believe anything they fancy" (p. 225). Immediately after this statement, which comes at the close of a chapter, Nina, without any transition, begins an account of a sail that she took with her cousin Jim during their adolescence. Jim insisted, in the face of storm warnings, on taking the boat out into open sea. Once out beyond the mouth of the estuary, their sailboat is nearly capsized by violent winds, but when they try to re-enter the estuary, they discover that they have little chance of doing so. "We'll never get back," Nina says. "Get back where? Did you think we were going back to the Long-water?" Jim answers. "What I thought," he continues, "was—with this lovely blow—we could do our Callacombe trip." And with this pretense of intending all along to take the ten-mile sail down the coast to this small fishing harbor, Jim is able to sustain Nina through a terrifying storm, so that she does not panic and surrender utterly to her fear. "By pretending he had made an enterprise out of the trip, for even if he was pretending (as I knew all the time) he was making a real difference by suggesting that we could *make* the whole affair rather glorious instead of a stupid escapade and a miserable struggle not to be drowned" (p. 229).

And now, concluding this episode from the past, Nina, in the next chapter, returns to Chester and maintains that he is no more a hypocrite in political life than Jim was in this adventure. "The truth is that a man like Chester, just because he had such a lot of imagination, such power of putting himself in other people's places and minds, was *nearly always sincere. . . .* Chester needed always to believe what he took up, he *needed to be sincere,* for if he had any doubts he could not 'put himself over' with effect. Sincerity (as he well knew) was the secret of his power as a speaker. . ." (p. 230).

What we have here, within the space of some eighteen pages in the novel, is Nina's pronouncement, expressed through a series of suggestive juxtapositions, on the fundamental irrationality of human behavior, on humanity's capacity for self-deception. The imagination, in her view, has its sweet way with the rational intellect, so that not only does the populace need to have its imagination soothed with images of decorum and authority in order that it not mislead itself, but, beyond that, all men, even the leaders, are victimized by their fancy and desire. Daisy and Goold have no understanding of the way in which simple desire creates a quite "reasonable" excuse—acceptable to an even more "reasonable" frugality—for a lavish expenditure. Chester's imagination, when he comes to appreciate the advantages which a pacifist position might bring him, has no difficulty subduing his reason and making him a sincere pacifist. And on the storm sail, sheer imaginative pretense is sufficient to redefine the real conditions of peril and terror, to make the mind and the limbs work purposefully in a mere postulated enterprise, and to redeem life itself. In this brilliant grouping of episodes, Nina makes her epistemological point, and even if, as readers, we are not prepared to invoke it ourselves as an adequate basis for judging or determining human conduct, we are at least in a position, from this point on in the novel, to understand the remainder of her moral evolution. She has equipped herself with a psychology of self-deception which, by appearing to explain all, comes insidiously close to forgiving anything.

But Nina is a complex figure—she needs to be in order to mirror some of the complexity of political life. Consequently, she balances tendencies precariously before she simplifies herself by succumbing utterly to confusion. On the occasion of Chester's next political crisis she reveals her characteristic ambivalence. After establishing himself as the leader of pacifist sentiment in England and pledging to resign from the Cabinet if it determined on war, Chester decides abruptly in July of 1914 to accept the Prime Minister's offer of the Ministry of Production in the War Cabinet. His statement in the newspapers justifies the betrayal on the grounds of his "never having believed it possible for any civilised people to be guilty of so dastardly a crime (the invasion of Belgium) against the very basis of civilised religious liberty . . ." (p. 267). Nina's justification has a schizophrenic ring:

> I was quite moved by his words [in the newspapers]— they made me feel (like thousands of his supporters who had been raging against him) short-sighted and narrow-minded, lacking in vision.
>
> And I told myself that Chester had really been surprised by the sudden attack on Belgium, that he had been indispensable in the War Cabinet, that it had been his duty, just as he had said, to ignore a pledge given under other circumstances; in fact, that in real life one cannot always keep pledges.
>
> And this is quite true. No one on earth can prove that Chester was not doing a rather noble act (risking his very honour) when he "ratted" on his pledges. Quite possibly (if he had time, in the middle of such important and urgent "public responsibilities", to consider the point at all) he believed it himself, even at the time. He certainly came to believe it afterwards.
>
> True, I was left with a very uneasy feeling . . . but this was not because of the "ratting"—it started from something quite different, his tone and look when he had said to me, "All this

fuss will be forgotten." I could not help seeing, behind these words, the calculator at work; they seemed to say, "I can break my word with impunity, because in the rush of new and important events, people will forget about the whole matter" (p. 268).

As always, Nina is torn between her fundamental admiration for Chester's political wisdom and courage, which overrides such conventional injunctions as keeping one's word, and her horror at Chester's utter moral indifference, his virtuosity at justification. We catch too the complication afforded by the self-deception motif—Chester's possible, indeed probable, sincerity. Because she is divided—and we must not, in fairness to the book, minimize the genuine knottiness of Chester's act and situation—she tends to drift into a kind of volitional paralysis which only perpetuates her self-divisive condition. She balks somewhat at Chester's cruel, devastating public attack on his old friend Goold, a political enemy since Chester's shift from pacifism to war; but she does not bolt. It is easier for her to bear the outrage as an internal wound of her own, than to allow herself to hate Chester. On the verge of a decisive break over Goold and Jim, who is now a district officer involved in a political fight over African administration, Nina and Chester pull back. "And then like an old married couple who, as if instinctively, turn aside from a serious quarrel, knowing how little good it can do and how easy it is to avoid it simply by going on with a routine (while free to think bitterness), we both hastened to give way" (p. 289). But the uneasiness, the bitterness, is there, and it is sufficient, at last, to turn Nina's sympathies more actively to Jim.

She visits Jim's family home at Buckfield and assists him in his agitation against the government on behalf of his beloved Luga tribe. But the defection from Chester is cut short by a ruthless emissary, Chester's physician, Sir Connell T., who threatens, on Chester's behalf, a scandal which would send the already sickly Jim back to his "punishment station" in Africa and certain death.

When Nina returns to Chester their relations are considerably strained, and her functions and responsibilities have largely been appropriated by her daughter Sally and Bootham, Chester's faithful secretary. Hatred of Chester, which for the first time Nina permits herself to feel, pushes her to a suicide attempt, but it ends in bizarre comedy and reconciliation. As she is about to jump at night from a balcony outside her bedroom she is delayed by Sally and Bootham's approach to the house. In an instant Chester is out of bed and at her side, preventing her. "But just then Chester's pyjamas (he had taken to them at last when he had begun to visit generals—but he did not manage them very well) began to slip down and he grabbed at them with such an offended look (as if they had tried to 'betray' him) that I had a horrible impulse to laugh" (p. 309). Full of a sense of the ridiculousness of the scene, Nina diverts Chester by pressing suggestively against him. " 'Very well,' he said, 'but I must get to sleep.' And he turned round and went back to bed while I followed like a Trojan captive on a rope, with a feeling of submission so acute and complete and sudden that it was comical, like something that happens to a clown at the circus." The episode gives Nina relief and allows her to see more fully the "worried haggard fierce old man" who as over-burdened Minister of Production is "giving his life to the country in a true sense." "And then," she says, "I was ashamed." Thus she becomes prisoner to him once again, now out of a sense of the greatness of his work, of his contribution, and of his need, as a "wounded soldier," for her care and comfort. Measured against these things, her own life and its pursuits appear trivial. But the relationship has not changed fundamentally; indeed it does not during their entire marriage, even after Chester is turned out of office in the election of 1922. Her inability to cope with Chester or to free herself from him remains. So too does her raging ambivalence toward him.

Preparing for the close of his novel, Cary has Nina return briefly but pointedly to self-deception. We are in a position now to begin

to apply the idea to Nina's own life, with its emotional splits and
beguiled morality, though she is herself thinking only of her son
Tom. A gifted professional entertainer, he has developed an act in
which he satirizes quite viciously a figure remarkably like Chester.
When Nina mentions this to Tom he denies the resemblance vehemently. She sees quickly that Tom "does not want to realize
what he is doing; the red nose and the whiskers are meant to deceive
him as well as the audience" (p. 344). A little later on she observes,
quoting Chester, that "happiness is all a matter of imagination. A
fakir on a bed of nails can be as happy as a bride on her wedding
day . . ." (p. 361). Nina's own capacity to escape from her sense
of decency and proportion, masking itself as an urgent acceptance
of divided allegiance, turns now into the booming pedal point of
the entire concluding section of the novel. It is here that we read
finally in her character the corrosion and perplexity that become
our measure of the human damage worked by her version of the
political milieu.

Tom's unfortunate death in Germany, after Chester has refused
to intervene to save him when he is picked up in a night-club
police raid, finally gives Nina the impetus to leave Chester. She
takes up her relationship once again with Jim Latter, settles with
him at Palm Cottage and, after thirty years of marriage, is divorced
by Chester. Carrying, once again, a child of Jim's, she enters into
an extraordinary peace, "madly in love for the first time" in her
life, only too willing to comfort Jim and submit to him in all
things, for he too is a defeated man, having lost his long fight on
African policy with the government and seen his own dear Luga
chiefs, whom he has tried to keep primitive, noble, and savage, turn
against him. Chester, however, does not keep away. He asks for
permission to call at the cottage in order to discuss Nina's letters,
which he wishes to publish. When refused, he connives to waylay
Nina at the Goold's home. He has already got into difficulty over
a sexual assault on a young woman in Kensington Gardens and

now proceeds to assault Nina. "In that moment," she says, "I felt
a new and deep fear of Chester, which comes to one in realising
that some creature, from sheer egotism or disease or age, has forgotten ordinary restraints and is so far mad" (p. 371). Chester is
interrupted by Sally and Bootham's return, but in their presence
he conducts a subtle conversation which has one meaning for his
daughter and secretary, and another for Nina. When on this
second level he charges Nina with corrupting him by introducing
him to decadent pleasures, she becomes annoyed and pauses for
a reflection:

> People who live together can't help changing each other
> —everybody in the world is "corrupting" everyone else. Even
> if one shut oneself up in a desert island, one bit of one's mind
> would "corrupt" another bit and try to "convert it" so that
> they would be able to work together (p. 374).

This generalized observation is as close as she comes to an awareness of her own corruption and its source in Chester. Occurring
at this juncture, it suggests at once Nina's degeneration and her
obliviousness to it.

After parrying Chester's pretenses for future meetings, Nina
takes her leave. She returns to her new son, Robert, and a Jim
who, deeply disturbed by his discovery of Chester's advances and
Nina's visit to Goold Manor, threatens to kill her if she "plays him
up." But soon after, Nina returns from a celebration of Jim's
extraordinary victory in a sailing race—he is now president of the
Longwater Club—which gives her, because her own pleasure is
linked with Jim's, "about as much happiness as anyone can possibly have," to find that Chester has installed himself, during
her absence, in Palm Cottage. Though Sally and Bootham arrive
to remove him, Chester, supported by crotchety Aunt Latter,
begins a series of cunning moves which culminate in a "heart
attack":

I realised then, at once, seeing Sally quite red with agita-

tion (and feeling very anxious myself), how difficult an old
man can be—like a wilful and delicate child who does not
care what happens to him so long as he gets his own way;
an autocrat and spoiled egotist who has to be humoured or
cajoled or he may kill himself out of perversity or mere pique.

And it was a moment of terror when he clutched himself
by the breast, gave a great moan, and fell gasping on the
sofa (p. 382).

In this solicitude and terror we catch a glint of Nina's eventual
submission. The situation, she suggests, is so ambiguous and intricate that even Jim, governed always by the strictest notions of
honor and straightness, when he walks in on the scene, hesitates
and forbears uttering an ultimatum. "But as [Jim] looked round
at us silently waiting for the explosion and then again at me, the
rage went out of his face—to be followed by a most strange and
unexpected look such as I had never before seen in [him]—of
confusion, even self-doubt" (p. 384).

Up and about shortly after and hard at work on Nina's letters,
Chester, on the very first occasion that he is alone with Nina, makes
a sexual assault on her within three yards of Sally, who is occupied
on the phone. It is done with a rapacity and inhumanity quite
new to Chester, whose sexuality had always before, despite its
intensity, had a spiritual and religious dimension. Nina is furious
and sends him a note declaring that she cannot see him again and
that he ought to return to the Manor. But the very next morning,
when an impatient Sally—who knows nothing of the assault—
comes to fetch her, because Chester is enraged at the interruption
in the letter project, she returns. Chester is now even more enter-
prising, though Bootham is present just out of sight, taking dicta-
tion at a typewriter. After dictating long rhetorical sentences which
set Bootham busily to work, Chester repeatedly swoops down on
Nina, imprisoning her in her chair, and forces himself on her.

At this point Nina attempts an explanation and justification
of her behavior which illuminates for us the extent to which she
has lost her moral bearings: "You say I should have turned him

out of the house. But I was extremely anxious to avoid any kind of contretemps which might upset Jim; and for another, I had Sally's firm promise that the whole miserable situation would come to an end that week" (p. 387). This is rather feeble as a justification. Jim, like any husband, would be a good deal more comfortable if Chester left than he can ever be while Chester remains; and the week's end is surely not a better time to call a halt to a profoundly distressing situation that the present moment. Out of a sense of the inadequacy of these remarks, Nina continues her defense; but it soon disintegrates into an appreciation of the comedy, an acknowledgment of Chester's sincerity and momentous needs, a disquisition on the transformations of old age—indeed anything that is calculated to blur the moral terms of her conduct. The complexity of the dilemma begins to appear more clearly as only a specious excuse for shoddy conduct:

I did indeed struggle with [Chester] (risking Bootham's hearing us), but the only result was to make him angry. He actually exclaimed aloud, "we haven't time to waste on this nonsense," and before Bootham could crane his neck backward to see what he meant, he was ten feet away, dictating again about the "true spiritual roots of the British Liberal tradition—the veritable protestant succession of the free soul." And though I wanted to laugh (I was much too angry at his "hypocrisy" to let myself *be* angry), I felt too that his impatience with my "nonsense" was quite real; he thought that my complaints were truly contemptible beside the tremendous ideas and anxieties which filled his mind night and day, until perhaps he simply had to let down the pressure by those sudden attacks on me.

I remembered all I had heard of other great men (and no one who knew Chester could deny that he had something of greatness about him) who in their old age seemed to forget the most elementary conventions (falling in love with little girls, like Goethe, ceasing to wash themselves, or talking, like Tolstoy, so coarsely that the roughest men blushed for them) simply because they were so overwhelmed by the fearful

tragedies and perils of humanity, at last made plain to them,
that they could no longer give much importance to rules of
"mere" propriety. Old age had not so much made them
wicked as changed the balance of their moral ideas.

I daresay you will think . . . that I am making excuses for
Chester simply to hide from myself my own weakness of
character and love of peace, but I am not pretending that
the man had lost his moral sense; he knew quite well that he
was doing something wrong and dangerous.

I think it was even a part of his pleasure. . . .

And I noticed that after one of these assaults—(and now
I did everything possible to give the man what he wanted as
quickly as possible, simply to get it over) he would seem ten
years younger, his eyes would sparkle, he would thrust out
his chest and strut about the room. . . . Looking at him then
(while still trembling at the danger just escaped and what
he had done to me) I was ready to laugh as well as rage (pp.
387-389).

But this is no laughing matter, however grotesque Chester may
have become. His behavior might be amusing enough if Nina
could simply observe it detachedly, but once she and the husband
she loves have become involved in it, its quality changes markedly.
Furthermore, Nina's groping for explanations is quite inapposite.
Chester is no longer the great man engaged in a great work with
power to impose meaningful obligation—prisonership to his grace
—on Nina, and we have not the sense that his demands on her
grow out of his being "overwhelmed by the fearful tragedies and
perils of humanity." Even if they did, they could not, for this
reason alone, escape moral scrutiny. When Nina touches on her
own weakness, she does so fleetingly and fixes quickly instead on
Chester's awareness of the impropriety of his behavior; but this
awareness she excuses straightaway as a part of his pleasure. As
readers, we find ourselves perhaps less ready to forgive simply out
of an appreciation for audacity. The next thing we learn is that
she is willing to yield completely to his demands, her explanation
being that the activity resuscitates him—comically at that.

What we appear to have here, then, in Nina's yielding is a kind of moral abandon fitted out with a number of shabby justifications. These are elaborated with a facility that Nina, we may infer, has absorbed from the life of politics. It is true that one of her intentions in the novel is to insist on the complexity of political activity and the intricate moral discrimination, modification, and flexibility that it demands. But gradually, through the course of the book, this kind of flexibility has entered her private life as well and has become a basis for marital relations. It is here, in the application of a political morality of expediency to her dealings with both Jim and Chester that she becomes more completely than ever the victim of a vitiating perplexity. She is not unaware of the transfer,[3] but she is unaware of its extent and its cost. She does, though, see some part of this cost in Jim:

> Of course it was obvious that Jim was suffering—he had suddenly been brought into a situation quite inconceivable to his idea of what was possible for himself. When Chester had stayed week after week, he even changed in appearance. He looked at me sometimes with so haggard and wondering an expression that I was ready to weep.
>
> He knew as well as I did that the whole place (in fact the whole country) was sizzling with gossip and curiosity; newspapers as far away as Aberdeen had paragraphs to say that "Lord Nimmo was staying with Captain and Mrs. Latter at Palm Cottage (Mrs. Latter was formerly Mrs. Nimmo)". To

[3] Nina has already drawn an extended parallel between the vocabulary of politics and marriage: "All this time there was between Chester and myself a 'situation'. I mean, an unusual tension. There is, I suppose, always a 'situation' between husband and wife (unless I have been 'corrupted' by living so long in a political atmosphere; I should suppose there is a situation between everybody) and 'relation' which need the equivalent of 'understandings' and 'spheres of influence'. In fact, it is a situation which changes three times a day at least. But with old married people who have a good 'understanding', the spheres of influence are so well marked out that they can be very free with each other and argue quite indignantly and have 'grave crises' without the least danger of an 'incident'. They are really quite comfortable with each other all the time, and their 'situation' can only 'deteriorate' if they show themselves 'ill-disposed' or, of course, form a new 'alignment' " (p. 286).

> a man like Jim who felt dirtied by such publicity, the posi-
> tion was agonizing, and every day I expected him to burst
> out and say that it must stop.
>
> But when I realised that he actually did not want to make
> a discovery, I felt such relief that I was, if possible, in greater
> love than ever for the man who could sacrifice his enormous
> pride (but Jim was perhaps too proud to admit that any such
> vulgar situation could hurt his pride) to his love for me. I
> knew then, in fact, that Jim did truly love me and could not
> bear to lose me (pp. 390-391).

After such knowledge, we may well ask, what forgiveness? Nina
seems willing to eat away at her beloved Jim's vital principle—his
honor and pride—and give him unbearable pain in the name of
an all but inexplicable allegiance to Chester, whom we know she
has never loved. Andrew Wright makes an astute observation on
Nina's emotional duality and its embodiment in the structure of
the novel. "At the end of the book," he says, "[Chester] has come
to her house and made his claims, which she cannot refuse. So the
formal device of the book clearly emphasizes the personal bound-
aries of Nina's life. She stands between the two men, sometimes as
mediator, but always as comforter to them both."[4] But in addition
to noting this formal device, we need to consider the whole nature
of Nina's mediation and of her dual commitment. We need ultimately to measure what appears to be Nina's failure to put first
things first.

Whatever our readiness to accept her frequent recourse to intricacy and anomaly when she deals with political conduct—her
insistence that conventional virtue is but a poor measure for men
who must lead nations—there is no question about the chaos that
such a morality introduces into Nina's domestic life. The closing
scenes of the book grow out of an intolerable acquiescence and
strike a note of authentic depravity. In these sequences we discover how too eager an understanding can terminate in irresponsibility and perplexity. And in discovering the inadequacy of such a

---

[4] *Joyce Cary*, pp. 138-139.

political morality in private life, we are turned back unavoidably to a reconsideration of the whole liberated ethic that Nina has been advancing all along, even in the public, political sphere. We see that her assertion of the imagination's power over the reason and of human vulnerability to self-deception may, in fact, characterize her own condition—her own deluded insistence on the intricacy and uniqueness of political difficulty, along with the specious excuses that follow from it. Out of her lack of awareness comes our awareness.

Eventually Bootham walks in on Chester molesting Nina in the kitchen and is outfaced by the wily old man. "Am I in a madhouse," Chester exclaims, "where idiots see visions? Go away, sir. I don't know what you are insinuating—I will not even guess at it before a lady" (p. 398). In the confusion which Chester thereupon creates, Bootham is dismissed along with Sally. When Jim demands to know if Nina is now going to turn Chester out, she cannot quite say yes.

> And I knew then that I should never get rid of Chester, that I dared not do so. And I saw that it was no good pretending that I merely tolerated an old man's whims because he was pitiful—I did not love Chester and I had never loved him, but now, more than ever, at the end of his life, I was in his power. When he fixed his eyes on me (it was perhaps the only time in a week that he even thought of me as a human being) and I felt myself shrink, I knew that he held me still with a thousand ties that I should never break—ties from a marriage of nearly thirty years that was all the more "part of me" because I had suffered in it (p. 400).

When, in torment, Jim asks for the truth, Nina summons up an awful lie:

> "Tell me the truth," he said in quite a soft voice. "What have you been up to?"
>
> My mouth was so dry that I could only whisper that I had done nothing.

"You mean absolutely nothing? You mean that Bootham is making it up?"

I nodded my head; and Jim shook my wrists as if to bring me to myself, but without hurting me.

"I want the truth this time," he said, "You've got to tell the truth. Do you mean that there's nothing in it—on your soul and honour?"

I nodded again, but Jim shook my wrists and told me to say the words, "I swear—by Almighty God—that this is the truth."

So I said the words, and then Jim, all at once, appeared at a loss (p. 401).

Well might he. Nina and her motives have become quite unfathomable, not only to Jim but to anyone not obsessed with, and enslaved by, the notion of Chester's greatness, or the unanswerable urgency of his needs.

A year after this episode, with Chester still at the Cottage, and Jim intruding on Nina and Chester regularly without warning as they work together, Nina sums up her present situation with these, the last words of the novel:

> The life which was going to be simple and restful, my "retirement from politics", is more difficult and complicated than ever, and also, of course, more "political". I have to consider every word I say and everything I do. The tension is like a perpetual crisis. I notice that my hair is turning white and I am so thin that my frocks hang on me. But what is strange is that I have never had so much happiness because Jim has never before been so much in love. You would say that neither of us has known till now what is meant by a grand passion—I suppose that Jim, like me, feels that every day may be the last.
>
> But how could I make him understand that it is because that happiness is so precious to me I dare not turn Chester out. For I should know I was committing a mean crime against something bigger than love.
>
> I should despise myself, which is, I suppose, what Chester means when he says that such and such a "poor devil" is

"damned". And I am terrified of "damnation", for it would destroy my happiness and all the joy of my life, and Jim can only shoot me dead.

It is the language of mediation, to be sure, but of woefully confused mediation. We notice first the characteristic insistence on difficulty and complication, and on the political nature of family life; but it has an unconvincing ring. The situation has come about not by fiat, not because of the nature of things, but as a result of Nina's refusal now to be non-political, her refusal to recognize a hierarchy of human obligation. She insists on ranking the remains of a dead and tortuous relationship equally with a new and rewarding one. But even the new one she views in questionable terms. Her happiness with Jim, like her love for him, is intensified by the morbid probability of death, as though, melodramatically enough, the relationship itself needs to be sustained by jeopardy. Still, she insists on the preciousness of that happiness, and gives it as her reason for not turning Chester out. But in her very next sentence there is, we learn, something bigger than this, bigger indeed than love; and it is in behalf of this something—thirty years of suffering? her own humanity? her need to serve the whole complex of weakness and greatness that she reads in Chester?—that she cannot repudiate the old politician. Then she drops Jim altogether from consideration in a sudden turning inward: if she sent Chester away she would despise herself, be "damned" and destroy her happiness. Her happiness, then, derives not only from her love for Jim but from her servitude to Chester. Indeed, so essential and inescapable is the latter, so much is she prisoner to her own conception of Chester and his public destiny, that "all the joy" of her life would vanish were she to cease to fulfil what she takes to be her obligation to him. But in view of such intense, compulsive, high-minded dedication, her willingness to indulge herself in a relationship with Jim—at terrible cost to him—is unfortunate, if not unforgivable.

Actually the passage is so skilfully contrived that out of the

constant bifurcation of feeling and loyalty nothing emerges very
clearly except Nina's perplexity. And her situation is indeed the
very emblem of a refusal to make authentic and responsible
choices, except for the choice to remain divided. There is an emotional equivocation in the writing that is worthy of Chester in his
best days, but it has none of the purposefulness, specious or otherwise, that policy can confer. She sees darkly, imperfectly, incom-
pletely. In the end, she is so much enslaved to what she can see, or
to what her imagination suggests to her, that she has no real room
for any consideration of Jim and what is, in all decency, due him.
"It is an illustration of the flexibility of Cary's writing," says
George Woodcock, "that her account should have even in its
idiom that taint of moral ambiguity which intensifies the atmosphere of intangible evil that hangs about her husband."[5] By the
time Nina's account closes, though, the taint has suffused her whole
being, and the moral ambiguity has become a moral chaos. To
have become an emotional and ideological prisoner to a man who
embodies the untrammeled ethic of politics, to insist repeatedly on
the insurmountable complexity of every important issue, we discover in Nina, is to become morally inept, to be disposed to an
indiscriminate, self-destructive emotional charity, to be a danger
to oneself and to those whom one insists one loves.

There remain a few more observations to make on Nina as
narrator. Cary takes great pains to fashion her character, for here
as everywhere in his work, character is fundamental to both his
conception and his execution. In his preface to the novel, he tells
of several false starts which he made on *Prisoner of Grace*. He
began with a Nina who carried tales about her husband and
carefully analyzed his motives; but Cary abandoned her because
she seemed mean and small. When he tried third person he was
dissatisfied with its effect on the key railway station scene (the one
on which so much of the Chester-Nina relationship is based).

[5] "Citizens of Babel," *Queens Quarterly*, LXIII (1956), 245.

Returning again to the first person, he gave the narrative to a brother of Aunt Latter's, but this narrator ruined it, for "everything was falsified and cheapened, the acuteness of the observer only emphasized the lack of real understanding, as sharp arrows will go right though a target and leave no mark" (p. 8). When Cary was about to abandon the whole attempt, the possibility of a Nina with parentheses occurred to him. "Nina, I said, is essentially a woman who can understand another's point of view, she has to be so to tell her story. All her judgments are qualified. And qualifications go into brackets [the British term]. . . . She had, in short, a brackety mind."

We have already examined enough passages from the novel to appreciate how accurate an analysis this is. Nina constantly employs the parenthetical qualification; it is the very badge of her honesty and her understanding. But it is more still. We come to see, after a time, that this readiness to admit another's point of view, and to allow it repeatedly to qualify her judgments, is ultimately what creates her uncertainty and indecision, her whole moral drift. Even this commendable play of mind and sympathy becomes a vice, allowing Nina to deceive herself with an excess of light, and to refuse none of the claims made on her. In meeting all claims, as prisoner and lover, in ceasing to choose, she ceases to be moral. Both Jim and Chester, by contrast, are narrower and more doctrinaire. Consequently, whatever their shortcomings, they are less susceptible to the forbearance and passivity which undo Nina. Cary is able to mirror this vitiating fairness in his brilliant parenthetical style for Nina, so that we read the very principle of her failure in her fanatical equity of expression.

Her language is not otherwise notable or distinguished in its details, but it occasionally offers us even larger patterns of her emotional divisiveness than the parentheses. When Chester is turned out of office in the election of 1922, Nina's comments on him are characteristically schizoid. On the one hand she sees him

quite non-politically and serves as our reliable point of view on a
fallen figure:

> He really was alone. It was impossible any longer to reach
> him. He had, so to speak, in thirty years of war, made such
> devastation round himself that to talk to him at all was like
> calling across a waste full of broken walls and rusty wire and
> swamps of poisoned water; full of dead bodies, too, like that
> of poor Brome [a young strike leader who was sent to the
> front despite a bad heart] (p. 334).

But just over the page, Nina speaks with a crass political calculation which reveals the extent of Chester's effect on her fundamentally non-political outlook. At the outset of her life this note would
have been quite impossible for her: "We were all agreed that it
would be an excellent thing if Chester took up religion again,
because he would certainly need all the chapel vote if he was going
to win another election." At this point in the novel, it has become
her idiom.

The last of Cary's techniques for conveying Nina's emotional
cleavage has to do with the design of the novel as a whole. We have
glanced at Andrew Wright's remark on the formal device which
places Nina between Chester and Jim as comforter to both, and
which reaches its climax in the *ménage à trois* at the close of the
novel. We ought, though, to see how fundamental this device is
to Cary's whole method, both here and elsewhere, and how much
it is responsible for the major effect of *Prisoner of Grace* as a
novel.

Cary's method of composition was a rather unusual one.[6] He
ordinarily began with a conception of a character in a situation.
If both seemed significant and useful to him, he tells us, he would
"write a few pages to show that character in that situation." From

---

[6] See Cary's discussion of his procedure in "The Way a Novel Gets Written,"
*Harper's*, CC (February 1950), 87-93. The quotations which follow above are from
this essay.

this sketch the general plan of the novel would grow, gathering subsidiary characters and incidents. "I may write," he explains,

> the end, the middle and the beginning, and very often in this order. That is, I decide how and where the book shall end, which is just as important to a book as a play; and then I ask myself where are the most difficult turns in the book. Then I might write one of these difficult passages to see if it is viable (p. 88).

We can understand several things about *Prisoner of Grace* from this explanation. Nina's moral disintegration at the end, her inability to distinguish among the claims being made on her, is crucial to Cary's conception, since the close of a book has very great significance for him and is a matter of first concern in his planning. We know in addition, from *Art and Reality*[7] and elsewhere, that the railway-station scene in which Nina first discovers her inability to desert Chester was the difficult passage in *Prisoner of Grace*. Once written successfully, it made the writing of the entire novel possible. It contained, for Cary, as he indicated in a B.B.C. interview with Jack Morpurgo several months before his death, the essence of the whole novel. That is, it was a viable rendering of a character in a situation.

In a sense, the novel never becomes anything more than a character in a situation—Nina, perpetually torn apart by obligation to Chester and love for Jim. The occasions of cleavage change constantly, of course; few novels of comparable length have so rich a profusion of events, difficulties, crises, stratagems, and compromises. Nina's subjection to Chester takes several forms, as we have noted, just as her displeasure with him does, moving from political considerations, to Tom's upbringing, to Chester's treatment of Goold. And her sympathy for Jim is enlisted in a variety of ways. But through all these variations, the underlying pattern of divided loyalty persists. We get, consequently, a constant rein-

[7] See p. 97.

forcement of her predicament by a kind of chafing, reiterative action. The amplitudes change slightly, but the arc of movement and countermovement remains similar. We ought not to see the novel as a *static* formal device or structure; like an engine it is wholly dependent on its inner, cyclical moving parts. Everything, including the basis, in Nina's character, of her predicament, is intensified by repetition, so that through the course of the novel Nina wears herself more deeply into her situation. Only at the close, when we witness the wildest reaches of her moral incompetence, do we realize that she has all along been shuffling herself into a quite bottomless pit.

This use of an entirely reiterative action creates the novel's special atmosphere. Cary, we know, has used the same pattern of continuing, unresolved conflict elsewhere, for rather different reasons and, often, with considerable success. This time, though, in addition to yielding that extraordinary emphasis on character at the expense of plot which marks all his fiction, it provides precisely the climate of ceaseless dilemma which *Prisoner of Grace* must have. The demand for moral choice presents itself in a hundred guises. Out of Nina's oscillations between repudiation and acceptance, out of her restless ambivalence, out of her refusal, eventually, to choose at all, emerges the quality of the novel and the quality of political imbroglio which it projects. For this result Cary has had to sacrifice several things. There are no large structures of action which would provide a more linear kind of dramatic development. His characteristic short chapter is at work, too, quickly and deftly posing a multitude of situations and problems, bringing its special contribution of tension and haste. As a result of it, Cary cannot take time or space for detailed and extensive scenes; instead he relies heavily on summary. What remains, though, is far more important. The novel constitutes a grand design of agitation which mirrors an agitation within. By exploiting a subjective narrative mode, the book manages to convey what takes on the appearance of an objective truth. Our clearest apprehension of the obliquity of politics comes to us in our sense of Nina's tortuous moral deterioration. Out of her microcosmic end comes our macrocosmic revelation.

Knowing what we do of Cary's characteristic reluctance to judge, of his extraordinary moral liberality, we may suppose that his own reading of *Prisoner of Grace* would differ somewhat from the preceding one. He would probably be far less concerned to have us condemn Nina than to have us sympathize with her plight, to recognize, that is, the irreconcilable division between allegiances of feeling and duty which besets her. Indeed, he might even wish us to accept her pleas for a complexity in adult human intercourse, both political and familial, which eludes traditional and determinate moral judgment altogether. Nina, in this perspective, would be a far more reliable narrator than we have considered her, far less a victim. And what we have construed as a progressive moral degeneration would appear as something different too—perhaps a heroic attempt to meet exalted and difficult responsibilities in the face of imminent death.

One of the most remarkable things about *Prisoner of Grace* as a novel is that, in itself, it offers no very good reasons for not being read from this more generous standpoint. Cary employs the first-person mode with such skilful indeterminateness that either reading can be sustained, though one would need to be remarkably close to Cary's irresolute habit of mind to accept Nina's position, at the book's close, as either necessary, inevitable, or commendable. Within the limits of the novel itself, the moral disposition of the reader is left free, in the best Cary manner, to weigh Nina's testimony and Nina with it. Limits could be set, of course, by the other novels of the trilogy. Our evaluations of Chester and Jim, and the legitimacy and force of their claims on Nina, might be clarified in their own narratives. This clarification would help us, in turn, to judge the adequacy of Nina's perception and the decisions or evasions that follow from it. The whole, that is, might fall

into place at the close, and some judgment of its parts become
feasible. It is a hope for such illumination that will lead a reader
on into the remaining volumes of the trilogy. While Cary's indeterminateness will disappoint him in the end, he will have discovered three individually remarkable, if rather ambiguous, novels
—recompense enough, one would think, for almost any amount of
trouble.

# IV

## Except the Lord:
### *The Recourse to God*

As a separate autonomous novel, *Except the Lord* presents no serious problems. It purports to be Chester's sober account of his childhood, youth, and early manhood in Devonshire, ranging from his birth in 1854 to the close of the seventies. In it he is concerned primarily with his own intellectual, emotional, and spiritual beginnings and development. These are largely conditioned by the extraordinary poverty of the moorland farming and mining region, which makes life itself precarious, and by the two contending forces which seek in different ways to meliorate this situation: politics, or more specifically, trade unionism, and evangelical Christianity.

If we confine ourselves to *Except the Lord,* we can follow Chester's evolution clearly and sympathetically enough. He moves from a religious boyhood, as the son of an evangelical minister, through a phase as a union organizer, and, finally, politically disillusioned, to religious faith once again, as a preacher to his father's own congregation. But the trilogy will not allow us this easy comprehension. Both *Prisoner of Grace* and *Not Honour More,* in their own ways, insist that the Chester of *Except the Lord* is an imposter, a man who is, in his integrity, sincerity, and idealism, utterly unlike the figure that Nina and Jim Latter record.

In Chester's narrative, Cary has provided us with his most deliberate surprise in both trilogies. When, in the first trilogy, we turn from *Herself Surprised* to *The Horse's Mouth* and *To Be a Pilgrim* we are quite prepared for the whole flavor and quality of Jimson and Wilcher as persons; as we enter their worlds we experience, for the most part, a confirmation of Sara's intimations in the first novel. What we know of Chester from Nina's *Prisoner of Grace,* however, prepares us not at all for his own account of himself, or, better, prepares us so subtly that only after we have been shocked can we make the appropriate explanations. The contradictions between the two novels are imposing. For all of Nina's masochistic sympathy and readiness to defend Chester in her novel, his maneuvers, after the most impassioned and skilful justification—indeed, because such justification is necessary—inevitably suggest duplicity and ruthless calculation. The circumstances of his marriage to Nina, his opportune pacifism, his wily evasion of the Contract Scandal, his later repudiation of pacifism in order to accept a position in the War Cabinet, his treatment of his friend Goold, his threatening his wife with Jim Latter's death, and his sexual outrages against the newly remarried Nina at the novel's close—all these acts, even if we put the best construction on them, as Nina persistently does, make Chester, at the very least, morally suspect. Chester's adeptness at justification, whether it takes the form of public addresses, letters to the newspapers, or conversations with Nina, serves, again, like Nina's own explanations, only to complicate our uneasiness.

The Chester of *Except the Lord,* however, is a startling departure from the Machiavellian figure that Nina unwillingly portrays. He is a man of principle rather than expediency, of serenity rather than energy. He is inspired by faith, truth, and love, not by power. Indeed, he does not hesitate to repudiate politics itself, the activity which absorbs almost his whole being in both Nina's and Jim's narratives. Some part of this shift can be attributed to a shrewd, convenient limitation which Chester imposes on himself. His narrative in *Except the Lord* deals only with the first twenty-five years of his life, before he begins his relationship with Nina; he does not even venture a justification of the knotty, dubious later portion of his political career. It is conceivable that these early

years were a good deal more principled than Chester's life was ever
to be again. Then too, writing as an old man in semiretirement at
Palm Cottage, during the period between the First World War
and the General Strike, he is perhaps sufficiently removed from the
pressures of office to indulge himself in a sententious, facile, senti-
mental idealism. Consequently, both the early years about which,
and the later ones in which, he writes may be sufficiently atypical
of his career to account for the pretensions of *Except the Lord,*
for its Chester over against Nina's.

This, however, if we are to be fair to Cary, is too partial and
too superficial an explanation. The whole burden of the trilogies
and their first-person method demands a more responsible and
fundamental accounting. We should do Chester a considerable
injustice, for instance, to think him incapable of treating any part
of his career as persuasively as he does these beginning years—not
only because Cary has made him clever and elusive enough to
justify anything, but because his own motives, in Cary's view,
would have one kind of appearance and validity for himself and
another for the world, even for Nina, who knew him best of all.
Chester's subjectivity does not, of course, rule out the possibility
of self-deception, nor of any condemnation of him that objective
evidence can substantiate. But it does tend to undermine the probability of deliberate, calculated misrepresentation in *Except the
Lord,* and to allow the sincerity that moves through the whole
narrative its proper place; it would be, at the most, a deluded,
rather than a meretricious, candor.

As we have seen, Nina's narration in *Prisoner of Grace* hovers,
not like Chester's between the possibilities of sincerity and duplicity,
but between reliability and confusion. As a result, while Nina
emerges from her novel as a victim of the turbulence which she
describes, Chester conveys, in his, a mastery both of events and of
the meaning and value of events. His control is notable; it is his
novel, as we might have expected, that becomes the center of the
trilogy. Unlike Nina, he does not hesitate to weigh and judge, even

himself; and his judgments, uttered with a quiet, wise religious fervor, strike us as compelling and right. Cary, in providing Chester with a fixed religious standpoint, has enabled him to look out serenely and lovingly on the world of his youth and to speak of it with the tongue of an angel. To the extent that we can reconcile this angel with the apparent devil of *Prisoner of Grace* and *Not Honour More,* we gain the kind of insight into the nature of reality which Cary was at pains to impart. The reconciliation is presumably our task as readers, for Cary is scrupulous about not pronouncing upon the matter in the novels themselves; but it is a labor that we must, in its final implications, at least, put off until we consider the trilogy as a whole.

As we turn to *Except the Lord* to consider Chester's portrait of himself in detail, we can comfort ourselves with its relative simplicity. The complete control and understanding which Chester exercises over this part of his life relieves us of the kind of continual assessment that Nina's account demands even before we examine her novel in relation to the whole trilogy. Within the bounds of *Except the Lord* itself, we encounter a perfectly coherent memoir.

Chester's whole childhood is spent in an atmosphere of poverty and religion. His father, a former soldier turned evangelical minister, loses his farm shortly after the novel opens and turns to odd jobs, finally rising to foreman of a well-to-do widow's farm. From their childhood on, Chester and his brothers and sisters are accustomed to working in one difficult capacity or another, living a meager cottage life, and thanking God for such comfort as they have. When their beautiful, wise mother dies of consumption, leaving her five children exposed to the terrible jeopardy of an unmitigatedly impoverished existence, Chester expresses the religious perspective in which the misfortune, though financially avoidable, is seen by the family:

We certainly understood that if we had been able to send

my mother to the south of France she could have been saved.

But not my father, not one of us children, except perhaps Georgina, perceived this difference as an injustice. So that when Georgina suddenly exclaimed one day after the doctor's visit that his medicine was no good, the only proper medicine was some money so that "mother can go to France and be properly warm and drink plenty of wine," we stared at her in surprise. And before we could reflect on her meaning father said shortly, in the common phrase, that wishes never put shoes on a horse or meat in the pot.

And then, as if he had suddenly understood the desolation in our minds, and that deep question and anger half articulate in Georgina's exclamation, he raised his head from his book and said in a stern manner, "It is not for us to question the work of Providence, the Lord gives and He takes away. You did not earn yourself, Georgy, and you would have no right to cry if you were crooked."[1]

This is the religious acceptance in which Chester begins his life. His sister Georgina, though for a while somewhat outside the father's influence, is eventually drawn under it again, moving, curiously, in a direction counter to Chester's. Another episode reinforces and clarifies this early religious phase. Some time later both Chester and Georgina steal off to the Lilmouth Great Fair and, though forbidden by their religion to watch plays, see a performance of *Maria Marten*, the story of the brutal seduction and murder of a poor cottager's daughter by a rich gentleman. As Chester watches his first drama, he is overcome with horror, sympathy, and rage, more deeply moved than he could be by any tragedy in his own life; yet, at the same time, he is fascinated by the power and evil of the villain, and by the potency of the spoken word. On their way home Georgina is outraged at the injustice that they have witnessed and bitter, once again, over her mother's unnecessary death and the irresponsible waste of money on pleasure by men like Lord Slapton of the neighboring gentry.

[1] *Except the Lord* (London: Michael Joseph, 1953), p. 39. All subsequent page references are to this edition and will be cited parenthetically.

Chester, on the other hand, is still quite unresponsive to such promptings:

> I had not come to my moment of illumination, I had lived with inequality all my life—for me still the cruelty of social injustice was swallowed up in a vaster, more dramatic, more immediate fatefulness of life itself, of arbitrary death.
>
> One child was born crooked, another straight; one to bad parents, another to good; one man was stricken, another left. . . .
>
> We could not blame Lord Slapton, or that vague entity the rich, for such catastrophes as these. They fell upon my imagination as the deed of forces beyond my understanding, the decree of a God whose ways were not my ways (p. 100).

The conviction, both in the old man recalling, and the young man entertaining, these ideas, is unmistakable. Chester begins life in a religious milieu presided over by his saintly father, who waits confidently for the Second Coming of Christ, and who confronts death, deprivation, and evil with an awesome humility and obeisance. As much as a child is able, Chester emulates him in his devotions.

A sequence of events, however, soon commits Chester to the other possibility which his environment holds out, labor-union agitation. Cary seems to make it clear, as he traces this new major development, that Chester's sincerity and dedication are once again genuine and selfless. There is no discernible calculation in Chester which might degrade his idealism.

*Maria Marten* is, oddly enough, the beginning of Chester's political activism. On the same journey homeward with Georgina where we have heard him express a thoroughgoing religious quietism, we discover that something quite different is stirring in him as well, though he is unable to formulate these new feelings precisely. Their relation to his fascination with evil and oratory during the performance of the play is left for the reader to infer:

> And while Georgina raged at those who had injured her

loved ones, I walked in a dream. Something moved in me
that was not yet even an ambition—the mere ghost of aspiration. It was true that I had smiled [during Georgina's rant-
ing]. At what vision, or rather sensation of proud independ-
ence, I could not tell. Who shall set bounds to the secret unconscious appetites of a young soul starved of hope?

I was a king, a hero of the revolution. But without wrath
—without even revolutionary principles. I could not be
troubled with indignation on this wondrous night (p. 100).

Circumstances do not allow this "mere ghost of aspiration" to
fade. A short time later Chester attends two Adventist meetings at
dawn to await the Second Coming of Christ. The first is held on
April 15, 1868, the day calculated by the London headquarters of
the sect. When nothing but a glorious sunrise greets the assembled
worshipers, Chester is not significantly affected. But fifteen days
later when the Nimmo family stands in the rain facing a dawn that
appears "like a dirty rag" to await Christ at the hour appointed by
father Nimmo, Chester's religious faith receives "a mortal wound."
The complete trust he had hitherto had in his father's wisdom is
destroyed. Unlike Georgina who is drawn closer to her father by
this failure, leaving all her strong political feeling behind her,
Chester's way is now opened to political agitation.

Shortly afterwards Chester is pushed along by an atheistic pam-
phlet which repeats the argument that Richard, Chester's brilliant older brother, had advanced when Christ failed father
Nimmo: "either the omnipotent God was a tyrant or a devil or
there was no God at all. . . ." Or in Richard's terms, "If there were
a God . . . why did He not stop wars and why had He let our good
mother die so miserably." Armed with disbelief and abetted by an
extraordinarily absorbing otherworldliness in his father, Chester
falls easily into a fervent new way of life.

It is the brilliant orator Lanza, a former disciple of Proudhon
and trusted lieutenant of Bakunin in the League of Peace and
Freedom, who provides Chester with a new faith around which to
organize his life and his energies. Speaking on the Brotherhood of

Man, Lanza insists that the family love and goodness which we all
know and trust to, which is one of our deepest and truest experiences as human beings, must be the foundation of all happiness and
peace in the world at large. Chester responds with all the intensity of a religious nature starved for belief, newly provided with a
means of expressing its deepest intuitions:

> I had rejected God and with God, the love, the charity,
> the assured faith in goodness that I had learnt in my own
> home. Now under another name, that of humanity, He was
> restored to his full grandeur and majesty as ruler of the world.
> For the miseries of the world were shown as the just and
> inevitable punishment of those who had turned their faces
> from that fundamental law of brotherhood. How should the
> world have joy which lived in joyless fear for its possessions?
> (p. 141).

We notice here that Cary has Chester speak in religious terms,
has him embrace a religion of humanity, presumably devoted to
the establishment, in the manner of such faith, of heaven on earth.
Nothing in the language, feeling, or causation is spurious. Chester's
commitment strikes us as total and genuine, not only here, where
it springs full-blown from his heart, but in the episodes that follow,
where he seeks to implement it. Whatever devious game Cary may
be playing in the trilogy at large, we have every right, as readers, to
insist upon the plausibility of Chester's sentiments here, to believe,
utterly, his own report of himself. Cary has couched it in the very
inflections and cadences of truth. If Chester is falsifying anything
at this point in his novel, Cary provides little or no indication of
this within the novel itself.

From the time of his conversion, Chester's involvement in political affairs increases rapidly. Through Dr. Dolling, a nineteenth-
century republican in the Mazzini tradition living in exile in
England, Chester not only discovers the literature of revolution but
learns that already there are agents of the millennium at work in
his own neighborhood, Shagbrook. Under the tutelage of Brod-

ribb, chairman of the Tarbiton dockers' union, Chester organizes a secret farm laborers' union at Shagbrook, consisting, before long, of twenty-seven members. Several of them, including Chester himself, mysteriously lose their jobs in rather hard times, and it soon becomes clear that the membership is no longer either secret or safe. During this period, his father out of work and the family hard-pressed for survival, Chester confesses his feelings: "But above all, what enraged me at that time was the idea of conspiracy, the belief that behind all the façade of law and justice, hard enough as it was upon the deprived, there was a secret compact between owners, the rich and their hangers-on, against the dispossessed" (p. 212).

This anguish gives way to yet another when Chester is set upon by three of his own starving union men who accuse him unjustly of revealing the membership of the union in return for money. Although he is fortunate enough to escape with his life and a head wound, Chester's opinion of political endeavor turns rather somber. "I can truly say that the wound to my soul has never healed. It was the first time I had been made to understand the fearful condition of political life, the fundamental want of all security, the appalling risks of those who accept any large responsibility for their fellows" (p. 226). He learns, in effect, that the war against poverty and injustice is neither so simple nor so pleasant as he supposed while sitting at the feet of Lanza or Dr. Dolling.

At Georgina's insistence, after she has helped her brother recover from his terrible disappointment, Chester travels to London and introduces himself to Pring, a Marxist who is one of the most eminent figures in the English labor movement. Pring's dealings with Chester bring the political apprenticeship which we have been tracing to a disillusioned close. It is ten years before Chester re-enters politics again to begin the career described in *Prisoner of Grace*. Only the sincerity and idealism which Chester brings with him into his last relationship with Pring, even after his bitter experience with the farm workers' union, could account for the depth of his disillusionment and repudiation. More and more he takes on the lineaments of an archetypal political *naïf*, of a man whose deepest instincts, curiously enough, are not political at all.

Pring places Chester, now twenty-one, in the Lilmouth office of the dockers' union as a liaison officer between Brodribb, the head of the Tarbiton local, and Banner, the Lilmouth chief. When the dockers are called out on strike at Lilmouth and Pring himself arrives on the scene to take charge, Chester becomes his chief aide-de-camp, an important and powerful figure. After nine weeks of striking, the dockers and their families, with union strike pay down to half a crown a week, are starving and difficult to control, many of them ready to return to work on any terms. In the face of these difficulties, the union strike committee meets and under Pring's influence, formulates a new policy of "discipline," "pressure," "activity," and "private persuasion," which means in effect, violence against the union's own weakest members and against anyone interfering with the effectiveness of the strike. Chester consents with "relief that a decision has been made." After the meeting, Pring reveals to Chester that he has had in his pocket all the while a confidential offer from a number of small wharf owners at Allsend and Tarbiton, who have broken away from the owners' association, granting the union two-thirds of its wage demands. He explains to Chester that he has suppressed the offer because announcing it would mean a split in the strike committee and the end of any effective union in the Lilmouth area for years to come. Although Chester consents, Cary allows him a regretful look back at the maneuver, which expresses clearly the shame, guilt, and repudiation that surround the whole episode for him:

> This book would be worthless if it did not show how men, especially young and ardent men as I was then, come to do evil in the name of good, a long and growing evil for a temporary and doubtful advantage. . . . I know, I think I knew then, that [violence] had no real excuse at Lilmouth. The compromise offered was fair, the victory in sight was reason-

able. Pring's motive in the so-called active policy was violence for the sake of violence, cruelty to make hatred, in short, class war and revolution (p. 252).

But Chester goes further before he finally withdraws. When as a result of the new "active policy" three carters are ambushed with a volley of stones and turned back, Chester, for the first time, lies to Georgina about the union's responsibility for the attack and exults privately in his dedication to the cause. He falters, however, when his father, who abhors the violence, asks him probing questions about the settlement offer, and he ends by evading an answer. This, though, hardly hinders him. After a month of "private persuasion" in which both bitterness and savagery mount on both sides, Chester visits the scene of an "incident" in which two men chosen for example are beaten, one of them severely about the face, and their houses wrecked by union thugs. Chester, far from being horrified, submits a cool report to the union in which he announces that "there is no doubt that the new policy has had all the success we anticipated in bringing the scabs into line, B and L and party deserve high praise for the efficient manner in which the assignment was carried out" (p. 261). When the report is published in the newspapers after a police raid on union headquarters, Chester does not hesitate to deny authorship and maintain that it is a police forgery. But with these exhibits of Chester's depravity, this phase of his career comes to an end, for he now encounters a situation which is too much even for his naïveté to withstand.

Brodribb, the Tarbiton leader who liked to tell his men that "they were Christians first and workers second," and who is in no sense a Marxist, resigns from the strike committee after the first attack on the carters, and sends a letter to the press proposing a conference with the employers. When Chester rushes in to union headquarters and demands to know why, as the Tarbiton representative, he has not been told about the plans afoot to retaliate physically against Brodribb, he is informed that through an oversight he was not notified about the emergency meeting at which the decision was made. In the midst of the ensuing quarrel in which Chester insists that disastrous consequences among the strikers would follow if a man like Brodribb were hurt, Pring enters and Chester at last recognizes his situation for what it is. Pring contemptuously dismisses Chester's exclusion from the emergency meeting as a "technical point," since the resolution was passed unanimously. Chester is taken aback:

> But what had startled me still more than this scornful attitude towards the whole principle, as I saw it, of our democratic and representative constitution, was [Pring's] glance at me as I attempted to explain my grievance. In the cold stare of his blue eyes flashed upon me, his expression of bored and angry contempt, I perceived the truth about the man; a truth I had always known and even gloated upon, but never applied to my own case, that no one on earth counted with him beside the cause.
>
> I knew in that moment that I was less than nothing to Pring, I had become a nuisance to him, to be quietly got rid of, from the time when, by some intuition or guess, he had decided that I might oppose his will to make an example of Brodribb (p. 271).

It is only a moment before Pring forces Chester's resignation, and Chester after voicing a warning against any "precipitate action at Tarbiton," is pushed downstairs and out of union life. Returning to his lodgings he finds his belongings out on the street, and the door locked against him. He awaits a carter in the deserted street, oppressed by a sense of betrayal and defeat:

> And when I write betray, I am expressing something beyond human treachery. It seemed to me in this disaster of my youth that I had been tricked by fate itself, by a conspiracy of circumstances.... The very silence of the street, usually full at this time of women's voices and playing children, seemed to join in with the falling dark like an approaching doom—as if a vast dark mind was gradually thinking itself to the point of crushing me out, a bug, a nothing, a creature rejected (p. 273).

It is on this gloomy, overdramatic note that Cary brings Chester's political phase in *Except the Lord* to a close. The writing is quite deliberately inflated, like the feelings that oppress young Chester. The phrases "human treachery," "tricked by fate," "conspiracy of circumstances," "approaching doom," and "crushing me out" are disproportionate to the encounter with Pring and its outcome. They suggest the whole quality of Chester's naïve expectations when he excitedly substituted humanity for God and set out to make the world anew by means of a few simple, sincere negotiations with the neighborhood employers. Actually his demands on union politics have been utterly unreasonable. When he speaks of himself as "a creature rejected," when in the cold, contemptuous stare of Pring's eyes he discovers that as a man he is "less than nothing to Pring," he intimates to us the personal basis on which he has all along been proceeding. We gather that he has looked for nothing less than love, for the kind of human consideration in the political undertaking that he has known in a family context—the affection and concern which his mother, and Georgina, and later Nina give him. It is not for nothing that in the very first sentence of the novel Chester speaks of the "three noblest [women] I have ever known, my mother, my sister, my wife," nor that the book opens and closes with reflections made at Georgina's grave. There is every reason for this first political endeavor to end painfully; for Chester is not yet prepared to deal with the impersonality, the hard conditions and exactions of political life. He has not yet mastered any of the personal indifference and stolidity of a Pring. The conception of politics which Chester attributes to his younger self in this novel must give way to something less loving, more calculating, before Chester can become the redoubtable politician that we know in *Prisoner of Grace*. For the present, a more benevolent enterprise suggests itself to him as an alternative and he returns to his father's church. It will be characteristic of the later Chester, though, that politics and religion do not offer themselves as alternatives.

The sequence which we have been tracing in detail and which, with Chester's recovery from his disillusionment, all but brings the narrative of *Except the Lord* to a close, is merely the skeleton of the novel. Unlike Nina in *Prisoner of Grace,* whose story is in large measure the story of her husband's career, Chester is unquestionably at the center of his narrative throughout. Yet Cary has been careful to interweave the abortive political autobiography richly with religious and familial strands which, in the end, turn out to provide the novel with its most significant texture and pattern— which is to say that they enhance, in an essential way, Chester's portrait of himself and his world.

Once again, as before in Cary, the narrative is charged with incident. The memoir format allows the neighborhood concerns, the careers of father Nimmo, and of Chester's brother Richard and sisters Georgina and Ruth, as well as Chester's own wide and bitter youthful experience to find their place and their relevance. Since the book runs to only 287 pages in the English edition, it is a crowded novel. Incidents, as in *Prisoner of Grace,* are not fully and elaborately rendered, a fact which Saul Bellow regrets in his review of *Except the Lord.*[2] Major episodes, like the performance of *Maria Marten,* the wait for the Second Coming, and Chester's final break with the strike committee are not neglected, but much of their effectiveness is owing to the brilliant economy with which they are done. In contrast, however, to *Prisoner of Grace,* where the rush of incident acts to confound Nina, so that she gives large portions of her narrative time to defenses and justifications which must quickly give way to new defenses and justifications, *Except the Lord* proceeds at a stately, measured pace. Chester's authority and substantiality as a narrator is such that he does not need to render incidents for us in order that we may experience them. He is able, instead, to interpret, to comment, and to generalize with such force that we find ourselves willing to take the actuality of the matter from his hands instead of shaping it for ourselves. Time

[2] *New Republic* (February 22, 1954), pp. 20-21.

saved from elaborate scenic rendering is utilized for pronouncements on truth, delusion, value, and permanence which grow
naturally out of the brief episodes and confer the kind of verisimilitude on them that we ordinarily think reserved for the most
detailed narrative accounts. Chester, far from being overwhelmed
by his material, looks back at events fifty to seventy years old, and
passes unequivocal, deliberate judgment on them with the wisdom
that belongs to experience alone. The criteria of judgment, which
derive from religious conviction, are always certain and clear;
Nina's standards, on the other hand, consist largely of a wild, uncertain desire to do the decent thing. This mastery of the events and
their meaning pervades the whole of *Except the Lord*, a story
which Chester feels impelled to tell for no less a reason than that it
"throws light upon the crisis that so fearfully shakes our whole
civilization"—atheism joined with skepticism. It is true that the
memoir, because it ends its narrative in the 1870's may be construed as a shameless evasion of the troublesome by both Chester
and Cary. But this possibility does not affect the moral control
which we sense in its treatment of its chosen materials.

There are other notable differences between Nina and Chester
as narrators. We have remarked Nina's fundamental passivity, her
tendency to remain a character in a divided situation which
changes only superficially during the course of the novel. The
reiterative structure which follows from this conception is typical
of Cary and appears throughout the trilogies. As we shall have
occasion to notice, *Except the Lord* conforms somewhat to this
pattern; but it departs significantly from it as well. Chester is primarily an evolving, questing figure in his narrative. He moves
quite discernibly, in one sense, from childhood religious resignation, to a stage as an atheistic union agitator, and then back to
religious faith. That there are somewhat similar impulses at work
in him throughout this pilgrimage does not obliterate the primary
effect of progression and development. It is this effect, this sense of
willed movement, which sets *Except the Lord* apart from *Prisoner*

*of Grace,* and indeed, from the remainder of the trilogy novels as well. Structurally, the novel moves forward from illusion to disillusionment, rather than endlessly to and fro between obligations.

This evolving figure of the narrator, however, is not entirely autonomous. Growth, even in *Except the Lord,* is, to some degree, conferred on the narrator by other people, though they act here to guide rather than, as in *Prisoner of Grace,* to disrupt and tear asunder. For example, in the midst of his account of Dr. Lanza's inspiring speech on brotherhood, itself one of these decisive influences on his development, Chester inserts a chapter which deals with his first sight of Nina Woodville, who later becomes his beloved wife. It occurs years after the Lanza incident, but bears centrally on Chester's conversion to the "religion of humanity." It is his recognition of goodness, truth, and innocence in Nina, then a mere child, which reveals to him those needs of his own nature which underlie all his idealism. While Chester is rudely kept waiting at Palm Cottage by Aunt Latter, Nina, an extraordinarily beautiful child, enters with a book, gazes fixedly at Chester, and asks him to read to her:

> I perceived then that the candour and confidence of that gaze did not arise from the arrogance of class but from the frankness of childhood, of a soul fearless of man, because innocent of evil.
> I felt instantly such a revulsion of sympathy that the tears rose to my eyes. I hastened to obey the command of this princess, and Miss Latter, when she bustled in ten minutes later with a somewhat offhand apology for her lateness . . . found me in a placable mood. . . .
> That lucid and candid gaze which so powerfully affected the awkward and embarrassed young man was not only the revelation of childhood's natural innocence but of qualities unique in that child—an inborn truth—an essential generosity of affection which no cruelty of fate, no bitter experience of human perfidy, could ever tarnish. Faith, hope—the profound charity which in the truest sense of the word rests in

the love of God, and is indeed the very door of His grace—
were innate in that spirit. . . .

What is the purport of all this—that he who founds argument and policy upon our intuition of human goodness will
not be disappointed (pp. 139-140).

This intuition of human goodness is made possible for Chester,
as Cary is at pains to show, by the whole force and tendency of his
family life, acting deeply and lastingly upon him from his earliest
days. Formed by a relentless poverty which varies only slightly in
degree through the course of the narrative, the family situation
occasions acts of impressive sacrifice and love. In dealing with
some of these family episodes, Cary shifts to the present tense, not
merely, as Andrew Wright has observed, to suggest their immediacy,[3] but to convey their continuing power to shape Chester's
whole life and growth. Chester's mother, though she dies of consumption in the early sections of the novel, is a moving and saintly
figure. One of Chester's earliest memories is of running behind her
as a baby when Georgina chases him in vindictive rage; in his
triumph it seems to him that "the column of her skirts was like a
fortress against all pain" (p. 8). At another point Chester's remarks
on Mrs. Nimmo provide a key to the connection between sexuality
and religious inspiration which characterizes his later life:

For all her gaiety, her humour, my mother was a dedicated
creature. Her life was inward, and she trembled before a god
that judged the very heart. When I kneeled in her lap and
whispered my first prayers into her breast, I cannot tell what
ideas that bedtime ceremony stirred in my infant mind. But
was I wrong to feel that I knelt in a holy place and communicated with a spirit which was then in all its gentle and modest
service truly one with the most High?

Confused ideas they were in a small child, and more feelings than ideas. But all the deeper, all the more powerful to
guard me long after that lap and breast were dust (p. 11).

[3] *Joyce Cary*, p. 143.

She injects her quiet, generous, resolute piety into the life of the family and into Chester himself. When she dies, the family goes into debt for five years in order to provide her with a fitting funeral. The sum spent is not only father Nimmo's "statement before the world that [Chester's] mother was worthy of honour, but also, in the mysterious domain of our spiritual life, an act of gratitude and worship toward the dead. And how better to measure that gratitude than by a personal sacrifice" (p. 43).

Chester's father is more important still as an influence on the growing boy. A selfless, godly man, he is the source and focus of the evangelical Christianity which pervades Chester's childhood. Far from being ineffectual, he is a heroic man, "at once soldier and prophet," whose tendencies toward martyrdom command Chester's admiration. He has courage and integrity enough to denounce the richest member of his congregation, Mr. Newmarch, for separating from his wife, at a time when Newmarch's influence is crucially important to the Nimmo family's fortunes. As a treasurer of a mineworkers' union he is injured in a brave attempt to stop a labor riot. And late in the novel, partially crippled by arthritis, he gives up his position as foreman of Stonepit farm and the cottage that goes with it, because of the dissolute life of its owner, Fred Coyte. With no prospect of employment he refuses Newmarch's offer to take the Nimmo family in and settles, instead, at Ladd's house, a damp cottage which jeopardizes both his and Georgina's life, in order not to desert his congregation. At a time when Chester is most godless, he nonetheless falters, as we have seen him do, before his father's impassioned denouncement of union violence and trickery, and before his father's favorite biblical quotation, invoked against the transgressors: "Their webs shall not become garments, neither shall they cover themselves with their works: their works are works of iniquity, and the act of violence is in their hands."

Despite the older Nimmo's spiritual force and its indelible effect on Chester, Cary subtly conveys, too, his remoteness and extraordinary otherworldliness, which help prepare for Chester's defection from religion. "His own life was so entirely given to others," Chester says of his father,

> without regard for return that he hardly noticed the difference between the labourer who, like Georgina, worked all through the day, and those like us who came in at the end of it and did comparatively little. He had that blindness to common justice between man and man which is not unusual among saints, who see all men as sunk so deep in obligation to God that their various merits are as corn to the height of the sky. One reed shaking in the wind may be some inches taller than another, but what are inches in the abyss of the eternal contemplation? (pp. 74-75).

When this absorption, so total and so detached, comes once into question, as it does when Christ fails his prophet on the moor by not returning to earth, it is not difficult for Chester to dismiss it as a grandiose delusion and take up what appears to be a more realistic form of amelioration, labor agitation. This same insensitivity of father Nimmo's to the family's immediate circumstances and needs leads to an important emotional rift between Georgina and him, and helps to make clear Chester's indebtedness to his older sister, his deepest in the entire novel.

A fierce, passionate, loving girl who worships her father, Georgina, while still a mere child, goes to work for the Grocer G. and regularly on Saturday nights lays her wages, three sixpences—not to be despised in the family's circumstances—on the table before her father, who is all but oblivious, busy with his theological reading. "She hates to seek his praise," Chester tells us, "she loves him too much." After her mother's death, Georgina as the eldest child is compelled to assume responsibilities which are beyond her years. "Georgina's watchfulness of expense, so unnatural to her impulsive and rather reckless character, led to continual quarrels. She was not only too young for such cares, but she was in the difficult position of all such elder sisters who have to take a mother's place without a mother's natural authority" (p. 44). As a result of this situation she is gradually isolated from the family circle, cut off even from her father by a distressing incident. Chester's gifted older brother, Richard, implies, during a quarrel with Georgina, that she is allowing G., her employer, to take sexual liberties with her in return for family provisions. When her father enters and questions Georgina about G., she denies resolutely having mentioned G. at all. The enormity of the lie, and her inability to explain her position or her sacrifice to her truth-loving father, mature Georgina preternaturally and bring about a painful change in her circumstances:

> It was many years before Georgina could be called a complete woman.
>
> But that decision taken so suddenly, and supported with a resolution so astonishing in a child, did profoundly affect Georgina. It changed her relation with her father. She had always worshipped him. . . . Up till now she had never dreamed of criticizing any of my father's least words or acts; there was between them a tie so close that it seemed a wish of my father's became at once Georgina's without passage through her brain.
>
> But from this time he became to her a person who, like ourselves, sometimes needed to be handled, managed, who could not be trusted to know his own advantage. . . . She did not forget, neither of them forgot, all their lives, that immense lie that had come between them.
>
> Now, too, she studied his needs with a tenderness of which we had not thought her capable. She had been, and still was to us, a slapdash housekeeper; for him she was tidy and careful. She took trouble to see that he had what he liked to eat, that his clothes were mended and weatherproof, she became a wife to him (p. 52).

From this point on Georgina, keeping her own counsel, making her own decisions, becomes the strongest figure in the family. Unlike Chester, she is drawn closer to her father and his religious outlook after his Second Coming fiasco, and her natural selfless bent grows until she takes on impressive proportions. She allows herself to become engaged to the half-idiotic Fred Coyte, her father's employer, largely in order to help her family. When she falls truly in love with an ambitious young man named Wilson, she keeps deferring the marriage, partly out of a desire to tend her sick father and partly out of a sense of responsibility for Fred Coyte's subsequent death. Despite a warning by her doctor that her father's damp cottage would be fatal to her, in view of her consumption, she chooses to stay on nursing him, Wilson all the while urging her to come to London to marry him. Eighteen months later she dies, while still in her twenties.

Her effect on Chester is profound. Because she holds the family together and oversees its emotional life as well as its fortunes, Chester is able to experience in his home those intuitions of human goodness which become, as he explains, so fundamental to all his larger undertakings. She makes available to him, in fact, the major revelations of the entire novel. This process begins while Chester is involved in his disastrous attempt to organize the farm laborers. During this time his younger sister Ruth falls in love with a young groom named Simnel, a gambler whom her father is unlikely to tolerate as a son-in-law. Georgina gives Ruth active aid and encouragement, "walking about with a pale, tragic countenance for weeks, oblivious to all consideration but this love affair" (p. 213). Chester is puzzled and annoyed, caught up as he is in his own union activities. It is only years later, after thirty years of marriage to Nina have taught him to see the world "though a woman's soul," that he comes to see the true primacy of these concerns:

> Through [Nina] I look back fifty years to that time when Ruth laughed at her lover, but wept because she could not have him, and Georgina wondered and raged at me and said, "Everything isn't politics." And I understood how little I knew of the real world in which people actually live and make their lives.

> I know now that those two young girls, whom I thought
> so frivolous and small minded, whom you would think almost
> uneducated, were wiser than I, with a far deeper wisdom. . . .
> (p. 215).

Speaking now as the old politician in semiretirement at Palm Cottage, close to the end of his career, Chester elaborates the nature of this wisdom:

> It is not instinct that tells a young woman in love that
> politics deal with the ephemeral, the passing situation—while
> she is concerned with a permanent truth, with problems of
> loyalty and responsibility that never change their essence,
> with family duty, with the heaviest and most inescapable of
> responsibilities. She knows it by imagination and ex-
> perience. . . .
> The empires die and are succeeded by more ruthless and
> cunning, more mean and evil despots, the kings depart and
> presidents set new and crueller prisons for more efficient op-
> pression; the rack and boot are abolished, the scientist takes
> charge of the torture chamber; masks and catchwords
> change, the same mobs of fools and thugs, of hysterical boys
> and greedy, lying opportunists rush through the streets and
> cry; "Down with the government—down with the law"; auto-
> cracy with a sword is followed by democracy with a cheka;
> the capitalist with his wage slaves gives way to a minister of
> production and the concentration camp; but thug, student,
> minister, each has somewhere a home, and in every home,
> throughout the centuries in all the world, women ask them-
> selves the question: How shall we ensure peace? How shall
> love be served?
> Their politics are the everlasting politics of love and truth,
> beauty and cleanness (p. 216).

This eloquent rendering of value, with its exaltation of the
eternal womanly and familial impulses in human life at the expense of masculine affairs and politics, grows, as Cary makes clear,
out of Chester's observation of Georgina. During the latter portions
of the novel, she becomes a pervasive force in her brother's life in

more active ways as well. When Chester is attacked and beaten
by three of his own farm workers, Georgina nurses him back to
health and keeps him from falling into despair. It is at her contrivance and insistence that he goes up to London and meets Pring—
assistance quite at variance with her religious convictions, but not
with her love for Chester. Later, when Chester becomes an important figure in the dock-workers' strike, Georgina denounces to his
face the violence and injustice of the union's tactics. Yet she defends him fiercely before the community at large, even giving up
her beloved and necessary work at the Stonepit dairy at the mere
suspicion that its foreman has called Chester a liar and a crook.
It is after her brother's shattering disillusionment with Pring, however, when Chester has been forcibly expelled from union life, that
Georgina's influence becomes most meaningful in both an active
and an exemplary way. For at this time she opens to Chester not
merely the reality of goodness and the "everlasting politics of love
and truth," as these are manifested in the life of the family and the
home, but the conjuncture of these things with the realm of the
spirit, with the religious life.

Cary has Chester provide us with a transitional passage
which directly links the domestic and God, and prepares us for the
novel's fundamentally religious resolution. Annoyed at the spectacle of Georgina's and Ruth's adoration at the cradle of Ruth's
newborn child, young Chester contemplates his sisters dourly, before old Chester intercedes with theology:

> "Yes," I said to myself in my gloomy rage, "they are child-
> ren—the eternal innocents of the world, daughters of nature.
> They may play at thought, at politics, they may run a few
> yards from the nursery into the real world of men—but nature
> has them on a string, she gives one pull and they are back
> beside some cradle."
> And I did not see the meaning of my own thought. For
> what is nature if she teaches love and duty, what is goodness
> that was before all teaching, all doctrine? Was it the churches

and the parties who showed these poor girls how to devote
their lives—or the God who was before all churches, all states,
and will be after them in all eternity. . . .

I say that love and duty and freedom were in the world
before the thought and name of any god, before ever they
could name themselves, for God is and was and always shall
be, or there is nothing at all (pp. 222-223).

We know, in fact, throughout the novel that the older Chester
represents himself as a profoundly religious man. As we have
noted, Chester's narrative is conceived by Cary as a memoir rich in
interjected comments upon the significance of events and attitudes.
Many of these remarks are of a religious cast, so that, as readers,
we feel, even during Chester's atheistic phase, that in the end the
novel will resolve itself in an affirmation of faith. Four chapters
from the close, when he has just finished describing his expulsion
from the dockers' union and his alienation from Pring, Chester
speaks to us in such a passage, placing revolutionary politics, un-
equivocally, in a Christian perspective. He mentions first the power
of the printed word—Rousseau, Proudhon, Owen, Marx—"the
power of sorcerers." "And the fruit of their sorcery," he continues,
"is egotism and madness, war and death." Echoing his earlier
denunciation of the masculine as against the feminine preoccupations, he maintains that even the "splendid and noble" battle cry,
Liberty, Equality, Fraternity, "bred nothing but new and more
cunning, more hypocritical despots, better organized murder . . . ,
hatred not to be assuaged by the blood of millions and a century
of tears." "Trace now," he goes on,

the record of another, a modest and unconsidered force, an
influence little more noticed by the learned and the propa-
gandists, the word-wielders, than the play of the English
weather—the daily, weekly, ministrations of fifty thousand
servants of the Lord. I speak not here of the mighty Wesley
but of those humble and poor men who gave their lives to
oblivion. Yea, and  among them not only the so-called dis-

senting pastors, but many a vicar and curate of the English church, as poor and as ungratefully forgotten; above all that great anonymous crowd of witnesses, teachers of children, speakers in the way, lay preachers and readers, men like my father, who went among their neighbors speaking mercy, truth, kindness towards all men (pp. 274-275).

When in 1889, ten years after their failure in the Lilmouth strike, the dockers win a great victory in London, it is won, Chester says, "not with cannon but by the conscience of a nation, the active soul of a people."

Cary does not, in *Except the Lord,* account in detail for Chester's conversion. Too many of Chester's later experiences go into the formation of the religious attitudes which pervade the old man's narrative, experiences which the trilogy itself never deals with from Chester's point of view. We are provided, however, with the beginning of Chester's return to spirituality as against revolution. It occurs in a sequence at the close of the novel in which Georgina is once again crucial.

It is she who comes along with a cart to retrieve Chester and his belongings as he sits despondently before his lodgings, dispossessed by Pring and the union. When he falls ill shortly after, she nurses him once again, but his recovery is slow, and during the course of the following year nothing can dispel his sense of emptiness and failure. Then one night at family prayers, Chester hears his father read the psalm from which the book's title comes :

> Except the Lord build the house, their labour is but lost
> that built it;
> Except the Lord keep the city, the watchman waketh
> but in vain.
> Lo, children and the fruit of the womb are an heritage
> and gift that cometh of the Lord.

Suddenly something "deep beyond thought or will" in Chester responds with great force, a "strange convulsion in [his] soul":

I did not know then what had happened to me. I might say that it was years before I grasped the full significance of that profoundest of truths not only for the man but for all his endeavours—not only in his family life but in his political activity—that unless he aim at the life of the soul then all his achievement will be a gaol or a mad-house, self-hatred, corruption and despair (p. 284).

The holy feeling is consummated a moment later through a human agency. Georgina, already emaciated by tuberculosis, looking like "one released only a little while from the grave to do her work on earth," comes toward Chester, now ruminating in the garden, carrying his overcoat.

I felt a sharp annoyance at this typical family interruption at such a moment, and stepped back further into the shadow. But pity held me, Georgina had the privilege of the dying. I waited for her and silently allowed her to help me into the coat.

Then as I turned again she smiled at me in that serene and tranquil manner which quite contradicted her tragic looks, "Why are you so unhappy. Don't you see how proud we are of you?"

She was consoling me and it broke my heart—I felt then an indescribable shock of anguish and of exultation. And instantly among the turmoil of my senses a darkness fell away, great presences were revealed, things absolutely known and never again to be obscured, grief that I knew for love, love that I knew for life, joy that I knew for the joy of the Lord (pp. 285-286).

Months later, Georgina is dead, but not before she has conferred on Chester that realization of love and faith which sustains him his whole life long. It takes him almost a lifetime to measure her gift, for it is only when he begins his memoir, that he sees, standing at her grave, how his life is bound up with hers, how her heart "could not know despair because it forgot itself in the duty of its love." Indeed, the memoir itself is a result of this insight, as

Chester makes clear in the very last words of the novel: "And my way was made plain. 'Here,' I said, 'the story began and here it shall begin again, in the things I lived with this forgotten one, in the young cruelty of the world, in the making of our own souls' " (p. 287).

Thus, Chester will have it, the spirit triumphs. Whether it manifests itself in human goodness and innocence, such as Chester saw in young Nina Woodville, or in the family love, sacrifice, and piety which his father and mother moved in, or in the feminine affinity for what is permanent, valuable, and true in human life that he observes in his sisters, or in Georgina's love, which embodies the sum of these things, or in the existence of God, Who is their source—all become comprehensible to Chester under a religious dispensation which, whatever its imprecision, becomes the salient truth of the entire novel. Indeed, six months after hearing his father intone "Except the Lord build the house," and after coming to understand the heritage which has been God's gift to him, Chester delivers his first sermon to his father's flock, beginning an evangelical career which keeps him out of politics for ten years. This triumph of religious faith is, for the reader of *Prisoner of Grace*, the most remarkable effect of Chester's whole narrative. As Cary allows it to gather force through Chester's depiction of the family and his elderly interpolated judgments, we are prepared to see it sweep everything before it, not merely the politics of violence or revolution, but politics itself. For as Chester has it as the close of his life, the profoundest truth for man and for all his endeavors —political as well as familial—is that "unless he aim at the life of the soul then all his achievement will be a gaol or a mad-house, self-hatred, corruption and despair." Underlying every form of politics, pre-empting it, is the soul, its destiny and its God, grasped not merely as an acknowledged truth, but as an active principle.

This relegation of politics by religion is Cary's major contrivance in the novel, his most extraordinary stroke. We come from the apparently ingenious extemporizer and evader of principle in *Prisoner of Grace,* for whom politics is all in all and God, apparently, a convenient rationalization, to the holy man of *Except the Lord.* Chester's religious tone, in his own narrative, is, on the whole, so compelling, so persuasive that at first it might appear that Cary is allowing him to enunciate the kind of "supervening human bond above and beyond [political] ideas," the "moral order beyond ideology" that Irving Howe sees emerging from every great political novel.[4] Perhaps, we might think, Cary is trying to elicit a religious form of consent from us, an awareness that Chester has indeed put first things first and grasped the governing truth about himself, his career, about all human endeavor. We are tempted to feel that perhaps the politician of *Prisoner of Grace* is only a sheep in wolf's clothing, armed to fight God's battle in the tawdry, vicious world of politics. But it is an uneasy supposition, and too much stands in its way.

First, there are the contradictions between Nina's and Chester's narratives. Richard Hughes, reviewing *Except the Lord* in the *Spectator* (December 18, 1953), maintains that he is unable to reconcile the Chester of *Prisoner of Grace* with Chester's version of himself. And Andrew Wright reminds us that when Chester, in *Except the Lord,* writes his moving, pious eulogy of the fundamental nature of woman, with her "everlasting politics of love and truth," he is dictating to Nina Latter at Palm Cottage "and taking bold advantage of her sexually, whenever the two of them are alone together." Chester's reaction, Wright says, "is not only pious, it is also, and equally, lascivious."[5] Even if we hesitate to denigrate Chester's sexuality, which he regularly links with his religious impulses, still no direct acknowledgement or justification of his impositions on the newly remarried Nina occurs in *Except the Lord* at all. Furthermore, beyond the discrepancies between the two novels, which might be multiplied indefinitely, there are

---

[4] *The Political Novel* (New York: Horizon, 1957), p. 24.
[5] *Joyce Cary,* pp. 144-145.

doubts cast on Chester's piety and goodness by certain aspects of his own narrative.

We have noticed that Cary is successful in utilizing a large measure of evaluative comment and spiritual pronouncement by Chester in order to achieve verisimilitude and convey Chester's mastery over his experience. After a time, however, this mastery may come to seem suspect, and the pronouncements, with their spiritual insistence, perhaps a little forced, or hollow, or contrived, as if Chester were striking a pose. Chester's nineteenth-century, evangelical rhetoric occasionally corroborates this suspicion, for his language, ordinarily quite moving, is capable of a trace of fulsomeness. His remarks on womanly devotion begin in eloquence and end in excess:

> Was it the churches and the parties who showed these poor girls how to devote their lives—or the God who was before all churches, all states, and who will be after them in all eternity; the God to whom all churches are as the stammering words of children playing upon his doorstep; the God who is love and beauty at the heart of things, the Lord of creation whose freedom is the breath of the soul and the life of all existence (p. 222).

By his own account, too, he is something less than a saint. At *Maria Marten,* still a mere boy, he is fascinated by the "fearful glory" of the villain of the piece—indeed, comes to see him as the hero. Even as an old man reflecting on the experience, Chester speaks of the hypnotic force of power combined with the "guilt of blood" or "some horror of cruelty" as though he knows it well. His behavior during his union career also reveals questionable tendencies. His pride in his power, his exultant lie to Georgina and his routine lies to Wilson and his best friend Edward G., his heartless indifference to the brutal attack on two scabs and the inhuman report to the union which expresses it, all give us reason to wonder about Chester, if not to condemn him. It is true that such matters as Chester's homiletics, tone, and confessions of depravity arouse our suspicions primarily because of Nina's book; *Except the Lord* itself has, on the whole, a plausible, even authentic ring. The point is, however, that Cary intends us to read Chester's book in the light of Nina's and suffer the complications.

Chester's religious conversion at twenty-five is not necessarily spurious; it could easily overcome any moral or spiritual insufficiencies which preceded it, in the timeless pattern of such things. But the old Chester, dictating *Except the Lord*, with the career in *Prisoner of Grace* behind him, is more difficult to account for. In a sense it is misleading to say that Chester's book deals only with the first twenty-five years of his life, because, as we have seen, it deals as well, in an important way, with his religious attitudes at the time of writing, when he is about seventy. Indeed, the most considered and final expressions of religious insight belong exclusively to this later period. Yet we know from *Prisoner of Grace* that this is a time of defeat for Chester, when the country has repudiated his leadership and he is deprived of the power and adulation that were his during his ministry. By juxtaposing the first two novels of the trilogy, Cary may very well be implying a specious religious consolation in *Except the Lord*—a renunciation of the political for the religious which grows not out of conviction, but out of disappointment and pique. *Not Honour More* lends support to this possibility, because it deals with the period following the writing of *Except the Lord*, when Chester once again becomes actively, almost devilishly, political. Yet, for all this, the force and substance of Chester's narrative, his touching delineation of spiritual truth operating through family life and human love, is too urgent, too genuine to be put easily aside.

The problem of *Except the Lord*, like that of the whole second trilogy, is the problem of point of view, of the ascertainableness of truth, reality, and value. Cary employs the first-person narrative method, with its lack of suprapersonal dimension, almost as a means of keeping the problem insoluble, of injecting and multiplying contradictions. Whether Chester is consciously distorting, self-deceived, or utterly true to his own inner life, whether politics is an enemy, or a vehicle, of the spirit, are questions which the first two novels merely raise. We can but turn hopefully, once again, to the next, and last, volume of the trilogy, Jim Latter's narrative, *Not Honour More,* for whatever revelation of ultimate order and congruity Cary may vouchsafe us.

# V

## Not Honour More: *The Morality of Exasperation and the Indeterminate Pinnacle*

The essential characteristic of realism in medieval and modern western literature, Erich Auerbach tells us, has been the serious, problematic, or tragic treatment of random everyday life—an undertaking which goes counter to the classical rule of differentiated levels of style.[1] The novel has, of course, been an outstanding vehicle of such a realism, and Cary, for all his comic proclivities, belongs solidly to this tradition. In *Not Honour More,* however, and in the second trilogy generally, he undertakes the consideration and portrayal of a great public figure and public issue, in addition to private, everyday existence. He does not, it is true, achieve in Chester Nimmo anything like the nobility and magnificence of the public figure in Greek tragedy; this disparity arises, in some measure at least, out of the changes which public life has undergone over the centuries and is very much a part of the meaning of the trilogy. Modern democratic public life, that is, offers, on the whole, shoddier possibilities; but it serves, still, to enlarge the scope of *Not Honour More* and to confer on it a magnitude that we do not ordinarily associate with the novel of personal, or even social, life.

The significance of *Not Honour More* is very much conditioned by an interplay between public and private considerations. Cary has designed the novel in alternating sections which focus on the private problem of adultery and on the public problem of the

[1] *Mimesis,* trans. Willard Trask (New York: Doubleday Anchor, 1957), pp. 37-40 and *passim.*

General Strike of 1926. Andrew Wright notes that "in the course of the book the two focuses become one."[2] This is an astute and helpful remark; yet we cannot comprehend the whole burden of the novel unless we realize that it is, in a sense, equally true that in the course of the book the two focuses remain two. Out of a constant pull between public and private obligations emerges the terrible, murderous frustration of the novel's narrator, Jim Latter, the meaning of the novel, and what we must take to be its contribution to the trilogy.

The pattern of alternated focus is fairly clear-cut. Cary has Jim begin his narrative, which is dictated in prison while Jim awaits trial for murder, with a private episode. On May 1, 1926, Jim unexpectedly returns home to Palm Cottage from hunting. As we know from *Prisoner of Grace*, Chester Nimmo has been visiting the Latters for about two years, writing his memoirs—of which *Except the Lord* is a first installment—waiting for an opportunity to re-enter public life, and forcing himself sexually on a reluctant but cooperative Nina. As he enters the Cottage Jim catches Chester "interfering" with Nina and shoots, wounding Chester slightly. Jim escapes with Nina's help, makes a statement to the press, then discovers that Chester has publicly denied that any attempt has been made on his life. On the following day Jim confronts Chester again, but allows himself to be talked out of immediate revenge by the wily politician. Before he can satisfy himself about the true nature of Chester's relations with Nina and work out his personal revenge, Jim becomes involved in political developments in the restless Tarbiton area, and the novel enters a public phase.

Chester has seized the opportunity provided by economic unrest and the threat of a general strike and "wangled," in Jim's terms, the chairmanship of the Emergency Committee, a presumably neutral group created to resolve tensions. He appeals, through intermediaries, to Jim to take charge of the special constables in the Tarbiton area, and, in Chapter Eighteen, Jim, out of a sense

[2] *Joyce Cary*, p. 151.

of duty, does so. The public consideration overrides Jim's private spite, though he suspects that Chester is employing him merely to neutralize him and avoid being shot. From Chapter Nineteen through Chapter Thirty-three, the General Strike and its political complications enlist Jim's major energies and attention. Although Cary has Nina appear in several meetings with Jim in this section she acts largely in a political capacity on orders from Chester.

During this period, Jim's major concern as head of the specials is to preserve order by regulating picketing and preventing mob violence. With the General Strike under way, his greatest obstacle is the Communists and their local leader, Pincomb, who are eager to exploit all the possibilities of agitation and revolution which the Strike affords. Jim begins to suspect, after Nina has been seen at Pincomb's headquarters, that a bargain has been struck between Chester and Pincomb. The suspicion is eventually confirmed. Jim learns later that in return for Communist support, Chester has agreed to allow the Communists to picket, and thus destroy, Potter's, a very old independent shipbuilding firm which is on the brink of financial ruin, but whose employees do not wish to strike. On May 10, Pincomb, after inciting a Communist crowd in front of Potter's and encouraging a menacing revolutionary situation, is injured and arrested by Maufe, one of Jim's specials. The Communists immediately charge Maufe with an unprovoked criminal assault, though there is evidence that Pincomb and his two bodyguards have resisted arrest. The Emergency Committee, however, suspends Maufe for his action. Jim, who considers Maufe a heroic benefactor of the community and the nation, resigns his position in protest. So ends the first public phase.

After resigning Jim returns late at night to Palm Cottage expecting to find Nina, with whom he has become reconciled, alone. Instead, he finds her with Chester in her bedroom. After hearing Chester's torrential rambling defense, Jim, now resigned to Nina's infidelity and indifferent to Chester, agrees, out of pity, to drive with them to the Town Hall, where Chester claims that the polit-

ical errand which brought him to the Cottage can be corrobo-
rated. Just before they enter the Hall, Nina, to whom Jim has not
spoken at all, attempts suicide by leaping under a moving vehicle.
As Jim waits, with Chester, for news of her condition, he consoles
himself with Nina's ultimate honesty: she refused to enter the
Town Hall, he thinks, because she was through with lies and
tricks. Full of forgiveness, he invites Nina to accompany him to
Africa, after her recovery, where they can escape the corruption
and complication of English public life. She agrees. Before they
leave, while Nina is convalescing, they seek refuge from publicity
in the loneliest spot that Jim knows.

> We wanted peace for a week. We were sick of the rackets
> and the ramps.
> Sick of the gimme game, the grab boys, the bunkum and
> the spoof. But we found pretty quick that in England you
> can't get out of it. Perhaps not in Europe. It's soaked into
> everything. It's crept into the last cracks.[3]

A photographer sneaks up on them as they lie in the sun and
"Nina's thin white face with her great eyes, looking as terrified as
a child who's seen a ghost, went all round the world." So the
desperate attempt to withdraw into private life fails.

The closing section of the novel occurs, consequently, in a public
context. Although the Strike is over, Maufe has been brought to
trial for his assault on Pincomb, who is now permanently disabled
by a blow to his head. Nina is summoned to testify, for it develops
that she has played a crucial role in the affair. The key witness for
the defense, a man named Bell, asserts that Pincomb struck
Maufe first, resisted arrest, and injured his head by falling and
striking it against a curb. Bell maintains that he passed this infor-
mation on to Chester and that Chester must have received it
because he sent Nina to see Bell and confirm the testimony. Since

---

[3] *Not Honour More* (London: Michael Joseph, 1955), p. 189. Subsequent references will be made to this edition, with page numbers cited parenthetically.

Chester is supporting the charges against Maufe, this is highly embarrassing evidence. However, Nina's testimony at the trial saves the old politician. She recalls hardly anything of her conversation with Bell; and when Chester's letter instructing her about the Bell interview is read in court, it turns out to be not the least incriminating, though Bell's original report to Chester is missing. Jim is suspicious, but he does not press her; since her suicide attempt she seems to have put all chicanery behind her.

Shortly before the trial ends and just a few days before their departure for Africa, Nina and Jim are sorting their belongings at Palm Cottage. Jim notices that two collections of letters—Chester's and Nina's to each other—have been lying about, and that Nina seems unable to make up her mind about disposing of them. Jim takes the line that they are none of his business, though he suspects that they contain the whole truth about the Maufe affair. Nina, to her credit, does not destroy or hide them, though she has a number of opportunities to do so. This restraint comes to an end when Jim receives a phone call informing him that Maufe has been convicted and given a three-year sentence. Just as Nimmo's car pulls up—he has come to collect his letters—Jim asks Nina for permission to examine the correspondence, knowing that this is his last chance to uncover the truth about the Pincomb-Nimmo-Maufe affair. She consents, asking him only to remember that it was all before "the accident"—her word for the attempted suicide. The correspondence reveals that Bell's report was actually received but that Chester has hinted that it be suppressed; that Chester refused Bell police protection, though Bell was threatened by the Communists; and that Chester was quite eager to have Maufe convicted in order to gather for himself the support of the Labor Party while he was trying to form a new government in London.

Filled with a kind of public rage at the way in which Maufe has been victimized, Jim turns on the newly arrived Chester with a razor and chases him into a lavatory. Chester manages to lock himself safely in, but he dies soon after from a heart attack. When Nina, not knowing this, pleads with Jim for Chester's life, Jim indicates that he is going to execute her as well. She says that he must not mind the letters since they were written before her "accident," in effect, before her conversion to honorable dealing and truth. But Jim interrupts to explain, in the manner of an inarticulate Othello, that there is nothing personal in his proceeding:

> "My darling," I said, "it isn't what you said about me— it's about the fearful thing you and Nimmo have done. Perhaps you think it wasn't very much to betray Maufe and to join in with the liars and cowards and tricksters against an honourable man, against the honour of England. But that only makes it worse—it only proves what I say, that the rottenness has gone too far" (p. 221).

And a moment later he reflects, "[Nina] couldn't understand she was up against something bigger than either of us or anyone's happiness. The truth. And nothing could change it."

Despite the banality and bombast of Jim's utterance here, it is clear that he conceives of himself as a disinterested instrument of justice, cleansing, in one supreme necessary gesture, some part of the public life of England. Not adultery, not sexual jealousy, he tells us, but political corruption and subversion of the truth impel him. Although Jim's disinterestedness, like Othello's, takes some of its vehemence from personal considerations, on the whole, his willingness to forgive Nina before the Maufe conviction must persuade us that his motives are largely those that he all but inarticulately expresses. It is the public Nina, the conspirator with Chester for Communist support and for the sacrifice of the courageous Maufe, whom Jim kills, not the unfaithful wife. Her attempt, from the time of her "accident," to withdraw from the machinations of political life, to flee publicity and England altogether, is a touching indication of her decision to purge herself of trickery and maneuver; so too is her refusal to destroy the incriminating letters. Jim is aware of this effort and prizes it. But Nina enters upon it too late in life and is not prepared, even after resolving to live honorably and privately, to deny her assistance to Chester. We know that her suppression of evidence at the trial in order to save Chester occurs after she has resolved to make a new life with Jim. She cannot repudiate her public role even in the full sweep of her private retreat.

This alternating focus—from the private matter of adultery to the General Strike, then to Nina's attempt at suicide and extrication from public life, and finally to the Maufe trial and its consequences—gives the novel its structural outlines and creates the pull which, as we shall see, acts decisively on its major figures and on our view of them. We would do wrong, though, to suppose that Cary is making anything like a mechanical or absolute separation between public and private interests. Throughout the novel charges of private interest in public decisions, as well as the reverse, occur. The intermingling acts to reinforce the main conflict by making it ubiquitous. It also provides the conflict with specific occasions on which to manifest itself in Nina, Chester, and Jim.

Nina's situation in this novel culminates her development in *Prisoner of Grace,* where she first becomes a victim of the divisiveness which works her moral destruction. Cary makes it fairly clear that her allegiance to Chester is essentially a public allegiance to a great leader. She becomes so completely a prisoner to his political efficacy that at the close of *Not Honour More,* when she knows that Jim is at the point of killing her, she has courage and devotion enough to beg Jim to remove the dead Chester from the lavatory because it is horrible that so great a man, revered by millions of people all through the world, should be left in such a place. Yet we gather that she does not love Chester; her sexual services to him are merely a vouchsafing of inspiration to the public man. Her love, her personal feeling and allegiance, are presumably all for Jim. She asserts this in *Prisoner of Grace* and Jim accepts it in his own narrative. The private attachment, however, is consistently overcome. She protects Chester through all the adulterous sequences in *Not Honour More,* runs shoddy, fawning errands for him during the Strike, seeking to reconcile the alienated Jim and keep him from discovering too much about the Pincomb-Nimmo bargain, and, in the end, perjures herself in order to convict Maufe. In sum, the public consideration—that is, Chester's career, his mission to save a tottering England—is powerful enough to impose a public morality on most of her private life. Expediency, trickery, deceit, the justification of means by ends infect all her dealings with Jim. Her two efforts to recover the decency and truthfulness appropriate to a love relationship—her suicide attempt and her reluctance to destroy the letters—are merely the last remains of that fatal divisiveness in her nature which she can never completely elude, even when it threatens Chester's career. Cary conceived her in division. At the close, he has Jim kill the public aspect of her and ask forgiveness of the private.

The public-private pull affects Chester as well. It is from him, after all, that Nina learns to forgive herself almost any transgression in the name of some larger, higher dedication. We have seen this dedication take the form, in *Prisoner of Grace,* of an obeisance to God, with Chester making political decisions as the appointed instrument of his Creator. In *Not Honour More,* however, he pitches his justifications in a lower key, for they are largely directed at Jim, who is likely to be more revolted than persuaded by religious claims. Instead of invoking God, Chester invokes the public cause, the public danger, as his sanction. His importance to the nation during the General Strike crisis must excuse, he implies, any merely personal consideration. Thus, when Jim, pistol in hand, confronts him after catching him with Nina the first time, the question of adultery drops quickly out of Chester's sight. "Don't talk about your honour," Chester says to Jim, "what is it worth? The country is tottering on the edge of revolution and you seize this moment to gratify a private spite. At last you see your chance to ruin the man who has never done you anything but kindness—a man over seventy, in any case condemned to die. But you can't wait to dance on my grave and vilify my memory, like all the other jackals who have preyed upon me in life—you are resolved to drag me in the dirt during my last months. And this at the cost of your country. My dear Jim, at least allow yourself to believe that I am not speaking a vain thing. You saw the Press this morning—if not, the papers lie there on the bed. I have some influence still. Say if you like that I have done nothing to deserve this position, but you can't deny or ignore it. Since this last week the whole picture has changed, at this moment my intervention could be decisive. Forgive me if I say that you don't realize the situation" (pp. 66-67).

And again, when Jim returns to Palm Cottage after resigning as head of the specials and finds Chester with Nina, Chester wanders, during the course of his excuse, into the public domain. He has just returned from London, he says, where the Prime Minister would have nothing to do with his proposal to form a new government to deal with the Strike emergency. Forgetting completely the immediate issue—his presence in Nina's bedroom—he gives what amounts to a public speech:

"For this is war. War for the soul of England—the very heart of liberal Europe. And we are ready. Lloyd George will serve. I will serve. In any capacity. We do not demand guarantees. This is not a time for haggling. And always remember this, if we threw our weight with the workers we could tell the Tories to get out, we could toss them into the Thames. And make such a revolution the world has never seen—it would transform history—and who would dare to say we were not justified. We have been flouted and ignored —the men who brought this country through the agony of the war—the most tremendous, the most bloody in the history of man. Our experience is despised by the miserable pettifoggers and timeservers who are paltering with a crisis equally beyond their imagination and their powers" (p. 166).

Characteristically, Cary makes it quite impossible to tell whether Chester is genuinely distressed by, and preoccupied with, his recent public failure in London—which, to add to the difficulty, has its own personal aspect as well—or whether Chester is merely trying to distract Jim's attention from the issue of adultery. In *Not Honour More* Cary allows us our closest look at the mature Chester; but the wily old politician remains, despite this, a mystifying figure. Chester's dialogue, at its lengthiest and most eloquent, is quoted verbatim by Jim, whose own narrative style verges on a kind of headlong military illiteracy. The improbability of such accurate recall and duplication may be something of a threat to the novel's verisimilitude, but the danger is well worth the gain. Chester's genius for intrigue, persuasion, and manipulation is fully rendered. We come to understand the greatness, even if it is nothing more than inspired audacity, which Nina responds to and which enslaves her. And Cary conveys, too, the way in which Chester, as a public figure, can at once trample the personal lives of others, vindicate himself to himself, if not to Jim, yet all the while be desperately dependent upon the private ministrations of a woman like Nina, who is willing, at terrible cost, to replenish and restore him. There is something of Zeus's need of the mortal Leda in Chester's proceedings, and something, too, of Zeus's inhumanity.

Cary has the public-private theme reach its climax in the novel's first-person narrator, Jim Latter. It is not for nothing, as Mark Spilka has pointed out, that Cary's very name for his protagonist makes him an unmistakable spiritual descendant of Conrad's Lord Jim. A gentleman soldier, Cary's Jim has ordered his life around such conceptions as duty, truth, love, justice, and honor; and he insists, sometimes frenetically, upon their reality and their survival even in a corrupt and ugly age. If this makes him appear, at times, antiquated and ludicrous, the fault, we are often inclined to feel, is not entirely his own. While Chester and Nina have allowed the looser morality of public life to govern their personal relationships,

Jim steadily insists on the reverse. He wishes public life, even the national life, to base itself on the same code which governs a gentleman's conduct. The whole novel takes its title from what Jim calls "Colonel Lovelace's great poem." At fourteen he had explained its meaning to ten-year-old Nina, who, at that time, he says, "didn't laugh at an idea because it was true or fine" (p. 126). Whatever the new wisdom that Nina has imbibed, for Jim "I could not love thee, dear, so much, Loved I not honour more" is still the climax of "the most beautiful and true of all poems." As an essentially private person with a history, in *Prisoner of Grace*, of ineffectual and frustrating dealings with the British government, Jim is bound to be outraged by Chester, and by Nina too, at least to the extent that she puts on Chester's knowledge with his power. Since the book is narrated by Jim, we view most of its events with his sense of outraged honor, and we share, if only tentatively, in his violent denunciations of a corrupt world. Our commitment to Jim and his code may be a little uncertain and uneasy, but the narrative mode tends to insist on it, at least for the duration of the novel. The trilogy is perhaps another matter.

Jim's opinion of Chester is simple and violent. Chester, for him, is an irresponsible scoundrel who will say and promise anything to anybody for political power and gain—the very emblem of a corrupt national life. Jim's remarks on him invariably draw heavily on the language of disease and putrescence. When, for example, Chester charges Jim, as we have seen, with losing sight of Chester's public importance in mere personal spite, with not realizing the nature of the situation, Jim answers him in one of his typical phillipics:

> "God damn it," I said, "I think of nothing else. Fifty years of it. Since you and your gang set out to pimp for every gimme in the game. And bought your first ponce's pants with Nina's money—and Nina's soul. The situation. A whoreshop for syphilites—everything goes because you'll all get it. And how smart we are in the dirt. You've poisoned everything

you touched and it's still working. A living shanker. And you think no one will notice if you talk big enough. You think you can talk it away. Like a bill in your talky house. Good or bad—talk it out—talk out the loyalty and the truth. Talk out the man who dares to have some faith—some principles" (p. 67).

After Chester shouts that he is not blaming Jim, Jim continues:

> "No," I said, "you don't blame anybody for anything. That's the password for politicos, that's the pill for punks— that's the joy call to the love feast. Come on, boys and girls, we understand each other. We're a putrid lot. Let's get together and sing unto our putrefying lord the hymn of the putrid. Don't blame anyone for anything. You don't blame me," I said, "because you want me to let you off. But I know bloody well what I was and what I am. . . . And I know what you are—a poor old fester on a dying ramp. A shit-merchant who's so buried in filth he can't smell himself" (pp. 67-68).

These are not the accustomed accents of honor and truth, but they do convey the tone of exasperated morality that Cary has devised for Jim in the encounters with Chester. For Jim, Chester is almost beyond belief—a dangerous fraud who has succeeded in deceiving an entire nation. When the evidence in Nina's letters has convinced Jim that Chester is responsible for the conviction of Maufe, that is, for the surrender of a private person in the interest of a public gain, Jim undertakes to make a public gesture of his own, though in the name of personal integrity and honor. As he prepares, at the book's close, to kill Chester, Jim says, "You've sold Maufe to the mob. You've made an example and put yourself right with the gang of gimme-boys and commies who mean by hook or crook, but chiefly crook, to smash this country first and then take it over. The gangs you're now sucking up to. Well, . . . there's only one answer. You run your show on publicity for the mob and that's what I've got to do. To hit the headlines in a big way. To make an example" (p. 219).

In much the same way, Jim's decision, at the last, to kill his
wife is a protest against the general rottenness of things:

> I say I never loved this sweet woman so much as now
> when I knew she had to die. Because of the rottenness. Be-
> cause of the corruption. Because all loyalty was a laugh and
> there was no more trust. Because marriage was turned into
> a skin game out of a nice time by safety first. Because of the
> word made dirt by hypocrites and cowards. Because there
> was no truth or justice anywhere any more. Because of the
> grabbers and tapeworms who were sucking the soul out of
> England (p. 220).

It is his "great duty" laid on him by a "cruel fate," a last attempt
to impose on public life the decency and truth that have governed,
as he likes to think, all his personal transactions. As he kills the
public Nina, the woman who suppressed evidence in order to
convict Maufe so that the Communists would be pleased, he
anticipates public acknowledgment of the significance of his act,
his gesture. Seeing himself as guardian over the life of England
at large, executing two of her worst offenders against honor and
truth, he looks to Nina and to the nation for recognition; but he is
disappointed by both. Of Nina a moment before her death, he says,
"But I knew it was no good talking to her. She kept staring at me
and saying that she was ready to die but she didn't quite believe
we couldn't go on as before—she wanted to so much. She couldn't
understand she was up against something bigger than either of us
or anyone's happiness. The truth. And nothing could change it.
She didn't want to understand. It was too big" (p. 221).

The nation, too, fails to understand the exemplary purgation,
the public rite that Jim intends:

> I say I knew even then that perhaps no one would want
> to understand. As happened. Look at the way the papers
> have handled this thing. As a sex murder. As a common
> adultery case. Suggesting I killed my wife because she was

unfaithful and a gold digger.... Only one of them ever quoted my words at the first statement when I said I killed her for an example because it was necessary. And in the same paragraph they put the statement by the doctor I was sane and responsible for my actions. So as to make the people see their real opinion I was mad as a hatter and didn't know what I was doing....

It has been a bitter thought to me in these weeks I'm going through hell for nothing. That I killed my darling to no purpose; that this great country is so blinded and bound, so hocussed and gammoned by the bunkum boys, the smart ones, the power and money merchants, it doesn't know where it's going or what it's going there for and it's too bewildered to care (p. 222).

Even Jim's statement to a reporter whom he knows, explaining why, "as an honourable man," Jim had to kill his wife and how "the trouble with the country was it was run from top to bottom by men without honour, men on the grab," is rewritten at the newspaper office with all the public claims suppressed.

As a consequence, Jim's deed becomes the crowning failure in his futile attempt to reform a whole time. It is he alone who tries to make the private and public focuses one, who tries, that is, to make public and political life over in the image of personal honor. Nina and Chester have long since abandoned such an endeavor; Nina's belated attempt to withdraw from the life of duplicity is rather vague, however touching. Jim's utter failure, his inability even to make his intentions known and achieve at least a gesture, is the measure of the distance between public and private morality in the novel. In Jim's futile murder of Nina, the public issue flies out the window and Jim is left, ironically, with a mere personal crime on his hands. The personal life, which was to be the source of a moral regeneration, is, instead, vulgarly discredited. None of Jim's indignation over public corruption breaks out of the private circle. Cary makes Jim an embodiment of political ineffectuality—a portent of the fate of intransigent virtue in a dynamic, evolving democracy, seething with special interests and adroit demagogues who use them.

Jim is not merely Cary's most significant example of the public-private conflict. As the first-person narrator, he is our means of knowing and weighing all the novel's substance. And like Nina and Chester in their narratives, he is himself an interesting and rather ambiguous figure—not the least because of his grasp of the other narrators.

Though he is charged by Nina and Chester with not being able to understand political transactions, and though his narrative style is impatient of ideas, commas, definite articles, and relative pronouns alike, his insight into Nina is remarkable. She is as elusive and difficult a figure as any in recent fiction; but the puzzling blend of honesty, loyalty, and deceit that characterizes her in *Prisoner of Grace* is not lost on Jim in *Not Honour More*. He recognizes, as we have seen, her refusal to continue lying to him when she attempts suicide, as well as her genuine good faith when she makes the incriminating correspondence available. His reflections on their adolescent relationship are filled with the memory of her uncommon "straightness," truthfulness, and goodness. Indeed Chester successfully exploits these memories to distract Jim from shooting him. Yet, for all this, Jim is prepared to recognize what has happened to Nina, even to diagnose it. And surprisingly, for so headlong a man, it is an interpretation which tallies nicely with the complex revelations of *Prisoner of Grace*. Early in his narrative, Jim remarks that Nina "was under the belief that [Chester] was a great man who had saved the country and spent his life in the service of the people." Jim, of course, takes rather a different view of Chester:

> I say he spent his life destroying the country and selling the people. I say he corrupted everything and everybody that came near him and stole this woman, my wife, from me when she was little more than a child and set to work to de-

stroy her body and soul. He wanted her money to get into
what he called politics, which was stirring up hatred and
envy and making promises he knew would never be fulfilled,
and when he caught her he proceeded to rob her and terrify
her into his slave. I say if a murderer should be hung, which
I agree to, then men like Nimmo should be hung twice over
because they don't only murder people's bodies but their
souls (pp. 8-9).

The language is, characteristically, violent; but Jim's insight into
Nina's evaluation of Chester, and into her enslavement, is accurate
enough. Elsewhere, Jim peers again at the relationship between
Chester and Nina with considerable acuteness. "Clever as she was,"
he says, "Nimmo could play on her like a piano. On her cleverness
and her pride. Even her bad opinion of herself. Building her up
as a noble free soul and knocking her down again as a light woman"
(p. 103). Or again, expressing for us one of the major threads of
*Prisoner of Grace*, he says of Nina, "It was only after thirty years
of Nimmo and London society, she found anything comic in a
word like duty and could use it to make a fool of her husband"
(p. 126). Jim is also quite aware of Nina's estimate of himself and
of her tactics with him: "She looks at me with a smile. Takes a bit
of fluff off my lapel, which wasn't there. Charming gesture.
Thoughtful wife. But her eyes are trying to see what's going on in
funny old Jim. Who doesn't understand politics" (p. 18). Sum-
ming her up as he awaits word on her condition after the suicide
attempt, Jim speaks with a heightened, but accurate forbearance:
"I said what I'd known for forty years though I wouldn't admit it,
this woman was more weak than wicked" (p. 179). Taken altogether, these insights constitute a considerable understanding of
an uncommonly intricate woman. Jim's final view of Nina's corruption, and of its connection with the age in which she lives, is
neither hasty nor unforgiving. Nor, once again, does it do violence
to the conception of her which we get from the close of *Prisoner of
Grace*.

We cannot say quite so much for Jim's grasp of Chester. His relentless view of Chester as a scoundrel and fraud clashes violently with Chester's pretensions in *Except the Lord* and with Nina's extenuations in *Prisoner of Grace*. Still, Jim's understanding of the old politician is not superficial. During the scenes in which Jim stands over Chester ready to kill him, he is conscious of a good many of Chester's subtle diversionary tactics, though, until the last scene, Chester rather consistently outwits him. This, however, we may take to be merely the superiority of the "wangler" over the honorable man. Jim is not always fooled by his redoubtable opponent. On one occasion when Chester is looking back over his life with Nina, Jim reflects acutely on Chester's relationship with her. He understands how Chester, years ago, when Nina was still his wife, loved to talk about her to Jim, not because Chester was exulting in his winning her, but because Jim had loved her and would appreciate her extraordinary graces and virtues. Commenting further on the thirty-year marriage between Nina and Chester, Jim writes:

> The truth was Nina was a kind of miracle to him. He'd never been with a woman before his marriage, and he'd had the luck to hit upon one who exactly suited him, who got over all his queer ideas about what was right and what wasn't right. Who showed him how to enjoy life. And so cleverly, so gradually, she never frightened him. Nimmo, as anyone could see from the beginning, was built for a good time. Full of blood and bounce, a bit hairy at the heels but any amount of go. Straining at the bit, bursting at the buttons. And Nina worked him loose. People think he was puritanical, all against the rich. But no one ever enjoyed splashing money about more, and Nina was just the woman to teach him how to do it. No one enjoyed more cutting a dash, giving a party, showing off a pretty wife (pp. 174-175).

It is not, of course, the whole Chester, but it is, we sense, a genuine perception that harmonizes with what we already know. At another time, when Chester, caught compromisingly with Nina, allows himself to rage at Jim, Cary permits Jim enough sensitivity to blend denunciation and repudiation with pity as he reflects on Chester. The combination owes much to the old idea of self-deception, applied to Chester, this time, by Jim:

> He really meant what he said. He'd really lost his temper. He was shaking all over, his face was all out of shape and blotched like a bad apple. I saw the real Nimmo, a miserable old wreck fairly coming to bits with his own putrescence. A canting mummy who talked of liberty and believed in swindling the people. A living lie who'd ended by lying himself into looking-glass land. And from that moment I began to be sorry for the old crook, thrown out on his neck (p. 164).

Jim's capacity for pity and his sense of Chester's self-deception are evidence of humanity and intelligence. Yet, like his other insights into Nina and Chester, they need to be reconciled with a ferocity and bluntness of temper which suggest rather a narrow understanding. When Chester calls him an "everlasting unlimited goddam wooden-headed fool," who can't be told anything because he would "get it all wrong," we have partly the public man's impatience with personal scruples; but we have, in addition, a reference to the inflexible innocence which makes Jim, in the end, rather a questionable representative of the moral life.

Before we make a full estimate of Jim as narrator, we must consider his politics and the style in which they are expressed. We know already that he is deeply committed to justice, truth, and honor and that he sees these everywhere disregarded in the England of 1926. Politics itself, with its inevitable organization of people into parties, unions, and governments interested in achieving programs and ends, he finds inimical to the kind of disinterested integrity which only a personal devotion to honor and duty can guarantee. He is as much revolted by Major Brightman's fascist movement as by Pincomb's Communists, and distressed to

see decent, honest people like his niece Sally moving in either
direction, under the pressure of the General Strike. When pressed
by a group of students on the need for constitutional reform, Jim
says, "The trouble was not institutions but the people who worked
them. The difference between a good regiment and a bad regiment was not the King's Regs. which was the same for both but
the colonel, officers and men and what they thought right" (p.
143). Yet to Jim's mind, the individual men who, in their up-
rightness and decency, are most capable of setting the moral tone
of a good society are the very ones that democratic public life
vilifies and crushes. Maufe, Sergeant Varney—his subordinate
in the specials—and himself, he sees as victims of the lies and
smears of political life, men who cannot hope to survive the
slanders and the swindles of a Nimmo or of any political person
uninhibited by righteousness. Jim explains that Varney and his
family are being deprived of a legitimate pension for Varney's war
injuries because it is in the nature of things for duty and decency
to be ignored: "Because [the Varneys] are the salt of the earth
and trust the nice gentlemen in black coats to do the right thing
by them. Because they won't complain when they're cheated. Because they don't shout for their rights but do their duty. Because
they are not gimmes but givers" (p. 84). Jim suffers much the same
kind of neglect himself. In his bitterness over Maufe's treatment,
he describes his own plight as a private person trying to ensure that
justice be done in the face of the Nimmo-Pincomb bargain. He
speaks of himself as "that nasty ex-soldier, making a ridiculous fuss
about some fellow called Maufe. Just one fellow, mark you. What's
more, a poor fellow. And what's more still, an absolute nobody. . . .
Not even in a union. The lowest form of animal life—an honest
freeman" (pp. 205-206). The terrible jeopardy in which the
"honest freeman" stands when he comes under the power of the
political man is the subject of another of Jim's reflections. On the
occasion when Varney receives verbal instructions to patrol the
dangerous dockside area without uniform, brassard, or truncheon

—"to act as a policeman without a policeman's powers"—Jim says,

> The racket was obvious. If there was any trouble and [Varney] tried to stop it, it was on his own responsibility. Suppose he stopped the Bolshies proceeding to the boat-yard with bottles of paraffin and pockets full of matches. There'd been threats to burn the boat-yards, because boat-yards didn't want to strike. All right. Local commissar runs special in, says unwarranted attack on private citizen taking home his weekly lamp oil. And Nimmo says, "Quite so. No authority from my committee. Sergeant Varney is an enemy of the people. Old soldier—brought up to butchery. Throw him into quod. Run him in for damages. Hold him up to public disgust and contempt. Turn on the Press gang—chew him up in best printer's ink all over the world." All right. But suppose he doesn't interfere and these boys go and set fire to the boat-yard. Why, then the committee wants to know why Sergeant Varney didn't do his duty. Duty of every citizen in such an emergency. Much more sworn special, even without instructions. Act of cowardice. Shocking dereliction. Old soldier too. Man with full understanding obligations of loyalty and discipline. Disgrace to the country. Blacken him. Hound him. Charge him full damages. Ruin him. He can't answer back because nobody will listen. And he's only got one vote (p. 85).

The almost paranoiac sense of exploitation, reminiscent of the cynicism and bitterness of the soldier in the ranks, is apparent even to Varney, who merely laughs and maintains that they must get on with the business anyway.

It becomes clear before very long that Jim's complaint against the unconscionable political man, and his solicitude for the survival of personal integrity and decency, are not really a politics at all, but an antipolitics. Jim is not recognizably fascist, liberal, or conservative. He is against sin, for honor. He expresses no real, explicit opinions on the General Strike beyond a desire for order, decency, and justice. The exigencies of democratic political life, the need to court large groups of people and to resolve delicate and complex conflicts by compromises and shifts of position—for these things Jim has no patience. They smack merely of corruption and decadence. His own world is simpler and his loyalties less ambiguous. Unlike Nina, who is sensitive, in *Prisoner of Grace,* to the political nature even of family life, Jim conceives of the private life as inhering solely in virtue and straightforwardness, the fountainhead of all moral criteria. The result of placing an antipolitical like Jim in the middle of a fierce political conflict is outrage and exasperation—moods which Cary manages to sustain in Jim quite skilfully, augmenting them with touches of ferocious satire. At a number of points he provides Jim with remarks that convey the man of honor's revulsion in a mode that we can only call the comedy of outrage. Of Chester making a public speech, Jim observes:

> When he begins to speak, noise gets worse. No one can hear a word. In fact there aren't any. He just moves his mouth, saving celebrated voice. Smiles celebrated smile, waves celebrated arms. Yells of, "Get out, Ches." But not so many yells. And some people near bawling for silence. See his celebrated mouth moving, see him grinning, think they're missing something (p. 17).

Of his own appearance at a gathering of Nimmo supporters, Jim says,

> All these people, as they gradually realized who I was, were quite as frightened as my wife. They stood round in rings, staring at me like a wild beast. They hadn't expected the audacious villain to return to his own house while red with the great man's blood. The low blackguard who dared to defend his home against the hero who was going to give them jobs (pp. 41-42).

Of the fascist leader Brightman's new home, he remarks,

> Brightman's place was an olde Englishe farmhouse . . .

built two years before with half-inch deal timbers nailed on brick and pebble-dash between. Steel casements with bottle-ends for panes. Roses round the door.... I ... walked into ye olde tyme lounge hall, panelled in Elizabethan linen-fold oak made out of chewed paper painted olde shitte colour. Full-length portrait of Brightman at east end, about eight foot high, as olde Englishe goodchappe, with shorts, open shirt and pipe. Slap-up bar underneath with olde chromium fittings (p. 73).

And on the general willingness to forget the violence and serious-ness of the General Strike as soon as it was over, he comments, "The idea was nothing much had happened, and anyone who reminded 'em of one or two little accidents, was worse than a dog who keeps on barking at the burglar when you want to go to sleep (p. 203)." These fierce satirical ejaculations are filled with the exasperation and despair of a man who is certain that he sees the terrible truth of things, the depravity that is everywhere, but that no one else can. He feels himself quite helpless to make others understand the vile pretense and imposition of democratic political life, largely because he despises the methods of publicity and propa-ganda which sustain it. Consequently, he expresses his frustration in the sardonic comic exaggerations which are perhaps the only recourse left to someone temperamentally and morally anti-political, yet caught up, out of a sense of duty, in a vehemently political transaction. One result of his frustration and rage is that he takes on some of the quality of a madman, or at least, of a para-noid personality. Indeed, some commentators, as we shall notice, have not hesitated to make madness the quality by which Jim is chiefly to be known.

As we have had occasion to observe before, first-person narra-tion can easily become a source of ambiguity. When we try to make an assessment of Jim and the terms in which he views his world, we need to proceed without the kind of help that Cary might have provided if he had seen fit to utilize the ordinary third-person convention. This mode would have given him a means of intruding on the action as commentator, or of entering the minds of several characters, even temporarily, so as to afford a perspective through contrast, or, finally, of filtering all the action through a comprehensive, definitive moral intelligence. In his last novel, *The Captive and the Free,* published posthumously, Cary, with characteristic boldness, returns precisely to this Victorian convention of the third-person narrative, with both free access to the consciousness of a number of characters and editorial remarks on his own part, though, predictably, some elusiveness remains. In the trilogies, however, he is preoccupied with a more strenuously multifarious obliquity. Although it is true that Nina and Chester speak their own pieces in their own narratives, the General Strike and the specific attitudes which it elicits are dealt with only in *Not Honour More,* and only by Jim. As a result our view of him in the major crisis of his life depends almost entirely on what he tells us. Such an arrangement makes rigorous demands on a reader's judgment without providing a genuinely adequate basis for judging. The results can be disconcerting.

Out of the autonomy that Cary allows both Jim and the readers of the novel arise widely disparate views. Andrew Wright, a careful and well-informed student of Cary, speaks of Jim, in his *Joyce Cary*, as a "madman" (p. 148) and a "fanatical man standing condemned on his own testimony" (p. 149). He maintains, too, that Jim "has a kind of simplicity which makes him in both private and public politics lamentably stupid" (p. 152). And when he considers the moral crux of the novel, Nina's suppression of evidence at the trial, Wright says, "To the reader of *Except the Lord* and *Prisoner of Grace,* her suppression is understandable. Fundamentally she trusts Chester's judgment. But to Jim, Nina's testimony is the ultimate evidence of betrayal" (p. 153). In much the same way, Maurice Richardson speaks of Jim as "very mad indeed" and goes so far as to diagnose his illness.[4] Edward Case, on the other hand, looks upon Jim as the embodiment of a noble conservatism:

> The view is cautious, believing in the wisdom of tradition and experience, aghast at the voracious appetite of the mob and the strong stomachs of its leaders, knowing that men are imperfect, that plans go astray, that power corrupts, believing that humane values and amenities are hardly won and easily lost, understanding that satisfactions are transient and judging, therefore, that progress is largely delusive, believing, finally, that order is a fundamental good and not a legitimation of current injustice.[5]

The disagreement is fundamental. It suggests that Cary has put his readers in the position of not being able to determine so crude and elementary a thing as the villain of the piece. Indeed, it ushers in the problem of the reader's subjective world, which has as much validity and reality as the novelist's and the narrator's, and which, consequently, the novelist must guard against with all manner of insistence and indication. Mr. Wright and Mr. Richardson make one kind of place in their scheme of things for uncompromising honor, truth, and the vehemence necessary to sustain them in a complicated world, Mr. Case another. It is true that Mr. Wright and Mr. Richardson are not sensitive to the provocation to which Cary exposes Jim, and that consequently they are disposed to misconstrue exasperation and outrage as mad-

[4] Review of *Not Honour More* in *The New Statesman and Nation* (April 23, 1955), p. 586. Elizabeth M. Kerr,, in "Joyce Cary's Second Trilogy," *University of Toronto Quarterly*, XXIX (April 1960), 310-325, joins in the denouncement of Jim, who for Miss Kerr "seems to be the real villain." She indicts him, though, by dealing far too generously with Nina and Chester in matters that concern them all equally, and by erroneously charging Jim with a failure to admit responsibility for the paternity of Nina's children. Actually, we have Nina's word that Jim does admit fathering Tom Nimmo, and that it is Chester who perversely denies the truth in the presence of those who know it best, Nina and Jim (*Prisoner of Grace*, pp. 39-41). Furthermore, Jim faces his responsibility squarely by asking Nina to come away with him, after Tom's birth, and give up "the old miserable false life" with Chester.

[5] "The Free World of Joyce Cary," *Modern Age*, III (Spring 1959), 118.

ness. It is equally true that the view which Mr. Case expresses owes more to his own politics, or to Edmund Burke's, than to any with which Cary has provided Jim. Still, it must be said that the novel does not really insist upon a particular, determinate view of Jim. There is even some question as to whether it makes one possible.

We can hardly escape being conscious of a thoroughgoing plausibility, even attractiveness, in Jim's position and behavior. Honor, truth, and justice have not lost their power to move even the most realistic of us; and the impassioned advocacy of such values, even in a world which seems to be governed by quite different considerations, is not necessarily an indication of madness. There is, after all, a sense in which those who yield to the world are themselves mad, or blind, or trivial. In this perspective, Jim's devotion to Maufe, to his own integrity, and to truth, is a noble, compelling virtue, perhaps the most meaningful kind of heroism possible in a backsliding, slipshod time. If he suggests Don Quixote, or the Boy Scouts, in his misconstruction of political reality, we may say that it is by virtue of such occasional innocent and willful misconstructions, or better, by such stubborn repudiations of duplicity, expediency, and corruption, that we are able to maintain our self-respect as men. This, after all, is the invaluable bequest of the martyr to the rest of us, the reminder of what we are capable of, but have forgotten or betrayed; and he confers it, always, at the risk of appearing ridiculous, naïve, or insane. "They think me mad," Jim says at the close of his narrative, in one of his characteristic contrasts between the human and the subhuman, "because I couldn't live like a rat." If we are mindful of the terrible subtle assaults on human dignity and personal integrity in which our age is so accomplished, we can measure Jim's performance with awe and admiration. Certainly his own narrative, apart from occasional impatience and excitableness, insists on this view. For a madman, he is a long time killing his wife and Chester, and he ex-

hibits, in the process, a startling amount of compassion and understanding.

Still, there is another view possible as well—that simple-minded
virtue, whatever its attractions, is utterly incapable of running or
understanding the world, and that, in the end, it can only suffer
ineffectually while complexity, manipulation, or chicanery is done.
Jim fails, in this view, to understand that Chester's cooperation
with Pincomb and the Communists may have saved the whole
Tarbiton area from widespread violence and revolution; that
Maufe's assault on Pincomb, apart from the actual circumstances
of the arrest, if ignored, would make the British government and
its Emergency Strike Committee appear insupportably tyrannical;
that the General Strike poses national problems of the first magnitude which transcend injustices to a few decent chaps like Varney
and Maufe; that Chester understands these larger matters and can
be trusted to work for their solution in the best interests of the
nation; and, finally, that Nina, regardless of her love for Jim and
the risk to her own life, will do anything necessary to help Chester
play this public role. If the novel is read this way, Jim emerges,
despite his justifications and denunciations, as a crank, a man,
whatever his loyalties and integrity, quite unfit to live in the
twentieth century.

The choice is one which Cary does not help us to make. *Not
Honour More* is Jim's apologia, and his indomitable honor and
justifiable outrage ring through every line of it. To find Jim wanting within his own narrative, we need to invoke some of Chester's
calculated replies to him at gunpoint or Nina's perfunctory attempts to explain Chester's position and her own with it. Neither
of these is thoroughly persuasive in the onrush of Jim's indictments.
The problem of Chester, like the problem of Jim, is quite indeterminate. Whether he is Jim's irresponsible demagogue, Nina's brilliant statesman, or his own man of God remains an insoluble
question, even when the trilogy is completed. In a political novel
like Robert Penn Warren's *All the King's Men*, the first-person

narrator, Jack Burden, ultimately makes discoveries and pronouncements about himself and Willie Stark which obviously have Warren's sanction, and which we can comfortably take to be the truth that the novel is concerned with expressing. But *Not Honour More* is too much a dramatic impersonation, and Cary too systematically noncommittal in the whole trilogy, to allow such identifications. In a very real sense Cary sanctions nothing in the novel, nothing in the entire second trilogy. As we have already noted, we are denied even the conclusions that we might reach in a novel where the author keeps aloof but invades the minds of several characters involved in a single action. Cary has planned the trilogy in such a way as to frustrate such a tally. Chester's narrative ends forty-seven years before Jim's begins, and Nina's, while close in time to *Not Honour More,* is concerned with totally different events. We do not have our narrators reacting around a common core of action which, by remaining constant, can afford us a true measure of their differences and their validity. The counterpoint and interplay are not sufficiently focused to cancel, qualify, and define. Consequently, the alternative, if we are concerned with resolving the dilemma, is to go outside the novels.

In a letter quoted by Andrew Wright, which responds to just such questions as we are raising here, Cary expresses his own position quite straightforwardly:

> What I believe is what Nimmo believes, that wangle is inevitable in the modern state, that is to say, there is no choice between persuading people and shooting them. But it was not my job to state a thesis in a novel, my business was to show individual minds in action and the kind of world they produce and the political and aesthetic and moral problems of such a world. In short (in the trilogy), the political situation as I conceive it in *my* world of the creative free individual.[6]

It is regrettable, to begin with, that such a declaration should be

[6] *Joyce Cary,* p. 154.

necessary; that is to say, that even so good a reader of Cary as Andrew Wright should need to resort to an obiter dictum in order to evaluate the figures of the trilogy. Even more disturbing is the general inadequacy of the explanation. In the novels Jim does not desire to shoot people as a means of running the state, but merely to proceed in all things truthfully, justly, and honorably, if a little inflexibly. Consequently, Cary's pronouncement misrepresents the actual conflict in the trilogy and awards the palm to Chester over a false issue. As we go further into the explanation, the considerations broaden significantly. Cary makes it clear, characteristically enough, that his business as novelist is not to state a thesis but "to show individual minds in action and the kind of world they produce." That is, he takes it as his duty to avoid precisely the kind of commitment within the novels which the reader of the second trilogy is most likely to look for as a help in imposing some final order and meaning on it. Presumably "the kind of world" which the individual minds produce is at once the private world of every human being, Chester, Nina, and Jim included, and the larger world—its objectivity rather indeterminate—resulting from the interaction of these individual minds, i.e., the world of the trilogy. The separate novels composing the trilogy set before us the private world of each narrator, as Cary hoped they would. But the effect of the whole trilogy is less certain. We are hardly in a position to compose from merely three testimonies a semblance of ultimate reality. Cary, we know, would readily concede this and proceed, as well, to deny the accessibility of an ultimate objective reality to any human being. The total world of the trilogy, then, must be a partial, subjective world. Even the interaction between the individual minds and worlds of the narrators is itself subjectively conceived in a single mind—Cary's own. He is consistent enough to tell us that what we have in the second trilogy is "the political situation as I conceive it in *my* world of the creative free individual." We know from Cary's metaphysic that his own world is theoretically as private and personal as anyone else's. Cary's is characterized, however, by a peculiarly profitless kind of subjectivity, for he insists on exempting himself, as a novelist, from the subjective commitments and evaluations which, in his view, define the human condition itself. It is as though he cannot put enough trust in his own subjectivity to utilize it in his fiction.

In the end, the world which the trilogy presents is not a coherent, explicit vision; it postulates only a plurality of beliefs and commitments. The three novels assert merely that there are people who see and judge like Chester, others who see and judge like Jim, some, like Nina, who, neither seeing nor judging decisively enough, are torn asunder by ambivalent inclinations. It is a spacious world, inasmuch as Cary is willing to suffer all fools gladly; but it is vitiated by a relativistic inclusiveness which makes it ultimately unsatisfying. Neither Jane Austen, nor Tolstoy, nor Dostoievsky, nor James fled from commitment to inconclusiveness so deliberately and systematically, and their novels gain immeasurably in their coherence, in their whole value as communications about human life, as a consequence. Even Conrad, Joyce, and Faulkner, who, like Cary, employ multiple perspectives, are far from surrendering their authority and prerogatives as novelists. We never have the feeling that Lord Jim, Leopold Bloom, or Jason Compson exist only to confound us, to perfect their creators in humility, or to testify to the utter intractableness of reality. A subjectivity which advances nothing but the prevalence of subjectivity may be philosophically defensible, but it results in a fiction whose substance and content are seriously impaired by the absence of specific shaping convictions. By writing with an unyielding relativistic, ultimately indeterminate, objectivity, by refusing to clarify Jim's inadequacy and sanction Chester's behavior unmistakably *in the trilogy itself*, Cary becomes guilty of a kind of novelistic dereliction of duty.

Although Cary's narrators are brilliantly realized and impersonated, they have the aimless vitality and unmasterable, impenetrable, mystifying complexity of figures from life, rather than the relevance and serviceability of characters who help to articulate a specific moral and aesthetic design. Such design as there is in the trilogy as a whole—this is not true of the individual novels—has philosophical, rather than dramatic, force. Cary is less concerned with the conflict arising from disparate views than with the fact that there are disparate views. Such a fact cannot make a work of fiction cohere. It substitutes for the novelist's peculiar conception of things—the greatest objectivity, after all, that he can summon— mere discordant atomies. It introduces an anarchic principle into fiction, which destroys the whole validity of selection, commitment, and personal vision, or, in Cary's own terms, of the kind of intuition into reality which art in general is concerned with expressing.[7]

We may say, in Cary's behalf, that the world of irreconcilable subjective visions and of an essentially indeterminate reality is precisely his own personal conception of existence, the very kind of commitment that makes fiction possible. And certainly the clashing first-person narratives which he employs in both trilogies constitute a perfect technique for communicating that conception— a superb instrument for projecting multiplicity of viewpoint. Yet we must, inevitably, judge the quality of a novelist's vision when we make our estimate of his work, even if we take into account Henry James's good counsel in "The Art of Fiction" about not quarreling needlessly with a writer's *donnée*. We respond, quite unavoidably, to the moral nature of Cary's conception and to the effect of the conception on the work which embodies it. Morally, Cary's neutrality, his dedication to the visions of his characters, is open to the customary objections to relativism : one does not make sense of the world by succumbing to its diversity. As a basis for fiction, the conception has related shortcomings. The novel need not exist at all if its version of reality is no more conclusive and meaningful that reality itself. In Cary's own aesthetic, the novelist's function is to impose meaning on what is essentially

[7] See *Art and Reality*, pp. 2-5 and *passim*.

meaningless. When the novelist's mind is too comprehensive, and, consequently, too indeterminate, this function is impaired.[8]

As we have observed in Chapter I, Cary's world is startlingly rich in its dualism and multiplicity. It encompasses chaos and order, matter and spirit, conception and intuition, art and reality, subjective truth and objective truth, the claims of the past and the claims of the present, inescapable anguish and triumphant joy. To the extent that Cary has succeeded in incorporating this richness into the second trilogy, he has fashioned some of the most vibrant, disturbing, and compelling fiction of his time. But his inclusiveness is a liability as well as a strength, for it impedes his ordering of his own energies and the energies of his characters. He fails to provide us with a reliable means of concluding from the novels themselves something more than that the world is senselessly divided and sustained by a compelling, frequently disastrous, vitality. Yet we must recognize that this failure is intimately wedded with what is most valuable in his work : the novels are filled with an indeterminate profusion of possibility and assertion which, as it were, both murders and creates. We do best, on the whole, not to disturb, not even to regret, the extraordinary impasse, the studied irresolution, of the second trilogy. Taken as it is, it constitutes an emblem of the deep uncertainty that we have allowed to haunt our time, and of a desire to assent to life on any terms whatever. It proclaims that value is rather a complicated matter, and that if we are to consider it at all, we shall need to be both guarded and magnanimous. Indecision, it suggests, is a way, at least, of life.

---

[8] In this connection, Jeanne Garant's observation in "Joyce Cary's Portrait of the Artist," *Revue des Langues Vivantes*, XXIV, No. 6 (1958), 476-486, is instructive. "[Cary] did not seek to interpret life," she says, "but to present it." Though spoken approvingly by an admirer, this condemns Cary as a novelist by his own criteria.

# Bibliography

*A Selected List of Joyce Cary's Published Work*

The considerable collection of Cary's unpublished manuscripts and papers, previously stored in the attic of his home at Oxford, is now in the possession of the Bodleian Library.

## 1 Novels

All but the last three of Cary's novels have been published in the uniform Carfax edition by Michael Joseph, each volume containing a preface by Cary written especially for this edition; *First Trilogy* also contains such a preface. The dates cited for the Carfax series indicate first printings in this edition.

*Aissa Saved*. London: Ernest Benn, 1932; London: Michael Joseph, 1949; Carfax edition, London: Michael Joseph, 1952.

*An American Visitor*. London: Ernest Benn, 1933; London: Michael Joseph, 1949; Carfax edition, London: Michael Joseph, 1952; New York: Harper, 1961.

*The African Witch*. London: Victor Gollancz, 1936; New York: William Morrow, 1936; London: Michael Joseph, 1950; Carfax edition, London: Michael Joseph, 1951; New York: Harper, 1962.

*Castle Corner*. London: Victor Gollancz, 1938; London: Michael Joseph, 1950; Carfax edition, London: Michael Joseph, 1952.

*Mister Johnson*. London: Victor Gollancz, 1939; London: Michael Joseph, 1947; New York: Harper, 1951; Carfax edition, London: Michael Joseph, 1952.

*Charley Is My Darling*. London: Michael Joseph, 1940; Carfax edition, London: Michael Joseph, 1951; New York: Harper, 1960.

*A House of Children*. London: Michael Joseph, 1941; Carfax edition, London: Michael Joseph, 1951; Harmondsworth: Penguin, 1955; New York: Harper, 1956.

*Herself Surprised*. London: Michael Joseph, 1941; New York: Harper, 1948; Carfax edition, London: Michael Joseph, 1951; Harmondsworth: Penguin, 1955; Universal Library, New York: Grosset and Dunlap, 1960.

*To Be a Pilgrim*. London: Michael Joseph, 1942; New York: Harper, 1949; Carfax edition, London: Michael Joseph, 1951; Harmondsworth: Penguin, 1957; Universal Library, New York: Grosset and Dunlap, 1960.

*The Horse's Mouth*. London: Michael Joseph, 1944; Harmondsworth: Penguin, 1948; New York: Harper, 1950; Carfax edition, London: Michael Joseph, 1951; ed. Andrew Wright, London: George Rainbird, 1957; ed. Andrew Wright, Harper's Modern Classics, New York: Harper, 1959; Universal Library, New York: Grosset and Dunlap, 1959.

*First Trilogy*. New York: Harper, 1958.

*The Moonlight*. London: Michael Joseph, 1946; New York: Harper, 1947; Carfax edition, London: Michael Joseph, 1952.

*A Fearful Joy*. London: Michael Joseph, 1949; New York: Harper, 1950; Carfax edition, London: Michael Joseph, 1952; Harmondsworth: Penguin, 1956; New York: Doubleday Anchor, 1961.

*Prisoner of Grace*. London: Michael Joseph, 1952; New York: Harper, 1952; Carfax edition, London: Michael Joseph, 1954.

*Except the Lord*. London: Michael Joseph, 1953; New York: Harper, 1953.

*Not Honour More*. London: Michael Joseph, 1955; New York: Harper, 1955.

*The Captive and the Free*. London: Michael Joseph, 1959; New York: Harper, 1959.

## 2. Short Stories

*Spring Song and Other Stories*. London: Michael Joseph, 1960. This recently published collection contains all the stories listed below with the exception of "Dinner at the Beeders'," "Happy Marriage," "Jubilee Christmas," "The Old Strife at Plant's," and the ten stories that Cary published in 1920 under the pseudonym, Thomas Joyce. It includes, in addition, five stories never before published.

"Babes in the Wood," *Evening News* (May 28, 1953), p. 9.

"The Bad Samaritan" [pseud. Thomas Joyce], *Saturday Evening Post* (July 3, 1920), pp. 40-46.

"The Breakout," *New Yorker* (February 2, 1957), pp. 28-36.

"Bush River," *Windmill,* I (1945), 120-125.

"Buying a Horse," *Punch* (December 2, 1953), pp. 654-656.

"Carmagnole," *London Magazine,* II (February 1955), 37-39.

"A Consistent Woman" [pseud. Thomas Joyce], *Saturday Evening Post* (August 21, 1920), pp. 30, 32, 81, 82.

"The Cure" [pseud. Thomas Joyce], *Saturday Evening Post* (May 1, 1920), pp. 30, 99.

"A Date" [also called "Red Letter Day"], *New Yorker* (August 1,1953), pp. 56-58; *Punch* (October 21, 1953), pp. 478-480.

"Dinner at the Beeders' " [excerpt from *The Horse's Mouth*], *Harper's,* CXCIX (September 1949), 38-46.

"Evangelist," *Harper's,* CCV (November 1952), 88-89.

"A Glory of the Moon," *Mademoiselle,* XLI (May 1955), 101, 156.

"A Good Investment," *Harper's* CCIX (December 1954), 64-72.

"Growing Up," *Vogue* (May 1, 1956), pp. 122, 123, 160.

"Happy Marriage," *Harper's,* CCXVI (April 1958), 65-68.

"A Hot Day," *Time and Tide* (June 16, 1956), p. 710.

"The Idealist" [pseud. Thomas Joyce], *Saturday Evening Post* (March 13, 1920), pp. 40-42.

"Jubilee Christmas," *Mademoiselle,* XLII (December 1955), 62-63.

"The Limit," *Esquire,* XLI (June 1954), 43.

"Lombrosine" [pseud. Thomas Joyce], *Saturday Evening Post* (January 31, 1920), pp. 30, 32, 62.

"A Mysterious Affair," *New Yorker* (January 28, 1956), pp. 28-34.

"None but the Brave" [pseud. Thomas Joyce], *Saturday Evening Post* (September 11, 1920), pp. 18-19, 100, 104, 107, 110.

"The Old Strife at Plant's" [a discarded portion of *The Horse's Mouth*], *Harper's* CCI (August 1950), 80-96; Oxford: privately printed with illustrations by Cary (1956).

"Out of Hand," *Vogue,* CXXVI (July 1955), 60-62.

"Period Piece," *Harper's Bazaar* (April 1958), pp. 110-111, 208.

"A Piece of Honesty" [pseud. Thomas Joyce], *Saturday Evening Post* (June 26, 1920), pp. 66, 69, 70.

"A Private Ghost," *New Yorker* (November 10, 1956), pp. 121-130.

"Psychologist," *Harper's Bazaar,* XC (May 1957), 140-142, 175-185.

"Red Letter Day." See "A Date" above.

"The Reformation" [pseud. Thomas Joyce], *Saturday Evening Post* (May 22, 1920), pp. 20-21, 124.

"Romance," *Time* (October 20, 1952), p. 119.

"Salute to Propriety" [pseud. Thomas Joyce], *Saturday Evening Post* (October 9, 1920), pp. 40, 42, 45, 46.

"A Special Occasion," *Harper's,* CCIII (September 1951), 97-98; *Cornhill,* CLXV (Winter 1951-1952), 387-389.

"Spring Song," *London Magazine,* I (March 1954), 29-31.

"The Springs of Youth" [pseud. Thomas Joyce], *Saturday Evening Post* (March 6, 1920), pp. 30, 32, 189, 190.

"Success Story," *Harper's,* CCIV (June 1952), 74-76.

"The Tunnel," *Vogue* (October 1, 1957), pp. 186-187, 226.

"Umaru," *Cornhill,* CLXV (Winter 1950-1951), 50-54.

"You're Only Young Once," *Encounter,* VIII (September 1956), 24-26.

## 3. Poems

*Marching Soldie*r. London: Michael Joseph, 1945.
*The Drunken Sailor: A Ballad-Epic*. London: Michael Joseph, 1947.

## 4. Essays and Treatises

"Africa Yesterday: One Ruler's Burden," *Reporter* (May 15, 1951), pp. 21-24.

"L'Art," New York *Times* Book Review (March 12, 1950), p. 8.

*Art and Reality* [The Clark Lectures 1956]. Cambridge: Cambridge University Press, 1958; New York: Harper, 1958.

"Barney Magonagel," *New Yorker* (June 19, 1954), pp. 27-31.

*Britain and West Africa*. London: Longmans, Green, 1946; revised edition, 1947.

"Britain Is Strong in Herself," New York *Times* Magazine (April 22, 1956), pp. 12, 32-33.

"Can Western Values Survive without Religion?" *Time and Tide* (July 9, 1955), pp. 901-902.

*The Case for African Freedom*. London: Secker and Warburg, 1941; revised and enlarged edition, 1944.

"Catching Up with History" [a review of Richard Wright's *Black Power*], *Nation* (October 16, 1954), pp. 332-333.

"The Censorship Plot," *Spectator* (March 11, 1955), pp. 275-276.

"Character on the Manhattan Boat," New York *Times* Book Review (June 6, 1954), p. 2.

"A Child's Religion," *Vogue,* CXXII (December 1953), 86-87.

"Christmas in Africa," *Esquire,* XL (December 1953), 101, 208.

"Cromwell House," *New Yorker* (November 3, 1956), pp. 45-67.

"Faith in Liberty," *Time and Tide* (July 16, 1955), pp. 933-934.

"The Front-Line Feeling," *Listener* (January 17, 1952), pp. 92-93.

"Gerald Wilde," *Nimbus,* III, No. 2 (1955), 47-54.

"The Heart of England," *Holiday,* XVII (January 1955), 26-31.

"Horror Comics," *Spectator* (February 18, 1955), p. 177.

"The Idea of Progress," *Cornhill,* CLXVII (Summer 1954), 331-337.

"Important Authors of the Fall, Speaking for Themselves," New York *Herald-Tribune* Book Review (October 8, 1950), p. 10.

"Including Mr. Micawber," New York *Times* Book Review (April 15, 1951), p. 4.

"An Interview with Joyce Cary" [conducted by John Burrows and Alex Hamilton], *Paris Review,* VIII (Winter 1954-1955), 63-78. Reprinted in Malcolm Cowley, ed., *Writers at Work: The Paris Review Interviews.* New York: Viking, 1958, pp. 51-67.

Introduction to R. S. Surtees, *Mr. Sponge's Sporting Tour* (Oxford World Classics, 1960).

"Joyce Cary's Last Look at His Worlds," *Vogue* (August 15, 1957), pp. 96-97, 150-153.

"Look Out for Labels," *This Week Magazine* (January 4, 1953), p. 2.

"The Mass Mind: Our Favorite Folly," *Harper's,* CCIV (March 1952), 25-27.

"The Meaning of England," *Holiday,* XXIII (April 1958), 117.

*Memoir of the Bobotes.* Austin: University of Texas Press, 1960.

"My First Novel," *Listener* (April 16, 1953), pp. 637-638.

"A Novel is a Novel is a Novel," New York *Times* Book Review (April 30, 1950), pp.1, 34; *Adam International Review,* XVIII (November-December 1950), 1-3.

"A Novelist and His Public," *Listener* (September 30, 1954), pp. 521-522; *Saturday Review* (November 27, 1954), pp. 11, 36-37.

"The Novelist at Work: A Conversation between Joyce Cary and Lord David Cecil," *Adam International Review,* XVIII (November-December 1950), 15-25.

"On the Function of the Novelist," New York *Times* Book Review (October 30, 1949), pp. 1, 52.

"Oxford Scholar," *Holiday,* XIII (June 1953), 96-101.

"Party of One," *Holiday,* XX (September 1956), 6, 89.

"The Period Novel," *Spectator* (November 21, 1952), p. 684.

"Political and Personal Morality," *Saturday Review* (December 31, 1955), pp. 5, 6, 31, 32.

*Power in Men.* London: Nicholson and Watson [for the Liberal Book Club], 1939.

*Process of Real Freedom.* London: Michael Joseph, 1943.

"The Sources of Tension in America," *Saturday Review* (August 23, 1952), pp. 6-7, 35.

"Speaking of Books," New York *Times* Book Review (June 26, 1955), p. 2.

"A Talk with Joyce Cary" [conducted by Harvey Breit], New York *Times* Book Review (February 18, 1951), p. 14.

"The Way a Novel Gets Written," *Harper's,* CC (February 1950), 87-93; *Adam International Review,* XVIII (November-December, 1950), 3-11.

"Westminster Abbey," *Holiday,* XIX (April 1956), 62-63.

## A Selected List of Commentary on Joyce Cary's Work

*Adam International Review,* XVIII (November-December 1950). The entire issue is devoted to Joyce Cary.

Adams, Hazard. "Blake and Gulley Jimson: English Symbolists," *Critique*, III (Spring-Fall 1959), 3-14.

———. "Joyce Cary: Posthumous Volumes and Criticism to Date," *Texas Studies in Literature and Language*, I (Summer 1959), 289-299

———. "Joyce Cary's Swimming Swan," *American Scholar*, XXIX (Spring 1960), 235-239.

———. "The Three Speakers of Joyce Cary," *Modern Fiction Studies*, V (Summer 1959), 108-120.

Allen, Walter. *Joyce Cary*. ("Writers and Their Work"; London: Longmans, Green, 1953; revised edition, 1954.

———. "Joyce Cary," *New Statesman and Nation* (April 6, 1957), p. 434.

Barr, Donald. "A Careful and Profound Thinker," *Adam International Review*, XVIII (November-December 1950), 30-31.

Bellow, Saul. "A Personal Record" [review of *Except the Lord*], *New Republic* (February 22, 1954), pp. 20-21.

Bettman, Elizabeth R. "Joyce Cary and the Problem of Political Morality," *Antioch Review*, XVII (Summer 1957), 266-272.

Case, Edward. "The Free World of Joyce Cary," *Modern Age*, III (Spring 1959), 115-124.

———. "In the Great Tradition," *Wall Street Journal* (June 6, 1955), p. 10.

"Cheerful Protestant," *Time* (October 20, 1952), pp. 118-130.

Collins, Harold R. "Joyce Cary's Troublesome Africans," *Antioch Review*, XIII (Fall 1953), 397-406.

French, Warren G. "Joyce Cary's American Rover Girl," *Texas Studies in Literature and Language*, II (Autumn 1960), 281-291.

Garant, Jeanne. "Joyce Cary's Portrait of the Artist," *Revue des Langues Vivantes*, XXIV, No. 6 (1958), 476-486.

Hamilton, Kenneth. "Boon or Thorn? Joyce Cary and Samuel Beckett on Human Life," *Dalhousie Review*, XXXVIII (Winter 1959), 433-442.

Hardy, Barbara. "Form in Joyce Cary's Novels," *Essays in Criticism*, IV (April 1954), 180-190.

Hatfield, Glenn W., Jr. "Form and Character in the Sequence Novels of Joyce Cary." Unpublished Master's thesis, Ohio State University, 1956.

Hayes, Richard. "Felt in the Head and Felt along the Heart," *Commonweal* (October 17, 1952), p. 42.

Hoffman, Charles G. "Joyce Cary and the Comic Mask," *Western Humanities Review*, XIII (Spring 1959), 135-142.

Hughes, Richard. "Joyce Cary," *Spectator* (December 18, 1953), pp. 738-739.

Johnson, Pamela Hansford. "Joyce Cary," in *Little Reviews Anthology* 1949, ed. Denys Val Baker. London: Methuen, 1949, pp. 200-209.

———. "Three Novelists and the Drawing of Character: C. P. Snow, Joyce Cary, and Ivy Compton-Burnett," *Essays and Studies by Members of the English Association* (1950), pp. 82-91.

Karl, Frederick R. "Joyce Cary: The Moralist as Novelist," *Twentieth Century Literature*, V (January 1960), 183-196.

Kerr, Elizabeth M. "Joyce Cary's Second Trilogy," *University of Toronto Quarterly,* XXIX (April 1960), 310-325.

Kettle, Arnold. *An Introduction to the English Novel*, Vol. II. London: Hutchinson's University Library, 1953.

King, Carlyle. "Joyce Cary and the Creative Imagination," *Tamarack Review* (Winter 1959), pp. 39-51.

McCormick, John. *Catastrophe and Imagination*. London: Longmans, Green, 1957.

[Maclaren Ross, Julian]. "Story of a Full Life," *Times Literary Supplement* (November 11, 1949), p. 732.

Meriwether, James B. "The Books of Joyce Cary: A Preliminary Bibliography of English and American Editions," *Texas Studies in Literature and Language,* I (Summer 1959), 300-310.

Monas, Sidney. "What to Do with a Drunken Sailor," *Hudson Review,* III (Autumn 1950), 466-474.

Murry, John Middleton. "Coming to London," *London Magazine,* III (July 1956), 30-37.

Owen, B. Evan. "The Supremacy of the Individual in the Novels of Joyce Cary," *Adam International Review,* XVIII (November-December 1950), 25-29.

Prescott, Orville. "Two Modern Masters: Cozzens, Cary," in *In My Opinion*. Indianapolis: Bobbs-Merrill, 1952, pp. 180-199.

Pritchett, V. S. "Books in General," *New Statesman and Nation* (October 27, 1951) pp. 464-465.

Reed, Henry. *The Novel Since* 1939. London: Longmans, Green [for the British Council], 1946.

Richardson, Maurice. [Review of *Not Honour More*], *New Statesman and Nation* (April 23, 1955), p. 586.

Rosenfeld, Isaac. "Popular Misery," *New Republic* (October 20, 1952), p. 27.

Ryan, Marjorie. "An Interpretation of Joyce Cary's *The Horse's Mouth,*" *Critique,* II (Spring-Summer 1958), 29-38.

Schorer, Mark. "The 'Socially Extensive' Novel," *Adam International Review*, XVIII (November-December 1950), 31-32.

Seymour-Smith, Martin. "Zero and the Impossible," *Encounter,* IX (November 1957), 38-51.

Steinbrecher, George, Jr. "Joyce Cary: Master Novelist," *College English,* XVIII (May 1957), 387-395.

Trilling, Diana. "Fiction in Review" [review of *To Be a Pilgrim*], *Nation* (May 28, 1949), pp. 618-620.

Van Horn, Ruth G. "Freedom and Imagination in the Novels of Joyce Cary," *Midwest Journal*, V (Winter 1952-1953), 19-30.

——. "Rx for Joyce Cary," *Nation* (May 11, 1957), p. 420.

Woodcock, George. "Citizens of Babel: A Study of Joyce Cary," *Queens Quarterly*, LXIII (1956), 236-246.

Wright, Andrew. *Joyce Cary: A Preface to His Novels*. London: Chatto and Windus, 1958; New York: Harper, 1958.

——. "Joyce Cary's Unpublished Work," *London Magazine*, V (January 1958), 35-42.

# Index

## DATE DUE

| | |
|---|---|
| | |
| | |
| | |
| | |
| | |
| | |
| | |
| | |
| | |
| | |
| | |
| | |
| | |
| | |
| | |
| | |
| | |
| | |